For Walter Smiley

with best regards

Bill Mayhue

7/9/85 Hot Springs

SHORT-TERM BUSINESS BORROWING:

SOURCES, TERMS, AND TECHNIQUES

WILLIAM A. MACPHEE

DOW JONES-IRWIN
Homewood, Illinois   60430

ISBN 0-87093-427-4
Library of Congress Catalog Card No. 83–70875

Printed in the United States of America

1 2 3 4 5 6 7 8 9 0 K 10 9 8 7 6 5 4

PREFACE

The concept of financial management focuses on orchestrating many variables to achieve corporate strategic objectives which includes managing short-term debt.

Noted management theoreticians, such as Igore Ansoff, the founding dean of the Graduate School of Management at Vanderbilt University, and Peter Drucker, have promoted the "take charge" managerial approach in their teachings and writings. Ansoff stresses that the present and future organizational culture will be driven by "managers of change" as opposed to "change agents" who react to environmental influences in a knee-jerk fashion.

Volatile interest rates and the uncertainty of money markets have underscored the importance of proper financial management. Our corporate and international financial consulting experience at MacPHEE and ASSOCIATES has revealed that many corporate treasurers are inundated with the rapid changes occurring in the money markets. Treasurers often rely on their bankers to provide insight and direction, which is an unfair expectation since most bankers are operating in the same ambiguous environment.

After making presentations to over 2,000 bankers and corporate treasurers, addressing various groups, including the American Bankers' Association, and conducting surveys and research for past publications and this book, we have concluded that the fundamental techniques and insight for managing corporate short-term borrowings have not been well defined. Further, there is considerable misunderstanding among bankers and treasurers about certain borrowing alternatives, resulting in the mismanagement of debt. Although the high interest rates of 1982 magnified the importance of properly managing short-term borrowings, the benefits of debt management have always existed, irrespective of interest rate levels. Specifically, a 2 percent savings on interest reduces interest expense by $20,000 per $1 million of debt per year whether the prime rate is 20 percent or 8 percent. The concept of hedging interest costs in a rising rate environment is more elusive, but the benefits have always existed. It took the shock of high volatile rates to encourage corporate treasurers to improve their "take charge" financial management skills. They could no longer simply react to changing money conditions.

To emphasize the significance of this topic one needs only to examine the trend and scope of short-term borrowings. As of December 1982 total U.S. short-term borrowings approached $1.5 trillion.* This exceeded the U.S. national debt of $1.3 trillion and was larger than the gross national product for all but the largest countries and exceeds the $520 billion of external debt of non-OPEC developing nations. Assuming an average interest rate of 16 percent, the debt service for these borrowings was approximately $240 billion for 1982. This was unnecessarily high, and any reduction could have influenced the degree of the present global economic malaise.

It is probable that short-term corporate debt is not consistently managed, resulting in higher interest expense than necessary and lowered efficiency. Such inefficiencies are often passed on to consumers in higher prices, placing upward pressure on inflation. The significance of interest expense has some accountants encouraging the entry to be made immediately after "cost of goods sold" on the income statement as opposed to burying it in other expense items. There are a number of reasons for the increasing importance of short-term debt. During the 70s, greater emphasis was placed on return on equity, through higher debt leverage. As long-term interest rates increased, treasurers were reluctant to lock in these rates for long periods and relied on short-term refinancing. The economic environment has forced treasurers to place stronger emphasis on cash flow which is read-

---

*This includes $800 billion in Eurocurrency loans which are also loaned to non-U.S. borrowers and sometimes on a long-term basis, but the figure does not include short-term multicurrency loans.

ily supplemented with short-term debt. This increasing emphasis on short-term debt has not been accompanied by equal focus on the fundamentals of debt management or alternatives to traditional borrowing plans.

The primary reason for this lack of insight rests with the academic and banking communities. Academia has a tendency to look at the "big picture," and few MBA programs deal with the mechanics of the micro arena. For the most part, financial textbooks provide little reference to the mechanics and application of short-term borrowing alternatives. Bank training has a tendancy to focus on credit skills and often ignores the fundamentals of borrowing alternatives. The emphasis is placed on the impact of debt and usually sacrifices the management of corporate borrowings. The student rarely explores the circumstances giving rise to debt or the available alternatives. The result is that many corporate borrowers mismanage their borrowing position and debt is not properly synchronized with the corporate needs.

The objective of this book is to bridge this technical gap of knowledge by focusing clearly on the five primary short-term borrowing alternatives: conventional loans, commercial paper, bankers' acceptances, Eurodollars, and multicurrency debt. Each topic will include a definition, brief history, characteristics, mechanics, applications, regulations, and documents. The text compares each alternative, emphasizing pricing calculations and historical relationships.

Since money is a commodity, this project would be incomplete without exploring recently introduced hedging practices which permit increased control over interest rate fluctuations. The hedging procedures are discussed as they pertain to each topic, although the fundamentals of futures trading are reviewed only in Chapter One, Short-Term Debt, to avoid repetition.

William A. MacPhee

ACKNOWLEDGMENTS

This book is dedicated with deep appreciation to Arthur B. Adams, retired president of Lawrence Systems Inc., who has been my mentor, my associate, and my friend, and whose character and thoughts will always influence my direction.

Special appreciation goes to Carol Iannacone for her support and tenacity in typing and retyping the manuscript and to Art Adams and Patricia Lewis, whose proofreading and suggestions were indispensable.

Personal thanks go to Margaret L. Coughlin, McLean Coughlin, and to the many banks and corporations I have been privileged to work with as a banker and financial consultant. These companies have taken me into their confidence and provided the opportunity to explore problems and introduce solutions. The net result is the publication of this book. Thank you J.J.M. for your support and encouragement.

W. A. M.

CONTENTS

CHAPTER ONE

SHORT-TERM DEBT

Short-term debt is usually associated with borrowed funds to finance inventory, receivables, and general cash flow. It is expected that these funds will be repaid within one year. However, to put it in proper perspective, we must discuss the relationship of short-term debt to financial statements.

Financial statements consist of the balance sheet and the income or profit-and-loss statement. These statements are the monitoring record of corporate performance. The balance sheet is a snapshot picture on a given day of the company's assets and liabilities, while the income statement is a moving picture showing changes that occurred between the balance sheets for two different accounting periods.

Short-term debt appears on the balance sheet under the category of current liabilities because it is expected that this debt will be repaid within the current year. The cash proceeds of this debt usually finance current assets, such as the purchase of inventory; pay salaries to employees whose labor converts inventories to finished goods for sale; and fund receivables due from customers.

This working capital cycle is well described by Charles H. Ludlow, vice president-treasurer of the Upjohn Company. Working capital management "emphasizes the control of the current assets and liabilities throughout the firm's natural business cycle.

This cycle begins with cash, which is invested in raw materials and merchandise as well as various supplies and services.... The inventory investment is converted to accounts receivable as the merchandise is sold to customers. The cycle is completed when cash is received from customers for payment on the accounts."[1]

The cash cycle is financed by corporate profits, trade credit provided by suppliers, and short-term borrowings. Since the cash cycle is imperfect, corporations rely on short-term borrowings to supplement the cash flow.

The balance sheet is divided into two general categories—current assets and liabilities and long-term assets and liabilities. The major distinction is that current accounts, like inventories and short-term debt, actively change during the year; while long-term accounts, such as buildings and long-term debt and equity, have a life expectancy beyond one year. In sum, long-term debt generally finances fixed costs, such as plant and equipment required to convert raw materials into finished goods. Short-term debt supplements cash flow to purchase raw materials, pay associated value-added expenses (variable costs such as labor and electricity), and finance trade credit. (See Table 1-1).

This process is measured mathematically by ratio analysis covering the gamut of financial relationships. We are concerned about short-term debt and focus only on relevant performance ratios. Keep in mind that ratios are used by different groups to measure performance.

The corporation uses ratio analysis as part of the strategic planning process in developing goals by which to measure various plans for achieving financial objectives. Bankers use ratio analysis to monitor the company's ability to repay debt. Security analysts apply ratios to assist in stock recommendations. Each group has its own standards for measuring present performance and future expectations.

Each industry is unique, and there is no absolute number for all companies to achieve. Generally, a company is compared with an industry average.

Although many ratios are affected indirectly by short-term debt, we will examine directly related ratios and the impact of short-term borrowing on the balance sheet and income statement.

1. *Liquidity ratios* measure the solvency of the firm to determine its ability to convert assets into cash covering debts. Asset convertibility to cash is presented vertically on the balance sheet, with cash at the top followed by securities, receivables,

---

[1]Weston, J. Fred and Goudzwaard, Maurice B., eds., *The Treasurer's Handbook* (Homewood, Illinois: Dow Jones-Irwin, 1976).

TABLE 1-1

Balance Sheet

Assets			Liabilities		
Current assets:			**Current liabilities:**		
Cash	$	100,000	Notes to banks	$	1,400,000
Securities		500,000	Trade payables......		1,072,000
Receivables.........		4,500,000	Current portion long-		
Inventory		3,200,000	term debt		500,000
Total current			Accruals		60,000
assets		8,300,000	Total current		
Property, plant, and			liabilities		3,032,000
equipment:					
Machinery		1,800,000	Long-term debt		9,100,000
Plant..............		2,000,000	Equity.............		3,400,000
Property		3,932,000	Retained earnings ...		500,000
Total property,			Total liabilities.......		$16,032,000
plant, and					
equipment		7,732,000			
Total assets..........		$16,032,000			

Income Statement

Sales	$18,000,000
Cost of goods sold....	12,000,000
Gross profit	6,000,000
Operating expenses:	
Administration	
expense...........	3,500,000
Salaries...........	1,200,000
Interest expense.....	300,000
Net profit before tax ..	1,000,000
Tax	500,000
Retained earnings	$ 500,000

inventories, and the least liquid asset, plant and equipment, at the bottom.

2. *Working capital* is the short-term liquidity position measuring the excess of current assets over current liabilities representing the short-term capital available for continued operations. An increase in short-term debt without a like increase in current assets will reduce working capital. The formula is: current assets − current liabilities or $8,300,000 − $3,032,000 = $5,268,000.

3. *Current ratio* measures the relationship of current liabilities to current assets and is calculated by dividing current assets by current liabilities. If the answer is less than 1, the company is technically insolvent because current liabilities exceed current assets. Any number above 1 represents positive solvency, but banks prefer a ratio of 3:1 to 4:1. The calculation is: current assets ÷ current liabilities or $8,300,000 ÷ $3,032,000 = 2.73.

4. *Quick ratio* measures the relationship of current liabilities to current assets minus the least liquid accounts (inventories). This ratio focuses on the ability of the firm to convert assets to cash covering current liabilities in the face of liquidation. Naturally, each current account must be closely examined to determine liquidity. The ratio is:

$$\frac{\text{Current assets} - \text{Inventories}}{\text{Current liabilities}} \quad \text{or} \quad \frac{8,300,000 - 3,200,000}{3,032,000} = 1.68$$

Banks prefer a ratio at least 1:1; however, it is not uncommon for the ratio to be below 1, especially for seasonal inventory buildup, i.e., agribusiness. Astute bankers will weigh each asset to determine the probability of liquidation.

Current Assets	Amount	x	Liquidation Probability	=	Asset Value
Cash/deposits	$ 100,000		100%		$ 100,000
Securities	500,000		90		450,000
Receivables	4,500,000		70		3,150,000
Inventories	3,200,000		60		1,920,000
Total	$8,300,000				$5,620,000

In the above example, the bank will use the weighted current asset figure of $5,620,000 and subtract $1,920,000 in inventories for calculating the quick ratio. The weighted answer is referred to as the borrowing base against which banks will loan money.

5. *Debt:equity* is a leverage ratio measuring the equity of the company to its debt, both long-term and short-term. The ratio is:

$$\frac{\text{Total liabilities} - \text{Equity}}{\text{Equity}} \quad \text{or} \quad \frac{16,032,000 - 3,900,000}{3,900,000} = 3.11$$

When the answer is less than 1, the company has more equity than debt. In most cases the answer is greater than 1, indicating that borrowed funds contribute more to the operations than funds provided from equity and retained earnings. Most banks prefer that this ratio not exceed 2:1, indicating that for every dollar the company provides, the creditors provide two dollars. As this number increases, the bank creditors assume a greater responsibility for the successful financial performance of the firm. This situation may create an unhealthy relationship between the company and the creditors. Since a greater share of the risk belongs to the creditor, it may attempt to influence the operations, especially if the firm, its industry, or the economy are unstable. Usually, lenders are not professionally equipped to assume this responsibility, since their primary function is lending money, not managing the daily affairs of a multitude of borrowers.

During the 1970s greater emphasis was placed on return on stockholders' equity as an investment criteria. Companies were seeking more debt since expansion and therefore greater sales and profits funded by creditors would increase returns for stockholders. The name of the game was higher leverage and the debt-equity ratio reflected this financing philosophy. During periods of prosperity, this works well; however, leverage is a double-edged sword. During periods of recession, debt service may eliminate dividends and cut sharply into funds needed for operations. In essence, "where [borrowed] assets earn more than their cost of debt, leverage is favorable. When assets earn less than the cost of debt, leverage is a hindrance."[2]

To personalize this fact, if an individual puts $10,000 down on a $100,000 house and sells the house one year later for $110,000, the return on the buyer's $10,000 equity is $10,000 or 100 percent. If, however, the same person puts down $20,000 on the same house, the return is 50 percent.

If the housing industry is in a recession and the same house declines in value by $10,000, the owner has lost all equity and the return is – 100 percent. If $20,000 had been put down, the $10,000 loss represents a – 50 percent return on equity. Therefore, during inflationary periods, higher leverage generates larger returns, but in a recessionary period higher leverage generates larger relative equity losses.

The role of short-term debt is most important since it has been contributing to the total debt picture at an increasing rate. It is believed that for every $1 of long-term debt there was $1.40 of short-term debt in 1981 compared to 1:1 in the early 70s.

6. *Interest coverage* calculates the net profit before taxes relative to interest expense. Also known as the debt-service ratio, it indicates the minimal profit required to pay interest expense. The before-tax profit figure is properly used in the numerator since interest is subtracted from revenues to determine the taxable income. The calculation is:

$$\frac{\text{Net profit before taxes} - \text{Interest expense}}{\text{Interest expense}} \quad \text{or} \quad \frac{1,000,000 - 300,000}{300,000} = 2$$

This calculation is directly impacted by borrowing. Since short-term debt represents a majority of corporate debt, proper management will minimize this expense account. Proper management will improve the interest coverage, increase profits, and strengthen cash flow through reduced interest expense.

7. *Return on equity* calculates the net profit relative to net worth. The investor is keenly interested in this ratio, which is calculated as follows:

---

[2]Weston, J. Fred and Bringham, Eugene F., eds., *Essentials of Managerial Finance* (New York, New York: Holt, Rinehart and Winston, 1971).

$$\frac{\text{Net profit}}{\text{Equity}} \quad \text{or} \quad \frac{500{,}000}{3{,}400{,}000} = 14.7\%$$

Improper management of debt may result in higher interest expense, reduced profits, and, ultimately, lower return on equity. This further impacts the price-earnings ratio and therefore may adversely affect the cost of increasing equity.

8. *Return on assets* is a measure of the efficiency of asset management. Any increase in profits will improve this performance ratio. Proper debt management and reduced interest expense will improve profits and positively impact the return on assets. The ratio is:

$$\frac{\text{Net profit}}{\text{Assets}} \quad \text{or} \quad \frac{500{,}000}{16{,}032{,}000} = 3.1\%$$

9. *Cash flow*, the life blood of corporate activity, is the calculation of liquidity, measuring actual cash inflow and outflow. It differs from working capital, which deals strictly with current assets and liabilities, but ignores dividends, compensating balances, long-term asset investment, and so forth.

The calculation includes current corporate generated cash, investments, and financing arrangements. Future projections (pro forma cash flow) focuses on planned investments, external sources of funds, and debt repayment. The calculation is integral to the overall strategic planning process, measuring future capabilities against financial objectives. It is the foundation for determining future borrowings and debt issues relative to working capital needs, investments, paybacks, and growth. The most common calculating method is

Net profits + Depreciation = Accrued cash

This approach has three shortfalls.

a.   It fails to eliminate accrual accounting, thus delaying actual cash receipts and payments.
b.   It does not include cash outflows for dividends, principal repayment or noninterest-bearing deposits (compensating balances) maintained against lines of credit.
c.   It does not identify interim cash shortages or surpluses.

For an accurate picture of the cash position, actual cash collections are used as opposed to the sales figure, and cash purchases are substituted for the cost of goods sold. See Table 1–2.

Annualized cash flow is nebulous since it reflects the accumulated cash flow of the preceding 12 months, failing to identify monthly or period cash positions. Specifically, a year-end cash

TABLE 1–2
Cash Flow

	Sources of Cash
	Beginning cash
+	Cash collections
+	Loan proceeds
+	Fixed asset sale proceeds
	Total sources
	Uses of Cash
−	Cash purchases
−	Salaries
−	Interest
−	Taxes (net depreciation)
−	General operating expenses
	Total uses
	Discretionary Uses
−	New equipment purchased
−	Dividends
−	Investments
−	Debt principal payments
−	Compensating balances
	Ending cash

position fails to identify interim cash shortfalls that must be supplemented with bank debt. Further, a year-end cash deficit does not reflect period cash surpluses.

Pro forma cash flow must include the monthly position, revealing period surpluses and deficits. This is the foundation for determining external lines of credit, monthly interest expense, and the real cash position. Failure to accurately calculate the monthly cash flow may result in negotiating lines of credit that are not properly synchronized with cash needs. Excess credit lines further reduce cash since banks charge fees or require the deposit of noninterest-bearing cash balances supporting the credit.

The strategic planning process includes long-term cash flow projections, determining investments and paybacks. The net present value, or discounted cash flow, formula is applied in order to compare alternatives on a current cash basis. This measures different alternatives with various payback periods, on the same current dollar basis since future cash does not have the purchasing power of present cash.

The actual factor is usually the projected inflation rate, the expected cost of capital, or the internal rate of asset return. Without arguing the merits of these approaches, suffice to say that the approach compares apples with apples by viewing alternatives on the same scale.

It is suggested that a worst case–best case approach be employed since the factor selected will undoubtedly be influenced by numerous contingencies not immediately known. Naturally the longer the period, the more the ambiguities surrounding the assumptions. Also, periods may be influenced by various issues, which should be reflected by applying different net present value factors.

LONG-TERM VERSUS SHORT-TERM DEBT

Short-term debt is due within one year and long-term debt is payable over a longer period of time. Only that amount of long-term debt payable in the current period is shown under current liabilities.

Usually debt is structured in balance with the offsetting asset. Therefore short-term debt finances current assets and long-term debt funds long-term or fixed assets such as plant and equipment. To finance long-term assets with short-term debt can create a cash flow bind. Long-term debt has traditionally been funded by commercial banks, insurance companies, and the bond markets. Major changes in the investment and capital markets have resulted in shorter long-term debt maturities, to the point where insurance companies are offering short-term borrowing facilities, corresponding more closely with their sources and cost of funds.

The long-term markets have become increasingly unpredictable. This volatile interest rate environment has lead many companies to refinance maturing long-term debt with short-term borrowings while waiting for long-term rates to drop. The effect has been to reduce the current ratio and therefore to create a liquidity problem for borrowers and lenders. When government short-term debt is added to this already distorted economic picture, the result is high short-term rates. This is tantamount to increasing the demand for any commodity while holding the supply constant. The commodity's cost will increase in the short-run.

HEDGING PRACTICES

Money is a commodity and its value is the interest rate reflected by supply-and-demand considerations, albeit the volume of money is regulated through the open-market committee of the Federal Reserve. As a commmodity, money is to a corporate borrower as grain is to a rancher or soybeans to a farmer, and the cost of the commodity may be hedged. A hedge is a protection against price movement, and in theory, it locks in the value of the commodity, preventing movements either way. In practice, however, most hedges may be undone for a price. This price is reflected by the difference of the prevailing market price of the commodity compared to the price when the hedge was effected.

The primary purpose of the hedge is to lock in a known price. In a rising grain market the cattle feeder wishes to freeze the price of grain in order to calculate the known costs of raising cattle. If cattle are previously contracted at a set price, grain fluctuations will materially affect his profit or loss. If grain drops in price, his profits will increase; if grain cost increases, it may ruin his business. Since it is impossible to have all the necessary information in a timely fashion to determine these moves, the farmer elects to freeze the price with a hedge and eliminate the guessing. The farmer may indeed lock out larger profits, but he also eliminates higher feed costs and he can accurately calculate total cattle costs against which to negotiate a sales contract.

A farmer who has no hedge is a full and unprotected speculator whose cost of feed is out of his control and totally influenced by market vagaries. This position is identical to a person speculating in the futures market, where enormous fortunes are made and lost in relatively short periods.

The corporate borrower is in the same position as the cattle feeder, since money is a commodity with wide and often unpredictable price (interest rate) fluctuations. If the borrower does not hedge, it is a full and unprotected speculator with an exposed position subject to market vagaries. When the corporation hedges this open position, it is freezing the net interest rate and preventing increases or decreases. Again, it is noted that if an obvious downward trend appears, the hedger may unlock its position for a price—the difference between the prevailing cash–spot price and the original price.

Like the rancher, the corporation may receive a large guaranteed order for its product. Realizing certain profit criteria, the company does not wish to reduce its return through volatile and unpredictable interest rate *commodity* fluctuations. Therefore, when the company plans future borrowing to build products, it enters a hedge to protect its otherwise exposed position. It may now calculate its costs of producing the goods and is positioned to negotiate the contract. In essence, by locking in costs, the company has guaranteed its profit on the sale.

There are numerous hedging procedures, but we will focus on the futures market. It is not our intent to delve into the mechanics of futures market in this text, although the recently established conceptual framework is critical for short-term debt.

Further examination of this topic is found in Edward Schwarz's book *How to Use Interest Rate Futures Contracts* (Homewood, Illinois: Dow Jones-Irwin, 1979).

Financial futures were established in the 70s and in 1981 they accounted for approximately 29 percent of all futures trading. The market is basically composed of two players, hedgers avoiding risk by protecting an open and volatile commodity position and speculators who are risk-seekers attempting to make a profit. Other intermediary participants include banks, traders, and brokerage houses who facilitate the hedge.

To introduce the topic, we refer to our farmer who is a hedger controlling feed costs. He knows his production costs, such as monthly mortgage, water, veterinarian, labor, transportation, and expected profit. His remaining unknown is feed cost. This is most critical, since his business is converting feed into beef weight. Assuming the cattle rancher has a contract to deliver cattle at a set price per pound and assuming he is aware of all the costs associated with raising cattle, the remaining variable that may influence his profit is the cost of feed.

If feed increases, it may result in a loss for the rancher. Conversely, if feed drops, the farmer may realize a greater profit. The farmer is not able to accurately predict the price movements and elects to hedge his open and exposed commodity position covering feed. This will theoretically eliminate any windfall gains, resulting in reduced feed costs while ensuring that increases in feed costs will not adversely affect his profits.

The farmer calculates the expected volume of feed required to fatten the cattle. He hedges his open feed position in the futures market and buys grain futures contracts, approximating the tonnage required to fatten the cattle with contract maturities corresponding to his actual grain purchase dates.

The market provides two avenues for clearing or settling the futures contracts:

1. The rancher may actually take delivery of the commodity covered by the futures contract.
2. The rancher may sell the contract back to the futures market.

The futures contracts are legal and binding and, unless offet by an opposite contract to sell, the grain will be delivered to the rancher. Approximately 98 percent of all futures contracts are offset by selling the contract back to the market, and delivery does not take place. The rancher certainly does not want to take delivery of grain purchased in the futures market, since he will pay shipping and insurance charges that are higher than buying grain locally.

The majority of ranchers hedge to prevent price movements of commodities needed at a future date. Gains or losses in the futures market will be offset by opposite moves in the cash–spot market price when the commodity is purchased locally. In the case of the rancher, if grain prices rise the farmer will earn a profit on the futures trade reflected by the purchase price of the futures contract minus the sale price of the contract. If he bought grain at $2.50 per volume and grain rose to $2.60 per volume, he earns 10 cents per volume on the futures trade. Since the $2.60 price reflects the prevailing grain cost, the gains on the futures contracts will offset higher actual feed costs and the net effect is zero. The following illustrates the offsetting transactions of delivered grain and futures contracts.

Rising Grain Market

Day 1	Day 180	Change
Sell cattle with expected feed cost of $2.50	Buy grain at $2.60	− .10
Buy grain futures at $2.50	Sell grain futures at $2.60	+ .10
Net change		0

In this case, grain prices rose. If the rancher did not hedge, his costs would increase by 10 cents. Since he hedged, he made 10 cents on the futures contract, offsetting his feed cost, which rose 10 cents, preserving his expected profits.

If grain prices dropped 10 cents, the rancher would lose 10 cents in the futures trade, but his actual feed cost would decline by 10 cents as shown below. In practice, the futures and cash–spot delivery prices are usually not identical, but the trend or direction of move is the same.

Declining Grain Market

Day 1	Day 180	Change
Sell cattle with expected feed cost of $2.50	Buy grain at $2.40	+ .10
Buy grain futures at $2.50	Sell grain futures at $2.40	− .10
Net change		0

If the rancher is fully confident that grain prices will fall, he may sell his futures contract back to the market before maturity and enjoy lower feed costs. He will lose an amount equal to the difference in the purchase price of the futures contract and the lower price at which he sells the contract back to the market.

Theoretically, the lower grain costs will more than offset his loss in the futures market. If he prematurely liquidates the futures contract he has an open and fully speculative position, and any increase in grain will reduce his expected profits.

This situation is identical to the corporation with a contract to deliver its product at a specified price at some future date. The corporation calculates all variable and fixed costs associated with manufacturing the item and negotiates a final sales price. However, unlike farmers, most corporations are unaware of the mechanics of hedging their cost of money, a volatile commodity.

Like the farmer, the corporation wishes to control interest rates in order to properly calculate all costs of production. Also, if the corporation does not hedge, it is a full and unprotected speculator with an exposed position subject to market changes.

The corporation therefore calculates its borrowing needs and buys futures contracts, approximating the amount of funds to be borrowed and the time of borrowing these funds. It is noted that not all borrowing alternatives have identical futures contracts. If the corporation's borrowings are tied to the prime rate, there is not a corresponding prime futures market. Therefore a complementary market, such as commercial paper futures or treasury bill futures, is used for hedging the prime rate. If the corporation's borrowings are directly related to the certificate of deposit or treasury bill rate, there is a direct hedging market. Eurodollars and commercial paper may be directly hedged in the futures market. The agribusiness community is faced with the same problem; for example, a tallow renderer hedges in the lard futures market. What is important is that the complementary futures contract moves in the same direction and with the same economic influences as the commodity hedged.

As the corporation borrows, meeting production requirements, it sells corresponding futures contracts purchased earlier. If the interest rate increases, the corporation will realize a gain on the futures contracts and a loss in its borrowing rate. The two rates will offset each other and the theoretical net change for the corporation will be zero. If the rate falls, the corporation will lose on the futures contract but gain by reduced borrowing costs. The following table indentifies this relationship.

In the event rates decrease, the corporation may prematurely liquidate its hedge by selling its futures contract back to the market. It will sustain a loss equal to the original futures price and the cash–spot liquidation price represented by its deposited margin with its broker.

It is critical to note that once the corporation prematurely liquidates the contract in order to gain with falling rates, it is again

Interest Rates Increase

Day 1	Day 180	Change
Sell product with expected interest rate of 16%	Borrow funds at 18%	− 2%
Buy interest futures at 16%	Sell interest futures at 18%	+ 2%
Net change		0

Interest Rates Decrease

Day 1	Day 180	Change
Sell product with expected interest rate of 16%	Borrow funds at 14%	+ 2%
Buy interest futures at 16%	Sell interest futures at 14%	− 2%
Net change		0

fully exposed and a rate rebound could easily offset gains. In this example, to prematurely liquidate the interest rate contract circumvents the entire purpose of entering the market initially.

Philosophy

This leads us to the most critical aspect of hedging: a corporate policy must be clearly expressed with the purpose and procedures strictly adhered to and routinely reviewed. It is not our position in this text to discuss the corporate policy on hedging, since each situation is different; but the highest level of the corporation must be apprised, must understand, and must approve the purpose and procedures of hedging. At least one person should be responsible for executing and recording contracts and daily positions in order to centralize control and minimize risk. Money is a commodity, an "inventory" item, which requires the same astute management and control as any other inventory. Failure to exercise this control may have serious consequences.

We are reminded of a Fortune 500 company which did not follow these critical guidelines. The company had $70 million in future treasury bills hedging $70 million in expected borrowings. An eager assistant treasurer, watching rates decline, prematurely liquidated the contracts, anticipating gains with reduced borrowing costs. The rates increased from 16 percent to 17.25 percent. The result was a 1.25 percent annual rate change, which resulted in a $874,000 loss to the company.

The real problem was not the assistant treasurer; it was the lack of corporate policy authorizing his conduct. He was without guidance. The amount of a commodity to be hedged is discretionary. Some companies hedge the entire risk; others calculate a percentage of risk. It is recommended that parameters be set by senior management, with some flexibility left to the actual traders. The traders deal with day-to-day data which influences their hedging posture. These data are available from numerous sources: government publications, the *Commodity Year Book*, private econometric firms, and brokerage houses. Again, no one person or entity has all the influencing information on a timely basis to execute contracts with 100 percent certainty of the trends. The best position is to have ready access to reliable data against which one calculates probabilities and executes accordingly within prescribed policy limits.

The process of hedging has its associated costs. Basically, the costs are the fee paid the brokerage house for executing contracts and the opportunity cost of margin accounts. The margin account is a percentage of the commodity's prevailing cash–spot value. Therefore a $1 million contract may require a $50,000 deposit with the broker, who in turn pledges this to the futures market. Daily market price changes increase or decrease the margin requirement. The daily requirement equals the difference between the original contract price and the prevailing cash–spot market price.

The purpose of the margin is to cover potential default positions. In the event of a default, the value of the cash commodity plus the margin account equals the original price, maintaining the market's financial integrity. The hedger's risk is the financial integrity of the Commodity Clearing Corporation, which represents the other side of the contract and has never defaulted.

A corporation may arrange for a standby letter of credit covering changes in the original market price. This reduces the administrative burdens and potentially lowers the cost to the corporation. The letter of credit insures the broker that in the event of default the bank will pay for the margin differences. In essence, the margin risk is shifted to the bank, which presumably weighs the credit risk of its client's ability to perform. The letter of credit price ranges from .25 to 1.50 percent per annum, depending on the creditworthiness of the borrower and the overall banking relationship. In any event, when interest rates are in the middle to high teens, this is an attractive alternative compared to maintaining cash margins which sacrifices interest income.

In summary, the critical issues are understanding when the corporation is hedging or speculating and awareness of the procedures for limiting risk. Most corporations, including banks, are unknowingly speculating when they do not hedge interest rate fluctuations. The fact that money is a volatile commodity whose changes may cause financial collapse, is exemplified by the faltering savings and loan industry, where long-term mortgage income is not sufficient to cover current borrowing costs.

Although there have been regulatory obstacles for S&Ls participating in the futures market, the basic problem has been a general lack of knowledge and recognition that money is a commodity inventory item just as cattle is a commodity inventory item to a rancher.

Our examples have been oversimplified by reflecting a true hedge where both the actual cash commodity and futures hedge have identical changes offsetting each other. A 100 percent pure hedge is not usually possible. Before participating in hedging activities, the corporate treasurer should become familiar with the procedures and mechanics of the market. Our purpose is to introduce the reader to the concept to improve overall management of short-term debt.

CHAPTER TWO

CONVENTIONAL

LOANS

Short-term conventional loans are funds provided by institutions (banks and insurance companies) to supplement corporate working capital. The institution is an intermediary or financial conduit through which funds are passed and loaned to corporate borrowers under prearranged terms and conditions. The debt is evidenced by a note.

The bank solicits deposits and the depositor loans money to the bank. These funds for the bank are tantamount to an inventory item for a production concern. Through the bank's corporate loan officers, these deposits are loaned to corporate borrowers.

Bank Note

Approval_____   Group_____

$_____   No._____   Due_____

Chicago, Illinois,_____

_____ after date, the undersigned, for value received, promises to pay to the order of
National Bank and Trust Company of Chicago, at its office in Chicago, Illinois,

_____DOLLARS

with interest thereon at the rate of _____ per cent per annum from date until paid. All interest shall be computed for the actual number of days elapsed on the basis of a year consisting of 360 days.

_____

_____

Address_____   _____

Presumably the interest paid the depositor is less than the interest paid the bank by corporate borrowers. The interest rate difference represents the bank's gross profit.

In theory, the system efficiently allocates excess cash from depositors to creditworthy entities requiring cash. The depositor is freed from the technical or financial responsibilities of determining the corporate borrower's ability or intent to repay the loan. The depositor's risk, then, is the creditworthiness of the bank which, in most cases, is supported by insurance provided by the Federal Deposit Insurance Corporation (FDIC) up to $100,000.

MECHANICS

Bank Selection

Bank selection is a critical first step and should take into consideration many issues aside from the actual lending of funds, which all banks do. Notwithstanding that the rate charged is a critical factor, the banking industry is product-oriented and should be judged accordingly. The key issue is how well it delivers and maintains its product. This is what differentiates one money vendor from another. In most cases, the corporate client's primary contact is the bank's corporate calling officer and not the chief executive officer. For this reason the following check list is suggested for gauging the bankers' performance.

1. *Is the banker astute and an active financial participant with the treasurer?* The treasurer should expect financial counseling and a reliable stream of timely data with which to make decisions. Unique financing techniques, procedures, and opportunities should be provided by the banker. A candid two-way communication is essential for an efficient, balanced relationship. The relationships should be complemented with at least two sessions to discuss the corporation's semiannual and year-end performance. This will provide the banker with corporate and industrial insight with which to better serve the client and understand the risks.

2. *Does the banker have a sound understanding of bank products available for corporate use?* Most banks provide a wide variety of products, such as trust and pension services, cash management, and international services. The banker should be the corporate liaison and plug the company into these products when appropriate. The corporate treasurer should not be shuttled from banker to banker in an effort to solve a problem, as often happens because the banker simply does not understand the related services. This results in a breakdown in communications and reduces corporate-bank continuity.

3. *Does the banker demonstrate insight into the unique corporate and industry characteristics?* In order to provide proper and timely information, the banker must be well schooled on the industry. This insight is most critical during difficult financial times, but lack of such knowledge leads to misunderstandings and improperly structured credits.

4. *Does the banker have decision-making authority?* The corporation should be confident that discussions with the banker will be relayed with authority. Although most banks have a credit-approving group or committee, the corporate treasurer should be confident that the individual banker will adequately represent the company before the credit committee.

5. *Does the banker properly represent the client's interest to the bank?* The above issues ultimately lead to this critical point. Without a solid rapport, good communications, product knowledge, industry insight, and authority, the banker falls short of properly representing the company.

This point often eludes bankers. Understandably, bankers are eager to represent their employers, but their representation falls short when they fail to understand and express the needs of the client. This equilibrium, however, is difficult to achieve. A common corporate complaint is that the bankers do not understand the industry and operating environment. Without this knowledge, bad loans are made or improperly structured, which may have devastating affects for the client and the bank.

The average banker works in a highly political environment through association with the volatile and passionate commodity of money. The industry is affected by regulations, stockholders, and depositors. Further, most calling officers are overburdened with a variety of corporate clients all clamoring for attention. Corporate indulgence therefore is required. We are reminded of a number of last-minute loan requests by major multinational corporations without regard for the banker. After many calls on a major Chicago corporation, the banker received a call on Friday at 2 P.M. The corporate treasurer, who hardly paid attention to the previous efforts of the banker, stated: "Recognizing your enthusiasm to enter our $3.5 billion credit picture, we have a $150 million loan request for disbursement on Monday at 9 A.M. to Angola. And we will not guarantee the credit."

Financial discretion is certainly in order for corporate treasurers, but far too often treasurers do not provide critical information in a timely and proper manner. This precludes the banker from analyzing and sponsoring the credit and creates an unhealthy relationship.

A Detroit corporate treasurer has a grotesque picture over his credenza in a well-appointed office. The picture is a detailed pencil etching of a witch with the words "Your Friendly Banker." Although humorous, this is not the recommended method for establishing harmony with the source of funds. The banker-client relationship is a two-way street requiring good communications and mutual understanding.

In selecting a bank, the corporate treasurer should be mindful of the bank's strengths. There are 14,000 banks in the United States, each with its own strengths. There are also political considerations. A company located in Corinth, Mississippi, with international banking requirements, should not choose a money center bank at the expense of a regional or local bank. These banks are critical to the financial health of the community, and corporate patronage is important. Therefore it is recommended that the corporate banking needs be assessed by the company and its banker. Services not provided by the local bank may then be referred to the appropriate bank that has corresponding financial arrangements with local banks.

It is a sound policy to have at least two banks. This ensures a competitive environment and diversifies the corporate source of funds. Most companies have multiple sources of raw material to ensure a steady and reliable flow of inventory and to encourage competitive pricing. This same principle applies to money vendors. Some corporations carry this policy too far, with an unnecessary array of banks, diluting communications with overdiversification. Further, by inviting more banks into a credit, the borrower is unnecessarily encouraging increasing scrutiny by the banks. Where five or more banks are involved, a lead or agent bank should be selected to serve as a representative of the banking group in negotiations and account management. This will improve communications and reduce repetition.

In summary, the decision-making process in bank selection should focus on the corporate needs, quality of bank services, financial diversification, and good communication.

In order to understand the banker's view of the world, we will explore some of the procedures and documents required for a loan approval. *The loan application*, prepared by the banker, is the focal point for the credit approval. It should be a well-written and concise (without sacrifice of content) exposé of the client. Although most banks have their own style for this report, there are critical points which must always be included. The application conveys a clear credit picture of the borrower to a reader who is presumed to be totally unfamiliar with the company. The credit-approving officers need to know that the borrower has the intent and capability to repay the loan.

The basic areas to be covered by the application are shown in Appendix One, a fictitious loan application. Fundamentally, the banker must identify the loan purpose and amount, interest rate, fees or balance requirements or understanding, security, repayment schedule, sources of repayment, and critical issues for the company affecting repayment.

The body of the application will describe the legal corporate structure, brief corporate history, banking history, financial analysis, marketing, competition, bank profit analysis for the credit, the nature and documentation covering security, and other probable banking services. The "critical issues" section is the most important part of the application. Without understanding the company, industry, and operating environment, the banker can not successfully complete this section. Every company has four or five major obstacles to its success; for example, the energy crisis for the auto industry; a new high-tech product entry for a computer manufacturer; or, more recently, the impact of high interest rates.

In most cases, the corporate treasurer will find critical-issues discussions insightful. They show that the banker is interested in the company and the industry. They force the corporate officers to face sometimes ambiguous issues and plan accordingly. Critical to strategic planning, the process serves to distinguish problems from symptoms.

Since a banker's success is based in part on the ability to generate loan and service revenues, there is a human tendency not to identify critical issues that may result in a loan declination. However, these issues exist, whether recognized or not, in the loan application. By identifying these areas, the banker shows perception and prevents problems. The credit should incorporate "what if" clauses identifying the company's and bank's response to certain contingencies affecting the company and, therefore, the loan repayment.

The basic rules covering loan applications are to make it clear and concise and allow it to stand on its own without further explanation. This is a difficult proposition and the new banker may expect many arduous hours honing writing skills.

Credit Analysis

This analysis focuses on the numbers and may be performed by the calling officer or a credit department. In any event, the calling officer should be intimately involved and should understand the analysis procedures and outcome.

It should be noted that where the analysis is performed by the calling officer other critical tasks such as business development may be sacrificed. On the other hand, when a credit department analyzes the company, there may be a tendency for the calling officer to avoid financial insight, since the analytical discipline has been removed. When this occurs, the credit risks increase. In sum, the banker is failing the client and the bank.

The actual *analysis* consists of three steps. The first is to display key financial information covering the balance sheet, income statement, working capital, and net worth in bank format. Appendix Two is a good representation of the layout. For the most part, this procedure is simply transferring data from the corporate-provided and CPA-prepared statements to the bank's format. Most banks prefer a five-year history to view corporate performance in various economic conditions. The second step is to collect industry data to permit comparisons. The third step is to perform various ratio calculations and note the narrative results.

For example, if a company's debt-to-equity ratio for five years is 2 to 1, 2.5 to 1, 2.7 to 1, 3.0 to 1, and 3.3 to 1, the narrative would reveal a 33 percent debt-to-equity increase over five years. However, this is insufficient unless the reader understands the change. Did debt simply increase, and why? Or did debt remain stable while declining profits eroded net worth, increasing the ratio? The ratio by itself is insufficient.

If the financial analysis is performed by the credit department, the calling officer should arrange to meet and thoroughly discuss the analysis with the credit technician. Following the meeting, the officer should append any insight he has that is proprietary and impacts the analysis. The completed analysis is then incorporated in the loan application and is ready for the credit decision process. The actual approval process may be formal, before a credit committee, or less restrictive, requiring the signatures of authorized officers. In any event, the first signature is that of the calling officer sponsoring the credit.

Negotiations

This is the process of agreeing on the terms and conditions set forth by the bank to the company. It may be a simple task or quite cumbersome, involving contractual covenants, extensive documentation, provisions for monitoring performance, and collateral. Most important, the result must fit two needs: it must be bankable, and the company must be able to live with the terms. Violation of either could certainly lead to conflict requiring additional work. The rule appears fundamental but it is often violated.

Attorneys may or may not be involved in the negotiations, but in most cases, they should not be. Attorneys are no substitute for a sound, well-structured loan. The negotiations should be directly between the client and the banker; for it is the banker who is called on the carpet for a bad loan, not the attorney.

We are reminded of a corporate treasurer of a major food processing company who was constantly flanked by his corporate attorney. It created confusion for the bankers who were unsure who they were negotiating with or who was the decision maker.

In a more dramatic case, 100 bankers met in New York with their attorneys to discuss the financing of a troubled U.S. automobile manufacturer. The discussions dragged on for days, with attorneys eagerly engaging in floor debate. The corporate treasurer requested the attorneys to leave the negotiation room, and the various issues were resolved in hours. This is not to dilute the importance of attorneys but to put their role into perspective.

Loan Agreement

The loan agreement reflects the bank's commitment to supply funds under specified terms and conditions as negotiated. This agreement may be a simple one-page commitment or an extensive contractual agreement.

This document is the reference by which the creditor and bank will live. It should be clear, concise, and direct. There is no room in this document or the loan application for ambiguity. It must reflect the verbal agreements, implied and stated. The agreement should focus on the particular performance expectations. The more common covenants focus on minimal working capital, current ratio and, the debt-equity ratio, with expansion where necessary. These goals must be clearly understood and achievable, since failure to comply may result in default under the agreement and demand for repayment.

An example of an inappropriate covenant was witnessed when a major money center bank required a debt-equity ratio not exceeding 3 to 1 for a major soybean processor. Surprisingly, the company did not contest the ratio and violated the covenant when its peak purchase period for soybeans required larger debt. The ratio soon exceeded 3 to 1, and all parties returned to the negotiating table.

Since the annual supply of soybeans was purchased during the fall harvest period with bank debt, the renegotiated covenant properly reflected this and default was avoided. Suffice to say that initial discussions should have focused on this issue at the outset, avoiding renegotiating the loan agreement.

Loan agreements should encourage performance. In the case where a bank requires collateral, the agreement should specify triggers for release of the security. Specifically, if the borrower meets certain financial tests for consecutive periods, then collateral release should be considered. To collateralize a loan simply to secure the bank is insufficient; the bank must justify its position, and creative solutions may be incorporated in the loan agreement.

A typical loan agreement is included in Appendix Three for review.

Drawdown

The actual disbursement of funds should be synchronized with the corporate requirements. The presentation of a note where multiple drawings will take place may physically be cumbersome. This is especially true when the lender and borrower are in different locations. A master, or grid note is often the solution, where the customer signs a note covering the entire credit amount at the outset. This way the lender's position is covered and multiple disbursements are made by telephone request.

Naturally, these requests must be made in a timely fashion. Most banks require that requests be received before 11 AM to allow for the funds to be wired through the Federal Reserve system. If a Chicago-based borrower requests funds from a San Francisco bank, the funds will electronically be transferred through four entities. The San Francisco lender will initially transfer funds to the San Francisco 12th district Federal Reserve Bank. The San Francisco Federal Reserve will then credit the account of its correspondent and transfer funds to the 7th district Federal Reserve in Chicago. The Chicago Federal Reserve will transfer funds to the borrower's Chicago bank, which finally credits the borrower's account.

Although the physical process is extremely fast, given modern electronics, two delays exist. The most obvious is the 2-hour time difference between San Francisco and Chicago. The second delay is the time required to physically enter the transfer. Since billions of dollars are transferred daily, backlogs exist.

On some occasions the lending bank may directly wire funds to the borrower's bank. This may occur if the borrower's bank maintains a corresponding account with the lending bank. In this case the lending bank, through coded telex, directly wires the borrower's local bank verifying that X dollars were deposited in the borrower's bank account for credit to the borrower's account.

Prepayment

Conventional loans do not have prepayment restrictions. Other fixed-term borrowings, like acceptances, are not readily prepayable without penalty. This flexibility may be important to the borrower and should be taken into consideration when negotiating the credit terms.

CHARACTERISTICS

A conventional loan is price-related to the prime rate of the bank and is usually contractually committed for a period of one year, subject to negotiated terms and conditions. The purpose is to supplement working capital and, more specifically, to finance cash flow shortfalls. The rate is tied to the changing prime rate.

The term *line of credit* refers to the maximum amount of the credit and implies a contractual agreement between the borrower and lender. These credits are usually on a revolving basis, allowing the amount to fluctuate, depending on the need, but not to exceed the stated ceiling. This offers the borrower the advantage of using only what is needed as opposed to borrowing the full amount when only a fraction of the availability is required. Therefore the actual outstandings revolve, depending on the need.

The line may be on an advised or guidance basis. An advised line is the amount of credit the company is told it may use, while a guidance line includes the amount advised plus additional credit the bank may be willing to extend if certain contingencies are realized. The purpose of the guidance line is to administratively review the total potential credit at the outset, anticipating expanding needs. The process minimizes credit approval time and allows for immediate response to interim credit needs.

An example will amplify the point. A major high-tech electronics manufacturer requested a $50 million revolving line of credit. The bank, anticipating possible increased usage, approved a $70 million line on a *guidance* basis and *advised* the company of the $50 million request. At a later date, after fully utilizing the $50 million credit, the electronics company requested an additional $12 million. The bank immediately disbursed funds since the total $70 million had been approved, based on the creditworthiness of the company.

One might ask why the company failed to request the larger amount in the first place. This is often a result of unforeseen contingencies, highly confidential strategies, or a company's desire not to pay bank fees or balances for a larger line of credit until actually needed. Banks often charge fees for their commitment, ranging from 1/8 percent to 1/2 percent, depending on the creditworthiness and length of commitment. Therefore, if the electronics company realized it needed $50 million for 10 months and $12 million additional for only the last 2 months, it might only request $50 million, against which it would pay a 1/8 percent commitment fee for 10 months and 1/8 percent for $62 million for the last two months as opposed to 1/8 percent on $62 million for 12 months.

There are risks associated with the strategy of intentionally delaying a credit request: The bank may not be able to deliver under restricted money conditions. When the company pays a commitment fee, it is giving consideration to the bank for providing funds irrespective of the money supply. This is tantamount to paying a vendor for his promise to deliver a certain amount of components over a year's time. The vendor establishes production schedules and sacrifices other business in order to meet the contracted supply order. The same holds true for the money vendors who prearrange sources of funds to meet corporate requirements.

Cost of Funds

The foundation of the prime rate is the aggregate or melded cost of bank funds. Specifically, the bank has access to "0" cost funds covering noninterest-bearing deposits and other sources with differing costs. These include borrowings from the Federal Reserve, federal funds, the bank's issuance of commercial paper, and various certificates of deposit.

These rates are weighted according to the amount of each source, to identify an average weighted or melded or blended cost of funds given various maturities. The bank then adds approximately 2–2.5 percent to cover the cost of processing, return on asset objectives, and perceived yield curves. The total is the bank's base rate, which is adjusted to the prevailing prime because of the competitive environment.

The total borrowing rate includes a factor reflecting the bank's risk perception. This is a nebulous area with many inconsistencies, depending on the individual banker's perception and ability to measure risk, which is a vague area. Therefore, assuming two institutions have identical costs and yield curves, the borrowing rate differs, subject-to-risk perception.

We are aware of four major banks bidding on a $20 million line of credit for a cattle feeder. The rates vary from prime to prime plus 1 percent per annum. Assuming the associated costs are similar for the banks, the 1 percent difference must be attributed to their differing risk perception and experience with the industry. Indeed, our involvement with the negotiations revealed that the banker offering prime is most insightful and experienced in the industry, while his competitor offering prime plus 1 percent does not have the same comfort level or experience. In this case, the borrower not only wants his banker to be aware of the unique characteristics of the industry, but he will also save $200,000 annually in interest expense at prime versus prime plus 1 percent.

The definition of interest is the cost of funds plus yield expectations plus the risk factor. Since there is a direct relationship between the risk factor and the rate, it is known that the greater the risk the higher the rate. During periods of economic stress, this formula has a tendency to backfire and become a Catch-22.

Specifically, smaller companies with marginal capital assume a larger absolute burden for higher interest costs, given the above definition. This not only hinders a company's success but may reduce or eliminate the company's ability to repay the bank. The bank must write off the loan, which will effectively reduce performance. Therefore the bank's definition of risk may result in a loan loss or a no-win situation.

We are aware of a company that defaulted on a $6 million loan when the prime was 20 percent. The risk definition adjusted the rate to 23 percent per annum. The company's financial advisors presented the bank with cash flow projections with differing interest rates. Although all agreed the company's cash flow breakeven point was at 19.5 percent interest cost, the bank, in light of its interest rate definition and risk perception, refused to lower the rate. There was no question that the bank was providing loans to major corporations below 19.5 percent, so we assume that the bank's cost of funds and expenses were covered at 19.5 percent. However, because of the interest rate definition relative to risk, the bank did not lower the rate. In the final chapter, the company folded and asset liquidation was 25 percent of loan outstandings. The bank wrote off $4.5 million. Flexibility may have been the optimal answer for both the company and bank.

We would be remiss in not carrying this point to conclusion. Given that banks establish a minimum return on asset objectives, critical to their performance and therefore their stockholders' interest, it may be concluded that smaller companies pay disproportionate rates offsetting lower rates paid by major corporations. This is to say that, in the face of competition, banks will provide subprime loans to major corporations. If these loans fail to meet the return on asset objectives, then higher rates charged smaller companies may offset the lower rates, and the average return is closer to the bank's return objectives. In other words, smaller high risk companies subsidize larger creditworthy concerns through the definition of interest relative to risk.

The subprime loan became a standard in 1982 for the strongest corporate borrowers. The rate is fixed for 30-day increments and is tied to CDs, bank-issued commercial paper, and other short-term, fixed rate bank debt instruments. Since these loans provide less than the desired return on assets and equity objectives established by the bank, other investments are affected. The bank has two fundamental options: reduce assets or increase profits.

Some banks are replacing branches with automatic teller machines for transacting routine business. This reduces assets and partially offsets the impact of subprime loans. In some cases, banks are increasing profits by lending to higher-risk borrowers. The problem with this approach is that it weakens the bank's loan portfolio and possibly increases loan losses. These losses are difficult to recoup with the low-yielding, higher-quality, subprime loans.

The interest rate calculation, excluding fees or balances, is as follows:

$$\frac{\text{Principal} \times \text{Rate} \times \text{Days outstanding}}{360} = \text{Interest}$$

The banking industry has historically used 360 in the denominator to represent a bank year. Naturally, increasing the denominator to 365 would reduce the interest cost. However, the industry's argument in favor of a 360-day figure is that it is consistent with its method for calculating interest for depositors. To emphasize the difference between a 360- and 365-day factor, consider the following comparison in which a company borrows $20 million for 90 days at 15 percent:

$$\frac{\$20,000,000 \times 15\% \times 90 \text{ days}}{360 \text{ days}} = \$750,000 \text{ Interest}$$

$$\frac{\$20,000,000 \times 15\% \times 90 \text{ days}}{365 \text{ days}} = \$739,726 \text{ Interest}$$

For the 360-day factor the interest expense is $750,000 compared to the 365-day rate of $739,726—a difference of $10,274 for the added cost of five days' interest charged on an annualized basis.

Conventional loans often include a compensating balance requirement. The company must maintain a prescribed noninterest-bearing deposit with the bank, providing the bank with a zero cost of funds, which are then loaned to a second borrower at the prevailing rates. Since the company does not earn interest, it incurs an opportunity cost for not having access to the cash deposit. There are two general approaches for calculating this cost. The first is by way of the company's internal rate of return. Specifically, the opportunity cost is that amount that could have been earned by corporate activity or a return on assets (profit ÷ assets). The theory is that if the company had access to the cash deposit, it would be applied to assets which would generate certain profits.

The second approach for measuring opportunity cost is the prevailing certificate of deposit rate covering deposits over a certain term. Specifically, this calculation quantifies the interest lost, resulting from the noninterest-bearing nature of the compensating balances.

If the prevailing certificate of deposit rate is 8 percent for one year and the company is required to maintain 10 percent of the committed credit line in compensating balances, the opportunity cost is calculated as follows:

10% Balances × Credit line × 8% CD rate = Cost

If the company's credit line is $10 million, the opportunity cost will be $80,000 per annum. If the company preferred to pay an equivalent fee for the commitment as opposed to maintaining balances, given cash flow considerations, the fee would approximate $80,000. In order to calculate the marginal percentage cost for the company's borrowings, we need to know what the average borrowings will be over the year. Since the balances are paid against the $10 million commitment irrespective of line usage, there is an incentive to maximize the $80,000 opportunity cost by fully utilizing the credit line. Again, we refer to the importance of accurately forecasting cash flow to avoid maintaining excess balances, which are costly.

To calculate the effective cost of borrowing when maintaining balances against the loan commitment irrespective of credit usage, the calculation is:

1. % Balances × Credit line × CD rate = Cost

    or

    10% × $10,000,000 × 8% = $80,000

2. Prime + Spread + $\left(\dfrac{\text{Opportunity cost}}{\text{Credit line}} \times \dfrac{1}{\text{Usage}} \right)$ = Rate

   12% + 1% + $\left(\dfrac{\$80,000}{\$10,000,000} \times \dfrac{1}{50\%} \right)$ = Rate

   13% + 1.6% = 14.6% per annum

This calculation is critical, since it enables the treasurer to effectively compare borrowing costs with alternatives and to more effectively manage the short-term debt position.

Our experience reveals that corporate treasurers are not consistent in calculating the true all-in cost of funds. Without this calculation the treasurer is blinded from more attractive alternatives. By manipulating the usage percentage, the all-in rate varies. The lower the usage the higher the rate, and vice versa. At 30 percent line utilization, the total cost is 15.42 percent per annum, while 100 percent utilization is 13.8 percent per annum. This stems from the balances being maintained against the commitment irrespective of usage.

Balances maintained against usage as opposed to the commitment, provide flexibility for the company; it pays for what is actually utilized. This is a more efficient application of balances and is calculated as follows:

1. % Balances × (Average usage × Credit line) × CD rate = Cost

   10% × (% Usage × Line) × 8% =

   10% × (50% × $10,000,000) × 8% =

   10% × $5,000,000 × 8% = $40,000

2. Prime + Spread + $\dfrac{\text{Opportunity cost}}{\text{Average usage}}$ = Rate

   12% + 1% + $\dfrac{40,000}{5,000,000}$ = 13.8

The total rate is predicated on a usage variable but is not based on the commitment.

In some cases a combination of balances is used where the firm maintains balances on the commitment and usage. These balances may be converted to a prevailing fee paid the bank as a function of the prevailing certificate rate or a bank's melded cost of funds, referred to as the intrabank rate.

More recently, banks are offering matched funding where the rate and time are fixed on a short-term basis. These funds are usually available in multiples of $1 million. As opposed to blending the bank's weighted average cost of funds, the lender sources a specific amount from an institutional depositor and quotes a rate competitive with investment alternatives available to the depositor. The bank adds a risk assessment factor plus a return on assets spread and quotes an all-in, or total rate, to the borrower.

The critical issue in matched funding is that the term for the borrower is matched with the term from the depositor and the rate is fixed in relation to the rate the bank pays the depositor. The matched funding loan may or may not require balances, and terms usually range up to 180 days.

We see advantages and disadvantages in using this instrument. In a rising interest environment, the fixed rate certainly reduces interest expense compared to a floating rate. Conversely, use of a fixed-rate note in a declining rate environment will lock in the high rate when prime is falling. Also, the borrower usually may not prepay matched funded loans, since the bank has contracted with the depositor for a specific amount, rate, and time.

The availability of the fixed and floating rate options will significantly increase control of interest expense in a volatile rate environment.

Table 2–1 identifies the 9-year cost history for corporate alternatives. The incremental components will be explained in the following chapters. What is significant is that the prime related borrowings were more expensive than alternatives available to the corporation. The cost differences averaged from 1 percent to 2 percent below prime borrowings and occasionally reached as much as 3 percent in favor of commercial paper or bankers' acceptances. This converts to a $30,000 savings per year covering $1 million dollars of debt.

As the prime changes, so will the rate to the company. This is a two-edged sword for the company while effectively hedging the bank's money inventory. We will explore this point in face of a rising prime rate and a declining rate. In any case, the bank is effectively passing its volatile cost of funds on to the borrower. This is a hedge for the bank, preventing it from losing money if rates are rising and precluding it from earning disproportionate profits in a falling rate environment.

For the company, the floating rate works to its favor when the base rate (average bank cost of funds) is dropping. As this rate declines, so does the rate to the borrower. If the company borrows when rates are at 20 percent on a fixed-rate basis and the prime then drops to 12 percent, as was the case in 1981–82, the borrower is paying 8 percent too much. This difference equates

TABLE 2-1
Rate Comparison, B-Rated Company (*90 Days, June 1973–1982*)

	90-Day Rate	Bank Commis-sion	Bank Balances	Discount Adjust-ment	Market Adjust-ment	Dealer Commis-sion	Total Rate
1973							
Prime	7.75	.00	1.16	.00	0	.00	8.91
Acceptances	7.90	.75	.00	.19	0	.00	8.84
Commercial paper	8.00	.00	.80	.19	0	.13	9.12
Eurodollars	8.81	.75	.00	.00	0	.00	9.56
1974							
Prime	11.75	.00	1.76	.00	0	.00	13.51
Acceptances	10.79	.75	.00	.32	0	.00	11.86
Commercial paper	11.18	.00	1.12	.00	0	.13	12.43
Eurodollars	12.04	.75	.00	.00	0	.00	12.79
1975							
Prime	7.00	.00	1.05	.00	0	.00	8.05
Acceptances	5.70	.75	.00	.09	0	.00	6.54
Commercial paper	5.67	.00	.57	.09	0	.13	6.46
Eurodollars	6.10	.75	.00	.00	0	.00	6.85
1976							
Prime	7.25	.00	1.09	.00	0	.00	8.34
Acceptances	5.77	.75	.00	.09	0	.00	6.52
Commercial paper	5.58	.00	.56	.09	0	.13	6.36
Eurodollars	6.22	.75	.00	.00	0	.00	6.97

TABLE 2-1 (concluded)

	90-Day Rate	Bank Commission	Bank Balances	Discount Adjustment	Market Adjustment	Dealer Commission	Total Rate
1977							
Prime	7.00	.00	1.05	.00	0	.00	8.05
Acceptances	5.39	.75	.00	.08	0	.00	6.22
Commercial paper	5.42	.00	.54	.08	0	.13	6.17
Eurodollars	5.78	.75	.00	.00	0	.00	6.53
1978							
Prime	9.00	.00	1.35	.00	0	.00	10.35
Acceptances	7.48	.75	.00	.12	0	.00	8.23
Commercial paper	7.75	.00	.78	.12	0	.13	8.75
Eurodollars	8.33	.75	.00	0	0	.00	9.08
1979							
Prime	11.50	.00	1.72	.00	0	.00	13.22
Acceptances	9.79	.75	.00	.25	0	.00	10.79
Commercial paper	9.77	.00	.98	.25	0	.13	11.13
Eurodollars	10.52	.75	.00	.00	0	.00	11.27
1980							
Prime	10.04	.00	1.51	.00	0	.00	11.55
Acceptances	8.31	.75	.00	.21	0	.00	9.27
Commercial paper	8.27	.00	.82	.21	0	.13	9.43
Eurodollars	9.41	.75	.00	.00	0	.00	10.16
1981							
Prime	17.87	.00	2.68	.00	0	.00	20.55
Acceptances	16.21	.75	.00	.40	0	.00	17.36
Commercial paper	16.24	.00	1.62	.40	0	.13	18.39
Eurodollars	18.00	.75	.00	.00	0	.00	18.75

to $80,000 higher interest expense per $1 million borrowed, assuming a weighted 8 percent average difference. On the other hand, if the company borrowed at 12 percent on a fixed-rate basis in the face of a rising rate, it would save on interest. If its rate is floating, it will lose, compared to a fixed-rate loan.

In sum, the bank does not lose or gain with floating rates, but the company pays more in the face of rising rates and less when rates are falling. It must be noted that banks usually charge a spread above their prime, reflecting their perceived credit risk. If this rate is fixed, in other words, P + 1%, the bank's return on assets or loanable funds will increase as rates drop and decrease as rates increase.

A truly hedged position, then, would be for a bank to change its spread according to prime changes. Specifically, if the bank requires a 20 percent return on loanable assets and rates are rising, the spread must be increased; if rates are falling, the spread must be decreased. This will stabilize the bank's return on assets, a key industry measurement. The following table illustrates the point, showing the impact of a fixed spread on a floating cost of funds and the various rates of return for the bank. The returns are on a net-after-cost basis.

Fixed Spread/Variable Cost Return

Variable cost	7.00%	8%	9.00%	10%	14.00%	16.0%	20%
+ Fixed spread	2.00	2	2.00	2	2.00	2.0	2
Borrowing cost	9.00	10	11.00	12	16	18.0	22
Variable % return	28.57	25	22.22	20	14.28	12.5	10

We conclude that a fixed spread over a floating cost of funds provides inconsistent returns for the bank as well as inconsistent costs for the borrower. When rates are increasing, the bank's return drops in favor of the borrower. When rates drop, the bank's return increases at the expense of the borrower. A solution is to price the loan on a complete floating basis where the cost of funds and the spread change, fixing the bank's return. The following table shows the spread change required to stabilize the return.

Variable Spread/Variable Cost Return

Variable cost	7.0%	8.0%	9.0%	10%	14.0%	16.0%	20%
+ Variable spread	1.4	1.6	1.8	2	2.8	3.2	4
Borrowing cost	8.4	9.6	10.8	12	16.8	19.2	24
Fixed return	20.0	20.0	20.0	20	20	20.0	20

We conclude that at a 7 percent cost, the bank will charge a 1.4 percent spread and earn a 20 percent return. In the first table the bank charged 2 percent, irrespective of its costs. At a 7 percent cost the return was 28.57 percent, disproportionate with the same risk. In this case, the bank's cash flow will decline; but its return, which is a critical performance ratio, will remain stable. For the company, which is concerned about cash flow, the rate reduction is positive.

Conversely, when rates increase, the bank must charge a greater spread in order to realize the same return, and the borrower will pay more. Naturally, the arguments around this approach differ according to whether one is lender or borrower and depending on a rising or declining rate environment. What is not arguable is that fixed spreads over variable rates result in inconsistent returns for the banks.

The prime rate is a nebulous term. Until the 1970s, it meant the most favored rate extended to the most creditworthy companies. However, given the competitive environment and explosion of alternatives, such as acceptances, Eurodollars, and commercial paper, the banking industry began offering subprime loans to creditworthy corporations. There is some irony in the competitiveness of commercial paper. Since bank credit lines are required to back up commercial paper, the banks are actively supporting their competition. Since commercial paper is generally cheaper than prime, major corporations actively borrow in the commercial paper market and avoid higher-priced bank loans.

The history behind the backup line stems from the Penn Central collapse. The commercial paper market was tainted when Penn Central's outstanding paper was in question. In order to maintain the fidelity of the paper market, rating agencies (Moody's and Standard & Poor's) required additional support. Today, bank credit lines are provided, comforting the purchasers of the paper. The corporations pay for such backup lines in the form of fees or noninterest-bearing deposits maintained with the bank. (Chapter Four, will delve into the pricing of paper, including the hidden cost of support lines.) Pricing prime-related borrowings is ambiguous at best when considering the various rates covering numerous sources of funds for the bank.

Secured versus Unsecured Loans*

Given the definition of interest relative to risk, a secured loan will be more expensive for the borrower and increase the bank's return on assets. This is a debated point since the security pro-

---

*This section was written by Arthur B. Adams, President Lawrence Systems, Retired.

vided presumably reduces the perceived risk and, therefore, additional interest should not be required. On the other hand, administrative costs increase.

An unsecured line of credit indicates that the bank is comfortable with the borrower's creditworthiness and no additional support is necessary. The purpose of securing the credit is to add comfort to the bank's exposure and provide a second source of repayment in the event of default.

Article 9 of the *Uniform Commercial Code* is entitled "Secured Transactions" and describes how a creditor can acquire and perfect a security interest in personal property (i.e., goods, accounts, chattel paper, instruments, documents, and general intangibles). The code was originally approved by its sponsors and the American Bar Association in 1952 and revised in 1958; during the period from 1958 through the 1970s it was adopted, usually with some minor differences, by all the states except Louisiana. Through the years, other revisions have been made and gradually the differences in the versions adopted by the various states have become somewhat more significant.

In general, however, a lender can acquire a security interest in a borrower's personal property by entering into an agreement to that effect with the borrower. The security agreement will describe the collateral, and the borrower will grant a security interest in the described collateral to the lender. This is all that is required between the two parties, but the lender's interest is not effective against other creditors of the borrower unless the security interest is "perfected." Perfection is accomplished either by filing a financing statement (UCC-1) with the appropriate state and/or county government agency or by taking possession of the collateral, depending upon its nature.

Of the six general categories of personal property mentioned above, perfection in each is accomplished as follows:

Goods:	Filing a UCC-1 or by taking possession.
Accounts:	Filing a UCC-1.
Chattel paper:	Filing a UCC-1 or by taking possession. (There are practical reasons why possession may be preferred.)
Instruments:	Possession is the only method.
Documents:	Filing a UCC-1 or by taking possession (again, possession may be the safest route).
General Intangibles:	Filing a UCC-1.

Where possession is the selected method of perfection, the lender may find it practical to bring instruments, documents, and chattel paper into the bank for safekeeping, but it is obviously not practical to put goods in the bank's vaults. Possession of goods is usually accomplished through a bailee—usually a field warehouseman. Field warehousing is a technical procedure used to bring the warehouse to the goods instead of bringing the goods to a terminal or public warehouse. The technical steps followed by the field warehouseman include

1. Leasing the storage area where the goods are held. Generally this is all or a portion of the borrower's storage facilities.
2. Securing the area with the warehouseman's locks.
3. Posting signs notifying one and all that the goods are in the custody of the warehouse company.
4. Selecting from among the borrower's personnel certain persons to act as the warehouse company's employees or agents. These people must be in a position to control the movement of the goods and account for all such movements.
5. Instructing the selected employees in the operation of the warehouse. These instructions will concern the procedure the lender has given the warehouse company relative to the goods to be included in the collateral borrowing base, how frequently the warehouseman is to issue warehouse receipts on incoming goods, and the conditions under which the borrower can remove goods from the custody of the warehouseman.

The field warehousing technique can also be used to perfect a security interest in instruments, documents, and chattel paper and may be the only practical approach if the borrower is not able to operate his business with these pieces of paper in the bank's vault.

The advantage in using the field warehousing method of taking possession is the added security provided by the field warehouseman and the legal liability and fidelity bond coverage he carries. When relying on a UCC-1 filing, the lender may have a legal right to dispose of his collateral in the event of a default by the borrower, but the financing statement does not guarantee that the collateral exists. The field warehouseman does make such a guarantee and may be liable to the lender for any loss suffered if he loses the collateral or through negligence misstates the amount he has in his possession. The prudent lender must also be aware that the revised Bankruptcy Act of 1978 may interfere with the orderly liquidation of collateral even if he has a perfected security interest.

Although security undoubtedly adds to the safety of the loan, the risk of collateral devaluation exists. Therefore creditors usually loan against expressed percentages, forming the borrowing base. In this case, the creditor may loan against 60 percent of the original inventory level and 80 percent against receivables. The borrowing base of receivables is usually higher than inventory, since the probability of liquidation is diversified and surer. But risks still exist for the lender—a company buying goods from the borrower may default.

The secured nature of a loan must be justified by the lender. It is not sufficient to secure a credit simply to be secured. Where the creditworthiness is marginal, the loan agreement should specify conditions under which the collateral will be released. Specifically, the purpose of collateral is to add support to the loan, but when performance reaches certain levels on a consistent basis, the security is no longer justified.

Recently an electronics company, which had been a fully secured borrower during its start-up period, entered into a loan agreement with its banks, providing for collateral release. The company's performance had been remarkable for a new business in an industry with intense competition. In recognition of this performance, the company requested that credit be extended on an unsecured basis. This required the preparation of a thorough report educating the lender on the company and industry and clearly showing sound financial performance.

The banks recognized the achievements but continued to insist on a fully collateralized and guaranteed credit line. The two positions were satisfied by loan agreement covenants stating financial goals to be achieved which would lead the bank to release collateral. In this case, the company had to maintain a current ratio of not less than 2.5 to 1 and a debt-equity ratio of not more than 2 to 1, and show stable profits for three consecutive quarters. This approach clearly identified the bank's comfort level while justifying its collateral requirements. It also provided the company with specific performance goals.

Guarantees covering the indebtedness of the company were handled in the same manner. The bank held the executed joint and several guarantees, but the agreement specified that the guarantees were to be held in abeyance until certain negative performance was achieved. In this case, the company's current ratio must drop below 1.5 to 1, debt-equity must exceed 2.5 to 1, and profit must decline for two consecutive quarters. (A standard guarantee is shown in Appendix Four.)

This agreement identifies certain performance triggers for the company while comforting the bank. It eliminates ambiguity and rewards the company for achievement. Most importantly, the agreement enhances the borrower-bank relationship through the execution of a document that is positive in nature.

Documentation is a critical aspect to any loan. It is the legal follow-up to the loan agreement, ensuring that the bank's position is legally enforceable. Sloppy documentation often leads to loan losses, as evidenced in the collapse of Oklahoma's Penn Square Bank, where the bank and numerous correspondent banks lost millions in the face of poorly executed or nonexistent documents designed to protect the creditors. Banking annals reveal numerous loan losses that were avoidable if certain documents, such as UCC-1, had been properly executed.

Recently, a major money center bank failed to obtain the guarantee of a borrower's parent company. The borrower was a domestic international sales corporation (DISC) set up as a separate company under the IRS regulations providing tax relief for international sales. The DISC company was negligibly capitalized at $1,000 and the bank extended unsecured credit to $10 million, supported by the parent company's guarantee. This guarantee was never executed and the demise of the DISC resulted in a substantial exposure for the bank.

FACTORING

Factoring is an extraordinary combination of professional services and financing. The essential characteristics are outright purchase (without recourse to the client) of the (trade) accounts by the factor and notification to the client's customers that the account is payable to the factor. Since the factor has purchased the accounts, it follows that the factor assumes the responsibility of credit investigation, collection of accounts, ledgering of receivables and assumes bad debts.[1]

It is important to distinguish factoring from secured receivable financing, a traditional bank lending function. Although the factor is comforted by the eventual liquidation of receivables, it does not have recourse to the client for customers' bad debts and there is no security, liens, or encumbrances against the client. In traditional receivable financing, the bank has a secured position, evidenced by a UCC filing and a claim to the proceeds of sales. The bank also has full and unconditional recourse to the client.

In receivable financing, the bank establishes a borrowing base which is a percentage of the receivables against which loans are made. The percentage is based on the client's historical provision for bad debts, the creditworthiness of the client, and the bank's perception of the industry. After the borrowing base is es-

---

[1] From Walter E. Heller's brochures and interview with AVP Ron Fox.

tablished, the client may borrow up to that limit but retains the responsibility for bad debts, customer credit assessment, and collections.

Factoring differs in that the client's credit department is supplemented by the factor which provides credit assessment and collections. The factor's credit exposure is the client's customers and not the client itself. The factor charges a fee ranging from 1 to 1⅞ percent for providing the credit and collection service. The fee is applied on a flat basis and is predicated on the overall volume of receivables, average size of the receivable, and credit quality of the client's customers. For relatively young companies or firms with expanding business, the fees charged may offset the cost of establishing or expanding the corporate credit-collection department.

Most factors offer the client two forms of payment for the purchased receivables. These are referred to as old-line, and maturity, factoring. Under an old-line arrangement, the client may receive immediate cash against the presentation of invoices to the factor. This is an advance from the factor without recourse to the client, and repayment is from the factor's collection of the receivables. The factor charges interest, related to the prevailing prime rate, which approximates prime plus 3 percent per annum. Interest is charged in arrears.

Under the maturity arrangement, the factor provides funds to the client based on a prearranged receivable turnover period. Sales proceeds are credited to the client's account irrespective of the client's customers' ability to pay when the receivable is due.

The history of factoring dates back to 3000 B.C. Although the transactional fundamentals have remained relatively the same, sophisticated factors are also involved in international arrangements. This is similar to domestic factoring and may eliminate the need for a letter of credit from the foreign buyer. Factors with overseas branches or affiliates may purchase a client's receivables under the same arrangements described earlier. There are a number of benefits in working with a factoring firm:

1. Most companies are in the business of providing a service or manufacturing a product. Ancillary to their primary business is the administration of providing credit and collection for sales. Few companies have credit collection departments on a par with banks or factoring companies whose primary business is credit assessment and collection procedures. A factor may eliminate the risks associated with extending credit and reduce the cost of collections for the client.

2. Since the factor's computer capabilities serve the company, overhead operating costs may be minimized and the company will eliminate excess computer time. This will increase the return on assets.

3. Collection of receivables may increase, reducing the client's debt burden by improving cash flow.

4. Since the receivables are purchased without recourse to the client, the working capital and debt-equity ratios improve, which may reduce the overall cost of borrowing. Depending on the arrangements with the factor, the return on assets, return on equity, and profit-to-sales ratios may also improve.

5. On-line terminal access to client-customer credit information may improve sales monitoring and may enhance the overall client-customer relationship.

There has been a misconception that a company involved with a factor is experiencing credit or finance problems. Our research and interviews indicate that, since the factor does not have recourse or executes liens against the client, there is no foundation for these assumptions. Further, a sophisticated factor may provide numerous savings and intangible benefits to the client that make good business and operating sense.

REGULATIONS

The primary focus of banking regulations, which are established by Congress and enforced by the Federal Reserve Bank and comptroller of the currency, is to protect depositors and to ensure bank solvency. Without belaboring the issue, the regulators provide lending parameters to include credit limits. Specifically, a national bank may not extend credit exceeding 15 percent of its unimpaired capital and surplus to any one company, so a bank with $1 million in capital and surplus may not extend credit exceeding $150,000 to any one borrower. This ensures that the failure of one borrower will not cause the bank to fail.

When a company requires credit lines exceeding a bank's lending limits, several banks may form a syndication, with the total credit less than the total lending limits. Because the number of banks may become quite large, one bank, usually the company's primary bank, is selected to act as agent or represent the entire banking group. This enables the company to deal with one bank as opposed to numerous banks. In the case of large credits, where hundreds of banks are involved, one can easily appreciate working with an agent bank. The disadvantage of a syndicated loan is that, unless otherwise specified, the competitiveness of the lenders is dissolved, since the borrowing rates are usually contractually committed.

SUMMARY

The conventional prime-related loan provides maximum flexibility as there is no fixed term or fixed rate. The company may prepay the loan at its convenience without penalties associated with other borrowing alternatives. In the face of a declining rate environment, the borrowing costs will move downward. As rates rise, so will borrowing costs.

The disadvantage of prime-related borrowings is that they are historically more costly than alternatives by as much as 2 to 4 percent, and it is impossible to accurately predict future interest expense. Since rates have exceeded 20 percent, the interest expense category has become extremely important. Some CPAs encourage the accounting entry to be moved under cost of goods sold, signifying the importance of interest expense.

In the event a company is bidding on a supply contract, the interest volatility may significantly erode profits. The vagaries influencing commodities in general affect the price of money and are unpredictable at any given time. Therefore two hedging options exist to eliminate the guess work: fixed-rate financing and offsetting the borrowing position, which is rate speculation, with a hedge in the futures market.

The following chart shows the 10-year history of outstanding conventional loans compared to alternatives: Eurodollars, bankers' acceptances, and commercial paper. For the 10-year period, conventional prime-related loans increased 118 percent compared to commercial paper at 297 percent, Eurodollars at 462 percent, and bankers' acceptances at 686 percent. Conventional loans lagged the alternatives because of their comparatively higher rates of interest and the introduction of Eurodollars and the increased use of bankers' acceptances. Although commercial paper is usually cheaper than corporate borrowing alternatives, few corporations qualify to issue commercial paper.

CHART I
Total Outstandings

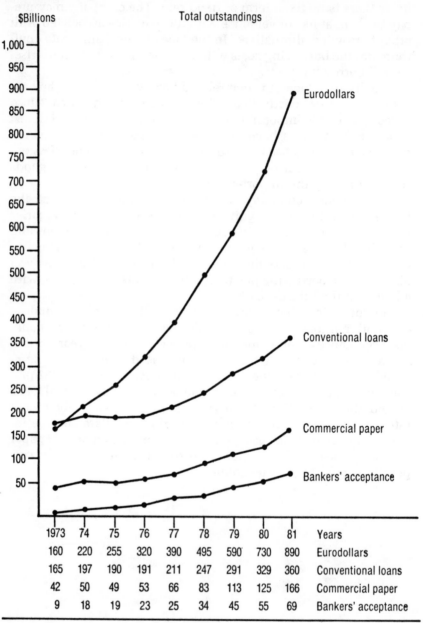

$Billions   Total outstandings

	1973	74	75	76	77	78	79	80	81	Years
	160	220	255	320	390	495	590	730	890	Eurodollars
	165	197	190	191	211	247	291	329	360	Conventional loans
	42	50	49	53	66	83	113	125	166	Commercial paper
	9	18	19	23	25	34	45	55	69	Bankers' acceptance

Source: Federal Reserve statistics.

APPENDIX ONE

LOAN APPLICATION EXAMPLE

Company: Graphic Engineering Inc.

Amount: $3,000,000 secured, revolving line of credit available under floating prime borrowings, eligible bankers' acceptances, or Eurodollars at the borrower's option.

Rate:

Advances:	Prime plus 1 percent per annum floating.
Acceptances:	Prevailing discount plus 1 percent.
Eurodollars:	Prevailing LIBOR (London interbank-offered rate) plus 1 percent.

Balances: Five percent compensating balances or equivalent fee on outstanding advances with no balances against Eurodollar loans or acceptances.

Security: UCC-1 filing covering receivables to be released when graphic's debt-equity ratio is not more than 2 to 1 and the current ratio is not less than 2 to 1 for three consecutive quarters.

Guarantees: Joint and several guarantees to be executed but held in abeyance pending two consecutive quarters when the debt-equity ratio exceeds 3 to 1 or the current ratio falls below 1.5 to 1.

Purpose: Supplement working capital.

Source of repayment: Continued profitable operations; refinancing with other bank debt; possible stock issue; or sale of corporate assets to existing suitors.

Other products: Graphic's growth and international sales will result in additional letters of credit through the bank and cash management services.

Historical profits: This relationship provided a 2 percent return on risk assets (RORA) for the bank in 1982, with gross revenues of $360,000 covering a $2 million line of credit. Pro forma 1983 revenues are expected to be less, since Graphic will be borrowing under an acceptance and Eurodollar line and rates are generally expected to drop. RORA is expected to be 2 percent or greater, given a 1 percent fixed spread over declining base rates.

Documents: Quarterly company-prepared financial statements.
Annual CPA-prepared financial statements.
Corporate resolution to borrower.
Loan agreement.
Documentary acceptance agreement.
UCC-1 filed.
Security agreement.
Grid note.
Presigned drafts.

Recommen-
dation: The undersigned sponsors this $3 million secured and revolving line of credit with concurrence of the general loan committee.

Bank Officer

COMPANY BACKGROUND

Incorporated December 14, 1977, in California, Graphic ranks second in the United States in the manufacturing of terminal graphic enhancement systems and represents the leading edge in product innovation, the critical industry advantage.

The company was capitalized at $5,000. Present equity is $3.9 million, with the founder and president, Bart Smith, controlling 57.3 percent; William Kent, vice president of marketing, 21.3 percent; and Bob Elliott, vice president of research and development, 21.3 percent.

Graphic's primary business is manufacturing terminal compatible graphic display systems, trademarked Fit-Graphics. This terminal enhancement system upgrades existing low-cost alphanumeric display terminals, enabling graphic formatting and display at the terminal. The system is fully compatible with industry software and hardware and is easily incorporated in existing terminals or with the original equipment manufacturer's product (OEM).

Graphic entered the industry in 1977, providing the first low-cost graphic display system at $2,500 for low-end users while

Tektronix, the industry standard, provided graphics incorporated in terminals to high-end users for $5,000. The CRT *Graphics Terminal* report, prepared by Venture Development Corporation in 1981, showed the graphics market represented 51,000 units; and a Standard & Poor's study shows this market will reach 210,000 units in 1984, valued at $641 million. Graphic's share of the existing market is 10 percent (volume) and is expected to hold or increase, given its technological lead.

These reports cited three strategic areas for product improvement: color display, high resolution (crisp images), and increased display speed. Graphic's third generation graphics (GEN III), recently available and two years ahead of industry standards, is color-capable, has the sharpest image, and provides the fastest display.

The company purchases raw materials (commodities), circuit boards, chips, etc., from numerous vendors, diversifying its supplier risk. These purchases are on a bid basis, ensuring that Graphic will not be contractually obligated to purchase commodities at a fixed rate when prices are falling or when products become outdated. Electronic commodity items rarely increase in price given production economies of scale and competition.

Commodity items are shipped to Graphic's Santa Clara plant, repackaged, and forwarded to 10 local subassembly firms. This minimizes Graphic's production fixed costs and labor variable costs, reducing its production break-even point, increasing sales margins, and providing pricing flexibility in the face of competition. With this production method, Graphic avoids large investments in production plant and equipment and risks associated with constantly changing production systems.

The finished product is returned to Graphic for inspection under a series of stress tests, packaged, and shipped.

Graphic markets Fit-Graphics through trade shows, industry publications, and major distributors. Eighty percent of products are sold through 100 suppliers, with no one distributor handling more than 15 percent of Graphic's sales. Eight major suppliers represent 60 percent of total sales. With the competitive nature of the distribution industry, the loss of any one supplier would not have an impact on company sales.

Graphic has a 50-day product lead time and schedules production 50 percent against firm orders and 50 percent anticipated orders. Forty-one percent of Graphic's sales are made through its DISC to international clients. The industry average is 25 percent international-domestic sales, further attesting to the demand for Graphic's product and diversifying its market risk.

International sales are executed against dollar letters of credit or open account with FCIA coverage, minimizing foreign credit risk and eliminating foreign exchange risk. It is noted that the international demand for Graphic's product has increased as the dollar strengthened, which proportionately increases the cost of U.S. goods to foreign buyers. This has not been the case for the industry in general and reaffirms the high demand for Fit-Graphics.

Ultimate users of Fit-Graphics include Texas Instruments, IBM, DEC, TAB, Tele Video, Advanced Data Systems, General Motors, Union Carbide, General Electric, Laurence Berkeley Lab, the U.S. government, the government of Israel, the naval postgraduate school, Dartmouth College, Indiana University, and the University of Illinois.

For the most part, graphics have focused on institutional users; however, the business community is expected to substantially increase demand through 1986, according to the earlier referenced Venture Development Corporation report. The high speed and duplicating qualities of graphics required by the business community are an integral part of Graphic's Gen III.

Graphic's inventory, production, and distribution cycle are integrated with its on-line computer-generated financial MIS. Considered state-of-the-art for the electronics industry, the system provides immediate information covering cash flow, balance sheet, and income statement relative to product cost accounting. The system provides immediate control, improves inventory-production cycles, minimizes lead time, and alerts management to potential obstacles; it also integrates production information with financial information, enhancing strategic planning.

INDUSTRY BACKGROUND

The electronics industry is marked by high technology, relatively short product life cycles, intense competition, and large capital investment, and performance is directly related to macroeconomic health.

1. *High technology:* Product innovation is critical to the industry. Graphic identified its graphics niche at the early stage and produced the first low-end user graphic enhancement system at a competitive price while maintaining its quality lead and its 22 percent pre-tax profit to sales, compared to 10 percent for the industry. Its continued R&D resulted in the development of its third-generation graphics two years ahead of the competition. It is expected that terminal manufacturers will increasingly turn to Graphic in order to maintain their respective product lead. With Graphic's new chip speed enhancement, its product will continue to outpace competition and position the company to enter the terminal industry.

2. *Short life cycles:* One-to two-year product life cycles are standard for the electronics industry and is a function of technology, competition, and user needs. Graphic's first-generation products had a four-year life, exceeding industry norms and attesting to the market's infancy and product quality. The Gen III product, developed in 1982 at a cost of $1.5 million, surpassed all expressed user needs for speed, clarity, and color. Further, Gen III is fully compatible—and may be installed in existing terminals or incorporated—with OEM in new terminals. Therefore it taps the old and new markets. Gen IV and V are under design.

3. *Intense competition:* Although competition is intense in the electronics industry there are few competitors in the graphics segment. The primary objective is to penetrate the terminal manufacturers who build their own graphics system and forestall Japan's intended invasion of the industry. The key to both obstacles is R&D. Graphic's existing two-year product lead and continuing R&D soundly position the company for the 80s.

4. *Capital investment:* Electronic companies traditionally have large capital investments; for example, a medium size chip plant costs $35–40 million. In order to channel scarce resources into R&D, which is required to maintain its lead, Graphic has minimized plant and equipment investment, preferring to use subcontracted assembly companies.

5. *General economy:* The electronics industry is generally tied to the economy. For 1982 the growth was sluggish. According to Standard & Poor's *Industry surveys,* (1982), the growth was 5 percent for 1981, and 8 percent is expected for 1982. This relatively slow performance is primarily attributed to the semiconductor industry, but areas important to Graphic are growing substantially: office equipment, 40 percent; and desk top computers, 60 percent through 1985. The report specifically identified the terminal segment for fast growth, citing the 12,000 units sold in 1978, the 51,000 units in 1981, and the 210,000 units, valued at $641 million and projected to be sold in 1983. Two separate approaches indicated the possibility that Graphic's sales may reach $60 million in 1984:

a. Graphic's current 10 percent volume of market share applied to S/P's $641 million industry terminal sales for 1984 is $64 million.
b. Graphic's historic 3-year trend projected forward to 1984 indicates its potential for generating $60–65 million in sales.

The primary reason for this growth is the recent introduction of graphics; the unlimited application to research through which most universities receive endowments; the innumerable applications of graphics for the defense industry, with its increased budget; the quickly developing business applications; and Graphic's product quality and full compatibility.

STRATEGIC RISK ASSESSMENTS

The following, which are critical issues to Graphic's continued success, identify the corporate awareness and management of these contingencies.

1. *Terminal manufacturers building graphics systems:* With the growth potential for graphics, many of the 61 terminal manufacturers may attempt to build their own graphics systems. However, with Graphic's strong R&D lead and product acceptance, it is likely it will continue its growth. Further, this obstacle may prove to be an opportunity for Graphic's stockholders, since R&D is often achieved through acquisition. There were 194 industry acquisitions in 1980–81, for $1.259 billion, and Graphic has been courted.

2. *Black market curtailing raw material availability:* It is doubtful that a materials shortage will occur similar to that of 1977 with IBM's unanticipated large purchase of computer chips. The number of raw material suppliers, including the Japanese, seriously precludes a repeat.

3. *Japanese competition:* Japan will probably encroach on the graphics niches. However, Graphic's R&D lead and quick life cycles will sustain the company's market. The primary competitive factors are product quality, compatibility, and price relative to production costs. Graphic is the leader in product quality and its products are fully compatible. Since it does not directly manufacture the product, it avoids production risks; but it will benefit from production economies of the scale employed by the competitive subcontractors.

4. *Corporate growth exceeding managerial capabilities:* This has been identified as a potential obstacle from the outset. The company prefers to maintain a lean but well-balanced team in order to quickly but prudently respond to economic or product changes while avoiding the bureaucracy associated with traditional corporate structures. Therefore the management-ownership team is comprised of Bart Smith, president; William Kent, vice president of marketing; and Bob Elliott, head of research and development. This team is further complemented by Mike

Adams, with an MBA in finance and eight years of financial and operational experience with IBM. Mike is responsible for finance and daily operations. The company has retained consultants to assist in establishing procedures and manage risks associated with growth, such as international sales.

5. *Competition:* Graphic has nine immediate competitors building graphic-enhancement systems. The larger producer, IBM, builds graphics for their own systems and do not consider graphics their primary business. Of the low-end graphics producers, Graphic has a clear product lead and believes it will have the largest market share. Competitive advantages include a two-year R&D lead, a sophisticated and thorough distribution system, an accepted product, low economies of scale, a low break-even point, and responsiveness to market and economic changes.

6. *Capital expansion proportionate with growth:* Graphic's four-year growth resulted in equity increasing 12 times proportionate, with a sales increase of 13 times and prudently exceeding its asset expansion of seven times. This evidences the importance of R&D relative to fixed asset expansion, which does not provide competitive advantages. This approach will continue with a moderate impact on debt-equity and working capital resulting from the strategic investment in R&D, expanding Graphic's technological lead. This will ensure future growth, profits, and ultimately service bank debt.

MANAGEMENT

The senior management team is lead by Bart Smith, 32; William Kent, 29; and Bob Elliott, 31. The team has well-balanced experience in management, research, and marketing. The group's extensive academic and field experience with graphic-enhancement systems, terminals, and computers enables the company to develop state of the art in terminals with a two-year competitive lead in graphics. Further, this talent will enable Graphic to develop new products for the 80s.

FINANCIAL ANALYSIS

Industry Comparison

The following three-year industry data, which was provided by Standard & Poor's (July 1982), compares Graphic's performance with its counterparts.

Category	Industry Average	Graphic (1982)
Pre-tax income/sales	10.7%	22%
Four-year growth rate (sales)	52.6%	239%
Return on equity	17.3%	51.3%
Return on assets	7.3%	15.4%
Current ratio	1.8 to 1	2.7 to 3
Debt-equity ratio	2.0 to 1	2.3 to 1

Graphic's performance, leading the industry composite, reflects the high growth of its niche, market acceptance of Fit-Graphics, and comparatively low overhead. The debt-equity and current ratio properly reflect the debt required to initiate the business and maintain its competitive edge vis-à-vis new product development.

Four-Year Company Performance

The following identifies critical financial data for Graphic.

	All Dollar Figures Times 1,000			
	1979	1980	1981	1982
Current assets	$610	$1,530	$ 3,796	$ 8,300
Current liabilities	$524	$1,210	$ 2,614	$ 3,032
Working capital	$ 86	$ 320	$ 1,182	$ 5,268
Current ratio	1.16:1	1.26:1	1.45:1	2.73:1
Debt (total)	$548	1,220	2,982	9,100
Equity	$142	604	1,772	3,900
Debt-equity ratio	3.85:1	2.01:1	1.68:1	2.3:1
Sales	$752	3,820	10,474	18,000
Profits	$124	456	1,432	2,000
Profit/sales	16.4%	11.9%	13.6%	11.1%
Profit/assets	18%	25%	30.1%	15.4%
Profits/equity	87%	75%	80.8%	51.3%
Total assets	$690	$1,824	$ 4,754	$13,000

FINANCIAL REVIEW

Graphic is in a growth mode of a dynamic industry and requires leverage to maintain its competitive lead. Although the company's performance generally exceeded industry achievement, Graphic's debt-to-equity ratio increased from 1.45 to 1 in 1981 to 2.3 to 1 in 1982. This resulted from Graphic's decision to expend $2 million for R&D in 1982 to cover its Gen III product. If the

	Achieved	Adjusted
Profits	$2,000,000	$3,000,000
Current assets	$8,300,000	$8,400,000
Current ratio	2.73 to 1	3.06 to 1
Debt-equity rato	2.3 to 1	1.85 to 1
Profits/sales	11.1%	16%
Profis/assets	15.4%	23%
Profits/equity	51.3%	77%

company had not undertaken this R&D it would have sacrificed its technological lead for an improved debt-to-equity ratio. The table above adjusts Graphic's financial performance by eliminating the $2 million R&D expense.

The company was unable to borrow the $2 million for R&D, given the skeptical view of institutional lenders towards high-tech R&D. Graphic did not pursue an R&D private partnership, since it was unwilling to share future earnings and the research was highly confidential. Graphic's funding of R&D in 1982 means future revenues for Gen III will not be diluted by capitalized R&D. Assets do not include intangibles resulting from the research.

In 1983 Graphic intends to build a new plant and office complex for $10 million. This will substantially increase debt and increase the debt/equity ratio. The investment will improve profits and cash flow, since monthly lease expenses are greater than pro forma debt service covering the building; and the investment will provide Graphic with an equity position in the building which it presently does not enjoy.

BANK RELATIONSHIPS

Graphic began its bank relationship with Bank of America in 1977 with a $15,000 short-term line of credit supplementing working capital. This line of credit has grown to $2 million and is priced at prime plus 1 percent per annum, with 5 percent balances on usage. The company, through its financial advisors, has requested a $6 million line of credit to be provided equally by two banks. Graphic has requested that the credit be available under a facility that includes prime, Eurodollars, and eligible bankers' acceptances. This will substantially reduce its interest expense and increase profits, since rates are declining and Eurodollars and acceptances are generally cheaper than prime borrowings.

Graphic has requested release of the receivable and collateral evidenced by our UCC-1 filing and release of principle continuing guarantees. We believe this to be premature but concur with their compromise. Graphic will accept a UCC-1 filed on receivables but released against inventory. The UCC-1 will be released when the company's debt/equity ratio is not more than 2 to 1 and the current ratio is not less than 2 to 1 for three consecutive quarters. Guarantees will be executed but held in abeyance pending two consecutive quarters of negative performance when the debt/equity ratio exceeds 3 to 1 and the current ratio falls below 1.5 to 1.

This credit is recommended, based on the company's solid and proven performance, Graphic's growth potential, bank earnings, and four viable sources of repayment.

CPA: Arthur Young

Financial Advisors: *MacPhee and Associates*

APPENDIX TWO

SPREAD SHEET

NAME: _____   BUSINESS: GENERAL

(000 Omitted) DATE SOURCE					
121	NET SALES				
122	REVENUES				
123	COST OF SALES				
124	COST OF REVENUES				
125	GROSS PROFIT				
126	SELL / OPER EXPENSE				
127	GEN / ADMIN EXPENSE				
128	SELL / OPER / GEN / ADMIN EXPENSE				
129	RESEARCH / DEVEL EXPENSE				
130	OPERATING EARNINGS				
131	INTEREST EXPENSE				
132	PROFIT SHAR / PEN CONTRIB				
133	G / L DISC OPERATIONS				
134	G / L CURRENCY TRANSLATION				
135	G / L FOREIGN EXCHANGE				
136	OTHER INCOME				
137	OTHER EXPENSE				
138					
139	NET INCOME BEFORE TAX				
140	INCOME TAXES				
141	EQUITY P / L				
142	G / L DISC OPERATIONS				
143	NET INCOME BEFORE EX'ORD				
144	EXTRAORDINARY ITEM				
145					
146	NET INC BEFORE MINORITY INT				
147	MINORITY INTEREST				
148	NET INCOME				
149	RETAINED EARNINGS - BEG				
150	PARTNERS CAPITAL - BEG				
151	ACCOUNTING CHANGE				
152	RECONCILING ITEM				
153					
154	OTHER - NET				
155	(PARTNERS WITHDRAWALS)				
156	(DIVIDENDS - STOCK)				
157	(DIVIDENDS - CASH)				
158	PARTNERS CAPITAL - END				
159	RETAINED EARNINGS - END				
160					
161					
162					
163					
164	DEPREC / AMORT / DEPL				
165	DEFERRED TAXES				
166	AVG NO SHARES OUTSTANDING				
167	CAPITAL EXPENDITURES				
168					
169					
170					
171					
172					
173					
174					
175					
176					
177					
178					
179					

INCOME STATEMENT

RATIOS

(000 Omitted) TO					
181 CURRENT RATIO					
182 QUICK RATIO					
183 % INVENTORY REQUIRED					
184 CASH, SEC REC PREM / AP PREM					
185 CASH FLOW					
186 WORKING CAPITAL					
187 WC / LTD					
188 DEBT (INC SUB) / WORTH					
189 DEBT / WORTH (INC SUB)					
190 CURRENT MATURITIES COVERAGE					
191 INT COVER BEFORE TAX					
192 CAPITAL EXPENDITURES COV					
193 SALES / WC					
194 AVERAGE COLLECTION PERIOD					
195 ASSET TURNOVER					
196 INVENTORY TURNOVER					
197 DAYS OF INVENTORY ON HAND					
198 ACCOUNTS PAYABLE TURNOVER					
199 ACCOUNTS PAYABLE / INVENTORY					
200 RETURN ON ASSETS					
201 RETURN ON STOCKHOLDERS EQ					
202 GROSS MARGIN					
203 OPERATING MARGIN					
204 NET MARGIN					
205 PRE - TAX MARGIN					
206 PAYOUT RATIO					
207 EARNINGS PER SHARE					
208					
209					
210					
211					
212					
213					
214					
215					
216					
217					
218					
219					
220					
221					
222					
223					
224					
225					
226					
227					
228					
229					
230					
231					
232					
233					
234					
235					
236					
237					
238					
239					
240 STATEMENT ANALYST					

RATIOS

07 - 224

APPENDIX THREE

LOAN AGREEMENT

This Agreement is entered into as of _____
_____ between Bank of America National Trust and
Savings Association ("Bank") and __Graphic Engineering, Inc.__
("Borrower") with respect to the following:

1. *Definitions*
1.1   "Acceptable Receivable" means an account:
   (a)   arising from the sale or lease of goods or the perform-
          ance of services by Borrower in the ordinary course
          of Borrower's business;
   (b)   upon which Borrower's right to receive payment is
          absolute and not contingent upon the fulfillment of
          any condition whatever;
   (c)   against which is asserted no defense, counterclaim,
          discount, or setoff, whether well-founded or other-
          wise;
   (d)   that is a true and correct statement of a bona fide in-
          debtedness incurred in the amount of the account for
          merchandise sold or leased and accepted by, or for
          services performed for and accepted by, the Receiv-
          able Debtor obligated upon such account;
   (e)   owned by Borrower and not subject to any right,
          claim, or interest of another other than the security
          interest in favor of Bank;
   (f)   that does not arise from a sale or lease to or perform-
          ance of services for an employee, affiliate, parent, or
          subsidiary of Borrower;
   (g)   that is not the obligation of a Receivable Debtor that
          is the federal government or a political subdivision
          thereof;
   (h)   that is not the obligation of a Receivable Debtor lo-
          cated in a foreign country;
   (i)   that does not arise from the sale of minerals or the
          like (including oil and gas) at the wellhead or mine-
          head unless Bank shall agree to the contrary in writ-
          ing;
   (j)   that is not in default. An account shall be deemed in
          default upon the occurrence of any of the following:
          (1)   The account is not paid within the _____
                 (___) day period starting on its invoice date;
          (2)   Any Receivable Debtor obligated upon such ac-
                 count suspends business, makes a general as-

signment for the benefit of creditors, or commits any act of bankruptcy; or

(3)   Any petition is filed by or against any Receivable Debtor obligated upon such account under any bankruptcy law or any other law or laws for the relief of debtors;

(k)   that does not, when added to all other Acceptable Receivables that are obligations of any Receivable Debtor obligated upon such account, at any time result in a total sum that exceeds _____ percent (__) of the total balance then due on all the Receivables; and

(1)   that is otherwise acceptable to Bank.

1.2   *Borrowing Base* means the lesser of:

(a)   _____

_____ Dollars (_____); or

(b)   _____ percent (__) of the balance due on Acceptable Receivables. For purposes of the foregoing computations, whenever Acceptable Receivables are used as a measure of advances under this Agreement, Acceptable Receivables and the advances shall be computed as of the time in question.

1.3   *Closing Date* means the disbursement date of the first advance under this Agreement.

1.4   *Collateral* means the property described in any Collateral Agreement.

1.5   *Collateral Agreements* means the security agreements required under Article 3 of this Agreement (individually a Collateral Agreement).

1.6   *Event of Default* means any event listed in Article 7 of this Agreement.

1.7   *Loan* means the loan described in Article 2 of this Agreement.

1.8   *Receivables* means all rights to the payment of money now owned or hereafter acquired by Borrower, whether due or to become due and whether or not earned by performance including, but not limited to, accounts, contract rights, chattel paper, instruments, and general intangibles.

1.9   *Receivable Debtor* means the person or entity obligated upon a Receivable.

1.10 *Tangible Net Worth* means the gross book value of the assets of Borrower (exclusive of goodwill, patents, trademarks, trade names, organization expense, treasury stock, unamortized debt discount and expense, deferred research and development costs, deferred marketing expenses and other like intangibles) less (a) reserves applicable thereto and (b) all liabilities (including accrued and deferred income taxes), other than indebtedness subordinated, in a manner satisfactory to Bank, to Borrower's indebtedness to Bank. All computations required hereby shall be made in accordance with generally accepted accounting principles and practices consistently applied.

2. *The Loan*

2.1   From time to time, between the date hereof and termination of Bank's commitment to lend under this Agreement, upon request of Borrower, Bank will advance to Borrower sums which shall not exceed in the aggregate outstanding at any one time the Borrowing Base.

2.2   Each request for an advance shall be made in writing on a form acceptable to Bank or in any other manner acceptable to Bank.

2.3   Each advance shall be made by a deposit to Borrower's commercial account no. _____ at the _____ of Bank, unless Borrower shall otherwise direct Bank in writing.

2.4   Principal, interest, and all other sums due Bank under this Agreement shall be evidenced by entries in records maintained by Bank (the Loan Account). Each payment on and any other credits with respect to principal, interest, and all other sums due under this Agreement shall be evidenced by entries to the Loan Account.

2.5   (a)   Interest on the total principal due Bank shown on the Loan Account shall accrue daily at a rate per annum _____ (_____) percentage point in excess of the rate of interest publicly announced from time to time by Bank in San Francisco, California, as its prime rate, with any change in such prime rate to take effect at the opening of business on the day specified in the public announcement of a change in said prime rate. Interest shall be computed on the basis of three hundred sixty (360)-day year and actual days elapsed.

  (b)   Bank may, upon five (5) days' prior written notice to Borrower, from time to time change the interest rate on the total principal due Bank under this Agreement. Bank need not give such prior notice of each change in Bank's prime rate (as defined in subparagraph (a) of this paragraph).

2.6   Borrower shall pay Bank on a day of each month designated by Bank interest for the preceding month in an amount equal to the greater of

(a) _____

Dollars ($_____); or

(b)   an amount equal to interest on the total principal due Bank at the rates specified in the most recent notice given under subparagraph 2.5(b), or if there be no notice given under subparagraph 2.5(b), at the rates specified in subparagraph 2.5(a).

Borrower understands and agrees that interest which is not paid when due shall, at the option of Bank, be added to principal and shall bear interest at the rates applicable to principal.

2.7   Borrower agrees that if at any time the amounts due Bank under this Agreement exceed the Borrowing Base, Borrower will immediately pay Bank the amount of the excess.

2.8   (a)   Bank's commitment to lend under this Agreement shall be terminated as set forth in Article 7 and may be terminated by Bank or Borrower upon at least _____ (____) days' prior written notice to the other.

(b)   All of Borrower's indebtedness to Bank under this Agreement shall be due and payable as set forth in Article 7, and, if Article 7 is inapplicable, by the close of business on the day Bank's commitment to lend under this Agreement terminates.

(c)   Termination of Bank's commitment to lend under this Agreement shall not affect Borrower's obligations and Bank's rights under this Agreement and any Collateral Agreement.

2.9   The line of credit under this Article is a revolving credit and Borrower may, subject to the provisions of this Agreement, repay and reborrow as Borrower may elect.

3.   *Security*

3.1   The Loan and all other sums due Bank under this Agreement shall be secured by security agreements, in form and substance satisfactory to Bank, executed by Borrower in favor of Bank granting Bank a security interest in or lien on Borrower's Receivables, and such other real or personal property (including but not limited to Borrower's inventory) as Bank may require.

4. *Conditions precedent*

4.1   The obligation of Bank to disburse the Loan is subject to the condition that, on the Closing Date, there shall have been delivered to Bank, in form and substance satisfactory to Bank:

    (a)   The Collateral Agreement(s);

    (b)   Financing statement(s) executed by Borrower;

    (c)   Evidence that the security interests or liens in favor of Bank are valid, enforceable, and prior to the rights and interests of others;

    (d)   Continuing guaranty(ies) in favor of Bank, each in the principal amount of _____ Dollars (_____) executed by _____

    _____;

    (e)   Subordination agreement(s) in favor of Bank executed _____

    _____;

    (f)   Evidence that the execution, delivery, and performance by Borrower of this Agreement and the execution, delivery, and performance by Borrower and any corporate guarantor or corporate subordinating creditor of any instrument or agreement required under this Agreement, as appropriate, have been duly authorized.

4.2   As a condition precedent to each advance (including the first advance) under this Agreement, Bank may, at its option, at any time and from time to time require that each request for an advance be accompanied or preceded by (a) a certificate, in form and detail satisfactory to Bank, setting forth the Acceptable Receivables on which the requested advance is to be based and (b) copies of the invoices of such Acceptable Receivables.

4.3   Each request for an advance under this Agreement shall be deemed a representation by Borrower that the representations and warranties contained in Paragraphs 5.1 through 5.6, 5.8, and 5.9 and in any other agreement, instrument, or document executed and delivered in connection herewith are then true and accurate in all material respects as though made on and as of the day of such request, and that no further action, including any filing or recording of any agreement or statement, is necessary in order to establish and perfect Bank's first lien on or prior perfected security interest in all the Collateral.

5. *Representations and Warranties*

Borrower represents and warrants that:

5.1   Borrower is a ___Corporation___ duly organized and existing under the laws of the state of its organization and the execution, delivery, and performance of this Agreement and of any instrument or agreement required by this Agreement are within Borrower's powers, have been duly authorized, and are not in conflict with the terms of any charter, bylaw, or other organization papers of Borrower;

5.2   The execution, delivery, and performance of this Agreement and of any instrument or agreement required by this Agreement are not in conflict with any law or any indenture, agreement, or undertaking to which Borrower is a party or by which Borrower is bound or affected;

5.3   All financial information submitted by Borrower to Bank is true and correct in all material respects and is complete insofar as may be necessary to give Bank a true and accurate knowledge of the subject matter thereof;

5.4   Borrower is properly licensed and in good standing in each state in which Borrower is doing business, and Borrower has qualified under, and complied with, where required, the fictitious name statute of each state in which Borrower is doing business;

5.5   Borrower has complied with all federal, state, and local laws, rules, and regulations affecting the business of Borrower, including, but not limited to, laws regulating Borrower's sales or leases or the furnishing of services to Receivable Debtors and disclosures in connection therewith;

5.6   All Collateral is owned by Borrower free and clear of all clouds to title and of all liens, encumbrances, and rights of others except the rights of Bank under the Collateral Agreements;

5.7   Except for the due filing of a financing statement with respect to any Collateral Agreement, the delivery to Bank of any Collateral as to which possession is the only method of perfecting a security interest in or lien on such Collateral, and recording of any Collateral Agreement describing Collateral that is real property, no further action is necessary in order to establish and perfect Bank's first lien on or prior perfected security interest in all property covered by such Collateral Agreement;

5.8   There is no litigation, tax claim, proceeding or dispute pending, or, to the knowledge of Borrower, threatened, against or affecting Borrower or its property, the adverse determination of which might affect Borrower's financial condition or operations or impair Borrower's ability to perform its obligations hereunder or under any instrument or agreement required hereunder;

5.9 No event has occurred and is continuing or would result from the making of the Loan which constitutes or would constitute an Event of Default or which, upon a lapse of time or notice or both, would become an Event of Default.

6. **Covenants**

Borrower covenants and agrees that so long as the credit hereby granted shall remain available, and until the full and final payment of all indebtedness incurred hereunder, Borrower will, unless Bank waives compliance in writing:

6.1 Pay principal and interest on the Loan and all other sums due under this Agreement or under any Collateral Agreement according to the terms hereof or thereof;

6.2 Promptly give written notice to Bank of:

(a) any substantial dispute which may exist between Borrower and any governmental regulatory body or law enforcement authority;

(b) any Event of Default or any event which, upon a lapse of time or notice or both, would become an Event of Default;

(c) any other matter which has resulted or might result in a material adverse change in Borrower's financial condition or operations;

(d) all litigation affecting Borrower where the amount involved is twenty five thousand dollars ($25,000.00) or more;

(e) any labor controversy resulting in or threatening to result in a strike against Borrower;

(f) any proposal by any public authority to acquire the assets or business of Borrower or to engage in competitive activities with Borrower;

6.3 Deliver to Bank in form and detail satisfactory to Bank, and in such number of copies as Bank may request:

(a) As soon as available but no later than ___Thirty___ (_30_) days after the close of each __Month__ ,
     Borrower's balance sheet as of the close of such period, and Borrower's income statement, _____

_____
for such period and for that portion of Borrower's fiscal year ending with such period, certified as being complete and correct and fairly presenting Borrower's financial condition and results of operations by a responsible officer of Borrower;

(b) As soon as available but no later than _____

(____) days after the close of each fiscal year of Borrower, a complete copy of Borrower's audit report, which shall include at least Borrower's balance sheet as of the close of such year, and an income statement, reconciliation of capital accounts, and statement of sources and uses of funds for such year, prepared and certified by an independent public accountant selected by Borrower and satisfactory to Bank. Such certificate shall not be qualified or limited because of restricted or limited examination by such accountant of any material portion of Borrower's records, and shall include or be accompanied by a statement from such accountant that during the examination there was observed no Event of Default or circumstance which, upon a lapse of time or notice or both, would become an Event of Default, or a statement of such Event of Default or circumstance if any is found;

(c)   If required by Bank, on a day of each month designated by Bank, a borrowing certificate setting forth amounts of Acceptable Receivables as of the last day of the preceding month;

(d)   On a day of each month designated by Bank, statements showing aging and reconciliation of Receivables and collections;

(e)   Each time collections are delivered to Bank, a schedule of the amounts so collected and delivered to Bank;

(f)   Such other statement or statements, lists of property and accounts, budgets, forecasts, or reports as to Borrower as Bank may request;

6.4   Pay or reimburse Bank for expenses incurred by Bank in connection with this Agreement or any agreement or financing statement or other instrument furnished in connection with this Agreement;

6.5   Perform, on request of Bank, such acts as may be necessary or advisable to perfect any lien or security interest provided for herein or otherwise to carry out the intent of this Agreement;

6.6   Maintain and preserve Borrower's existence and all rights, privileges, and franchises now enjoyed; conduct Borrower's business in an orderly, efficient, and customary manner; keep all Borrower's properties in good working order and condition; and from time to time make all needed repairs, renewals, or replacements thereto and thereof so that the efficiency of such property shall be fully maintained and preserved;

6.7   Maintain and keep in force in adequate amounts such insurance as is usual in the business carried on by Borrower;

6.8   Maintain adequate books, accounts, and records and prepare all financial statements required hereunder in accordance with generally accepted accounting principles and practices consistently applied, and in compliance with the regulations of any governmental regulatory body having jurisdiction over Borrower or Borrower's business; and permit employees or agents of Bank at any reasonable time to inspect Borrower's properties and to examine or audit Borrower's books, accounts, and records and make copies and memoranda thereof;

6.9   At all times comply with, or cause to be complied with, all laws, statutes (including but not limited to any fictitious name statute), rules, regulations, orders, and directions of any governmental authority having jurisdiction over Borrower or Borrower's business, including but not limited to laws regulating Borrower's sales or leases to or performance of services for Receivable Debtors and disclosures in connection therewith;

6.10   Cause all financial information, including information relating to Receivables, upon submission by Borrower to Bank to be true and correct in all material respects and complete to the extent necessary to give Bank a true and accurate knowledge of the subject matter;

6.11   Not engage in any business activities or operations substantially different from or unrelated to present business activities and operations;

6.12   Cause each Guarantor to sumbit annual personal financial statements to Bank within ninety (90) days after the close of each fiscal year of Borrower, each covering that portion of the calendar year ending no earlier than the close of such fiscal year;

6.13   Apply the proceeds of sales of its fixed or capital assets in excess of a cumulative total of Fifty Thousand Dollars ($50,000.00), at the option of the Bank, to (a) replacement of the assets sold or (b) a reserve for future purchases of fixed or capital assets.

7.   *Events of Default*

The occurrence of any of the following Events of Default shall terminate any obligation on the part of Bank to make or continue the Loan and, at the option of Bank, shall make all sums of interest and principal remaining on the Loan immediately due and payable, without notice of default, presentment or demand for payment, protest or notice of nonpayment or dishonor, or other notices or demands of any kind or character, except as hereinafter specified:

7.1   Borrower fails to pay, when due, any installment of interest or principal or any other sum due under this Agreement or any Collateral Agreement in accordance with the terms hereof or thereof;

7.2   Any representation or warranty herein or in any agreement, instrument, or certificate executed pursuant hereto or in connection with any transaction contemplated hereby proves to have been false or misleading in any material respect when made;

7.3   Bank fails to have a valid and enforceable prior perfected security interest in or lien on any Collateral;

7.4   An involuntary lien or liens in the aggregate sum of ___One Hundred Thousand___ Dollars ($_100,000.00__) or more, of any kind or character, attaches to the assets or property of Borrower, except for taxes due but not in default, or for taxes which are being contested;

7.5   A judgment or judgments is or are entered against Borrower in the aggregate amount of One Hundred Thousand Dollars ($_100,000.00__) or more on a claim or claims not covered by insurance;

7.6   Borrower or any guarantor of any of Borrower's obligations to Bank admits in writing Borrower's or such guarantor's inability to pay Borrower's or such guarantor's debts generally as they come due, commits an act of bankruptcy or involvency, or files any petition or action for relief under any bankruptcy, reorganization, insolvency, or moratorium law, or any other law or laws for the relief of, or relating to, debtors;

7.7   An involuntary petition is filed under any bankruptcy statute against Borrower or any guarantor of any of Borrower's obligations to Bank or a receiver or trustee is appointed to take possession of the properties of Borrower or such guarantor;

7.8   Borrower voluntarily suspends its business for more than _____Seven_____ (_7_) days in any _____Thirty_____ (_30_) -day period;

7.9   Any governmental regulatory authority takes or institutes action which, in the opinion of Bank, will adversely affect Borrower's condition, operations, or ability to repay the Loan;

7.10   Any default occurs under any other agreement involving the borrowing of money or the advance of credit to which

Borrower may be a party as borrower or guarantor, if such default consists of the failure to pay any indebtedness when due or if such default gives to the holder of the obligation concerned the right to accelerate the indebtedness;

7.11   Any guaranty, subordination agreement, Collateral Agreement or other agreement or instrument required hereunder is breached or becomes ineffective or any default occurs under any such agreement or instrument;

7.12   Bank, in good faith, considers any Collateral to be unsafe or in danger of misuse to the extent that Bank's prospect of or right to payment or performance under this Agreement or any instrument or agreement required hereunder is impaired;

7.13   Borrower breaches, or defaults under, any term, condition, provision, representation, or warranty contained in this Agreement not specifically referred to in this Article 7.

8.   *Miscellaneous*

8.1   This Agreement shall bind and inure to the benefit of the parties hereto and their respective successors and assigns; provided, however, that Borrower shall not assign this Agreement or any of the rights, duties, or obligations of the Borrower hereunder without the prior written consent of Bank;

8.2   No consent or waiver under this Agreement shall be effective unless in writing. No waiver of any breach or default shall be deemed a waiver of any breach or default thereafter occurring;

8.3   This Agreement, and any instrument or agreement required under this Agreement, shall be governed by and construed under the laws of the State of California;

8.4   In the event of any action by Bank to enforce this Agreement or any instrument or agreement required by this Agreement, Borrower agrees to pay the costs thereof, reasonable attorney's fees, and all other costs and expenses;

8.5   This Agreement and any agreement, document, or instrument attached hereto or referred to herein integrate all the terms and conditions mentioned herein or incidental hereto, and supersede all oral negotiations and prior writings in respect to the subject matter hereof. In the event of any conflict between the terms, conditions, and provisions of this Agreement and any such agreement, document, or instrument, the terms, conditions, and provisions of this Agreement shall prevail;

8.6   Upon the occurrence of any Event of Default, Bank may, at its option, without notice to or demand upon Borrower:

(a) exercise any or all of its remedies under any Collateral Agreement and under any applicable law;

(b) immediately take possession of all of Borrower's records relating to Receivables; and

(c) apply to any court of competent jurisdiction for appointment of a receiver to take possession of the Collateral, without notice to Borrower and without a prior hearing, to which appointment Borrower hereby consents.

Bank shall have the right to enforce one or more remedies partially, successively, or concurrently, and Bank's enforcement of any remedy or remedies shall not estop or prevent Bank from pursuing any additional remedy or remedies that it may have hereunder or by law. In addition to all other sums which Borrower may be called upon to pay be reason of the occurrence of any Event of Default, Borrower agrees to reimburse Bank for: (a) all collection costs incurred by Bank and (b) all reasonable expenses, including all attorneys' fees and legal expenses, incurred by Bank in establishing Bank's security interest in the Collateral in any legal proceeding, and in retaking, holding, preparing for sale, and selling the Collateral;

8.7 Until Bank exercises its rights to collect the Receivables pursuant to any Collateral Agreement, Borrower may continue its present policies for returned merchandise and adjustments. If a credit adjustment is made with respect to any Acceptable Receivable, the amount of such adjustment shall no longer be included in the amount of such Acceptable Receivable in computing the Borrowing Base;

8.8 The proceeds of collections of Receivables, when received by Bank, shall be credited to interest, principal, and other sums due Bank under this Agreement in the order and proportion determined by Bank in its sole discretion. All such credits shall be conditioned upon collection and any returned items may, at Bank's option, be charged to Borrower;

8.9 Borrower agrees to indemnify Bank against, and hold Bank harmless from, all claims, actions, and losses, including attorneys' fees and costs incurred by Bank, arising from any contention, whether well-founded or otherwise, that there has been a failure to comply with any law regulating Borrower's sales or leases to or performance of services for Receivable Debtors and disclosures in connection therewith.

IN WITNESS WHEREOF, the parties hereto have executed this Agreement as of the day and year first above written.

_____Fit-Graphics_____	BANK OF AMERICA NATIONAL TRUST AND SAVINGS ASSOCIATION

By _____   By _____

Title _President_____   Title _____

By _____   By _____

Title _____   Title _____

Address where notices to   Address where notices to
Borrower are to be sent: Bank are to be sent:

APPENDIX FOUR

BORROWER: _____

GUARANTOR: _____

CONTINUING GUARANTY

To **BANK OF AMERICA**
NATIONAL TRUST AND SAVINGS ASSOCIATION

(1) For valuable consideration, the undersigned (hereinafter called Guarantors) jointly and severally unconditionally guarantee and promise to pay to BANK OF AMERICA NATIONAL TRUST AND SAVINGS ASSOCIATION (hereinafter called Bank), or order, on demand, in lawful money of the United States, any and all indebtedness of _____ (hereinafter called Borrowers) to Bank. The word "indebtedness" is used herein in its most comprehensive sense and includes any and all advances, debts, obligations and liabilities of Borrowers or any one or more of them, heretofore, now, or hereafter made, incurred or created, whether voluntary or involuntary and however arising, whether direct or acquired by Bank by assignment or succession, whether due or not due, absolute or contingent, liquidated or unliquidated, determined or undetermined, and whether Borrowers may be liable individually or jointly with others, or whether recovery upon such indebtedness may be or hereafter become barred by any statute of limitations, or whether such indebtedness may be or hereafter become otherwise unenforceable.

(2) The liability of Guarantors under this guaranty shall not exceed at any one time the sum of _____ Dollars ($_____) for principal, together with all interest upon the indebtedness or upon such part thereof as shall not exceed the foregoing limitation (exclusive of liability under any other guaranties executed by Guarantors). Notwithstanding the foregoing, Bank may permit the indebtedness of Borrowers to exceed Guarantors' liability. This is a continuing guaranty relating to any indebtedness, including that arising under successive transactions which shall either continue the indebtedness or from time to time renew it after it has been satisfied. This guaranty shall not apply to any indebtedness created after actual receipt by Bank of written notice of its revocation as to future transactions. Any payment by Guarantors shall not reduce their maximum obligation hereunder, unless written notice to that effect be actually received by Bank at or prior to the time of such payment.

(3) The obligations hereunder are joint and several, and independent of the obligations of Borrowers, and a separate action or actions may be brought and prosecuted against Guarantors whether action is brought against Borrowers or whether Borrowers be joined in any such action or actions; and Guarantors waive the benefit of any statute of limitations affecting their liability hereunder or the enforcement thereof.

(4) Guarantors authorize Bank, without notice or demand and without affecting their liability hereunder, from time to time to (a) renew, compromise, extend, accelerate or otherwise change the time for payment of, or otherwise change the terms of the indebtedness or any part thereof, including increase or decrease of the rate of interest thereon; (b) take and hold security for the payment of this guaranty or the indebtedness guaranteed, and exchange, enforce, waive and release any such security; (c) apply such security and direct the order or manner of sale thereof as Bank in its discretion may determine; and (d) release or substitute any one or more of the endorsers or guarantors. Bank may without notice assign this guaranty in whole or in part.

(5) Guarantors waive any right to require Bank to (a) proceed against Borrowers; (b) proceed against or exhaust any security held from Borrowers; or (c) pursue any other remedy in Bank's power whatsoever. Guarantors waive any defense arising by reason of any disability or other defense of Borrowers or by reason of the cessation from any cause whatsoever of the liability of Borrowers. Until all indebtedness of Borrowers to Bank shall have been paid in full, even though such indebtedness is in excess of Guarantors' liability hereunder, Guarantors shall have no right of subrogation, and waive any right to enforce any remedy which Bank now has or may hereafter have against Borrowers, and waive any benefit of, and any right to participate in any security now or hereafter held by Bank. Bank may foreclose, either by judicial foreclosure or by exercise of power of sale, any deed of trust securing the indebtedness, and, even though the foreclosure may destroy or diminish Guarantors' rights against Borrowers, Guarantors shall be liable to Bank for any part of the indebtedness remaining unpaid after the foreclosure. Guarantors waive all presentments, demands for performance, notices of non performance, protests, notices of protest, notices of dishonor, and notices of acceptance of this guaranty and of the existence, creation, or incurring of new or additional indebtedness.

(6) In addition to all liens upon, and rights of setoff against the moneys, securities or other property of Guarantors given to Bank by law, Bank shall have a lien upon and a right of setoff against all moneys, securities and other property of Guarantors now or hereafter in the possession of or on deposit with

Bank, whether held in a general or special account or deposit, or for safekeeping or otherwise; and every such lien and right of setoff may be exercised without demand upon or notice to Guarantors. No lien or right of setoff shall be deemed to have been waived by any act or conduct on the part of Bank, or by any neglect to exercise such right of setoff or to enforce such lien, or by any delay in so doing, and every right of setoff and lien shall continue in full force and effect until such right of setoff or lien is specifically waived or released by an instrument in writing executed by Bank.

(7) Any indebtedness of Borrowers now or hereafter held by Guarantors is hereby subordinated to the indebtedness of Borrowers to Bank; and such indebtedness of Borrowers to Guarantors if Bank so request shall be collected, enforced and received by Guarantors as trustees for Bank and be paid over to Bank on account of the indebtedness of Borrowers to Bank but without reducing or affecting in any manner the liability of Guarantors under the other provisions of this guaranty.

(8) Where any one or more of Borrowers are corporations or partnerships it is not necessary for Bank to inquire into the powers of Borrowers or of the officers, directors, partners or agents acting or purporting to act on their behalf, and any indebtedness made or created in reliance upon the professed exercise of such powers shall be guaranteed hereunder.

(9) Guarantors agree to pay a reasonable attorney's fee and all other costs and expenses which may be incurred by Bank in the enforcement of this Guaranty.

(10) Any married person who signs this guaranty hereby expressly agrees that recourse may be had against such person's separate property for all obligations under this guaranty.

(11) Where there is but a single Borrower, or where a single Guarantor executes this guaranty, then all words used herein in the plural shall be deemed to have been used in the singular where the context and construction so require; and when there is more than one Borrower named herein, or when this guaranty is executed by more than one Guarantor, the words "Borrowers" and "Guarantors" respectively shall mean all and any one or more of them.

(12) This Agreement shall be governed by and construed according to the laws of the State of California, to the jurisdiction of which the parties hereto submit.

Executed this _____ day of _____, 19____

Witnessed

_____	_____
Witness	Guarantor
_____	_____
Address	Print Name
	_____
	Address
	_____
	Soc. Sec. No. or I.D. No.
_____	_____
Witness	Guarantor
_____	_____
Address	Print Name
	_____
	Address
	_____
	Soc. Sec. No. or I.D. No.
_____	_____
Witness	Guarantor
_____	_____
Address	Print Name
	_____
	Address
	_____
	Soc. Sec. No. or I.D. No.
_____	_____
Witness	Guarantor
_____	_____
Address	Print Name
	_____
	Address
	_____
	Soc. Sec. No. or I.D. No.

CORPORATE RESOLUTION TO BORROW

RESOLVED, that this corporation, ...
borrow from BANK OF AMERICA NATIONAL TRUST AND SAVINGS ASSOCIATION, a national banking association, herein-
after referred to as "Bank," from time to time, such sum or sums of money as, in the judgement of the officer or officers hereinafter
authorized, this corporation may require; provided that the aggregate amount of such borrowing, pursuant to this resolution, shall

not at any one time exceed the sum of ....

.... Dollars ($ ....),
in addition to such amount as may be otherwise authorized:

RESOLVED FURTHER, that

.... the ....

or .... the ....

and .... the ....

or .... the ....

of this corporation (the officer or officers, or officers acting in combination, authorized to act pursuant hereto being hereinafter
designated as "authorized officers"), be and they are hereby authorized, directed and empowered, in the name of this corporation,
to execute and deliver to Bank, and Bank is requested to accept, the note or notes, advance account agreements, acceptance agreements or other instruments evidencing the indebtedness of this corporation for the monies so borrowed, or to be borrowed, with
interest thereon, and said authorized officers are authorized from time to time to execute renewals or extensions of said note or
notes, advance account agreements, acceptance agreements or other instruments.

RESOLVED FURTHER, that said authorized officers be and they are hereby authorized, directed and empowered, as security
for any note or notes or any other indebtedness of this corporation to Bank, whether arising pursuant to this resolution or otherwise,
to grant a security interest in, transfer, or otherwise hypothecate to Bank, or deed in trust for its benefit, any property belonging to
or under the control of this corporation, and to execute and deliver to Bank any and all loan or credit agreements, grants, transfers,
security agreements, deeds of trust and other hypothecation agreements, which said instruments and note or notes and other instruments referred to in the preceeding paragraph may contain such provisions, covenants, recitals and agreements as Bank may require
and said authorized officers may approve, and the execution thereof by said authorized officers shall be conclusive evidence of such
approval.

FURTHER RESOLVED, that said authorized officers may, and they are hereby authorized, directed and empowered, in addition to the authorized borrowing set forth above (a) to discount with or sell to Bank, security agreements, leases, bailment agreements, notes, acceptances, drafts, receivables and evidences of indebtedness payable to this corporation, upon such terms as may be
agreed upon by them and Bank, and to endorse in the name of this corporation said notes, acceptances, drafts, receivables, and evidences of indebtedness so discounted, and to guarantee the payment of the same to Bank and (b) to apply for and obtain from Bank
letters of credit and in connection therewith to execute security agreements, applications, guaranties, indemnities and other financial
undertakings.

RESOLVED FURTHER, that Bank is authorized to act upon this resolution until written notice of its revocation is delivered
to Bank, and that the authority hereby granted shall apply with equal force and effect to the successors in office of the officers
herein named.

I, ..., Secretary

of .... , a corporation, incorporated

under the laws of the State of..., do hereby certify that the foregoing is a full, true and correct copy
of a resolution of the Board of Directors of said corporation, duly and regularly adopted by the Board of Directors of said corpora—

tion in all respects as required by law, and by the by-laws of said corporation, on the..day

of ...., 19..........., at which meeting a majority of the Board of Directors of said corporation was present
and voted in favor of said resolution.

I further certify that said resolution is still in full force and effect and has not been amended or revoked, and that the specimen
signatures appearing below are the signatures of the officers authorized to sign for this corporation by virtue of this resolution.

IN WITNESS WHEREOF, I have hereunto set my hand as such Secretary, and affixed the corporate seal of said corporation,

this .... day of ...., 19...........

AUTHORIZED SIGNATURES:

....
(Signature)

....
(Signature)

....
(Signature)

....
(Signature)

Affix

corporate seal

here

....
(Signature)

....
(Signature)

SECRETARY OF

A CORPORATION

N-243   1/80

CHAPTER THREE

BANKERS'

ACCEPTANCES

A bankers' acceptance is a time draft or an order to pay a specific sum of money at a specified date. The draft is presented to the bank, which stamps the draft "Accepted," engaging the bank's liability. It is then held in the bank's portfolio as a loan or sold in the secondary market, the investment community.

Unlike conventional loans, where interest is paid monthly or quarterly in arrears, the interest on acceptances is paid at the outset. Specifically, the bank advances the borrower the face value of the acceptance less the interest rate. This procedure is known as discounting. At maturity, the company pays the face value of the acceptance to the bank. If the bank sells the acceptance to an investor in the secondary market at a rate below the discount rate, the bank is immediately paid interest. The difference between the rate charged the borrower and the rate paid the investor is the bank's commission for adding its obligation to pay the investor at maturity irrespective of the borrower's ability to pay the bank. An acceptance is the direct obligation of the bank and it must appear on both sides of the balance sheet. To amplify, this process is tantamount to an individual presenting a personal check (also a draft) to a bank. As opposed to the current date placed on the check, the date is for some future time, in other words, 30, 60, 90, or 180 days hence. The bank advances the amount of the check less the interest, or discount rate, to the customer. The bank stamps the check "Accepted," which is similar to its endorsement, and sells the accepted check to an investor who pays the bank the face value less the market discount. At maturity the investor presents the check to the bank, which pays the face value. The bank then presents the check to the customer, who in turn pays the face value. The following flowchart identifies the acceptance life cycle. The numbers correspond with the narrative.

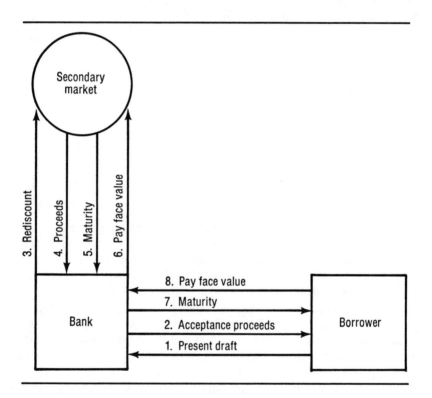

1. The borrower presents the draft to the bank.

2. The bank stamps the draft "accepted" and pays the borrower the face amount less the interest (discount).

3. The bank rediscounts the accepted draft (acceptance) in the secondary market to an investor at a rate less than its discount.

4. The investor pays the bank the face value less the market discount. Specifically, if the market discount is 9 percent and the bank charges 10 percent to the borrower, the 1 percent difference is the bank's commission fee for engaging its liability, adding its creditworthiness.

5. At maturity the investor presents the draft to the bank for payment.

6. The bank pays the investor the face value of the acceptance.

7. The bank presents the acceptance to the borrower for payment.

8. The borrower pays the face value of the acceptance to the bank.

As the chart shows, "The bank may hold the acceptance in its own portfolio or rediscount (liquidate) it in the secondary market. This decision is based on the bank's capitalization, liquidity, cost of funds and alternative investments."[1]

The secondary market was established in 1913 through the adoption of the Federal Reserve Act, which encouraged the Fed to discount acceptances, financing international commerce. The market today is comprised of money market paper dealers, individual investors, corporate investors, and correspondent banks. This market is well established and structured, and an investor has never lost its investment.

During the last decade, bankers' acceptance financing has achieved remarkable growth. Acceptances outstanding in 1973 were $8.8 billion, increasing to $65.6 billion in 1981. This 686 percent growth compares to a 118 percent growth for conventional loans for the same period, which were $165.6 billion in 1973 and $360.1 billion in 1981.

"Why this soaring growth? Bankers' Acceptances are one of the oldest funding instruments known to the banking community. They enable the banking industry to meet customer needs with investor funds, as opposed to deposits or retained earnings and they benefit both banks and borrowers. Yet bankers' acceptances did not receive notable attention in the U.S. until 1973–75, when the tight money climate spurred bankers to search for alternative sources of funds."[2] Acceptance financing was further encouraged by corporate treasurers who appreciated the significant interest savings.

HISTORY

The bankers' acceptance has its roots back to 1100 B.C., with the use of bills of exchange and trade acceptances. During the early

[1]MacPhee, W., "Bankers' Acceptance Finance," *The Journal of Commercial Bank Lending* (1978).

[2]Ibid.

Draft

No._____

San Francisco, California _____ 19____

Pay to the order of _____

$_____

_____ Dollars

CROCKER NATIONAL BANK
SAN FRANCISCO, CALIFORNIA

ASSISTANT VICE PRESIDENT

ASSISTANT VICE PRESIDENT
INTERNATIONAL BANKING OFFICER

CROCKER NATIONAL BANK

Registered by _____

This bill was secured at the time of acceptance by
independent warehouse, terminal or other similar
receipt conveying security title to

_____ stored in _____

No. _____

$_____

ACCEPTED

Date _____

TO

CROCKER NATIONAL BANK
INTERNATIONAL DIVISION
1 SANSOME STREET
SAN FRANCISCO, CALIFORNIA 94104

years a seller would accept a buyer's note covering goods with a promise to pay a specific sum on a specific date. This form of trade credit allowed the buyer to process and sell the goods with payment flowing back to the original seller. We speculate that this trade credit procedure worked well in local or regional communities where buyers and sellers were known to each other. As trade regions expanded, buyer-seller relationships were more distant and credit terms less flexible.

Trading houses developed where an independent third party known to the buyer and seller would guarantee the buyer's credit to the seller. This guarantee was evidenced by the trading house's endorsement of the note or bill of exchange, which became a trade acceptance. This procedure engaged the trading house's obligation to pay the seller in the event the buyer defaulted.

Occasionally, the seller required funds before the maturity of the trade acceptance. The seller would present the trade acceptance to the trading house or another businessman looking for a short-term investment. The investor would advance funds, less the interest rate of the trade acceptance, to the seller. When the trade acceptance matured, the buyer paid the trading house, which, in turn, paid the seller, who repurchased the trade acceptance from the investor.

One can readily see that these procedures laid the groundwork for bankers' acceptance. Eventually the trading house's guarantee function was replaced by banks, adding their acceptance to the draft, and the secondary investment market developed into a market for liquidating acceptances.

> It was through this medium of bankers' acceptances that central banks traditionally exerted influence on the balance of payments and domestic economic conditions.... By manipulating their discount rates, central banks influenced the acceptance rate at which both domestic and international trade was financed, thereby affecting the cost and availability of credit.[3]

Until 1913, only the well-established and creditworthy London banks enjoyed universal recognition for their bankers' acceptances. "Financial institutions in the United States were not as well known or as trusted as London (banking) houses, and more significantly, there was no U.S. central bank that could guarantee liquidity of U.S. (corporate) obligations and convertibility of (U.S.) currency into gold—a feature then necessary to attract for-

---

[3]Master, D. V., "Acceptances Practices and Regulations" (Unpublished Master's Thesis, 1970), University of Washington.

eign short-term funds to the U.S."[4] Also, international trade transactions in the 19th and 20th centuries have been, for the most part, settled in sterling.

Before 1913, American businessmen relied largely on a few private banking houses and on the British banking institutions for acceptance financing. Few American banks were active in foreign trade, and there was no open market for bankers' acceptances in the United States prior to the passage of the Federal Reserve Act. Acceptances were sometimes created by banks, but there was no specific authorization for national banks to create acceptances. Further, there was no open discount market for bankers' acceptances in the United States, and banks which did create acceptances were obliged to hold them in their own portfolios. As a result, large American banks financed their customers' international transactions, particularly imports, by arranging commercial credits with foreign banks in foreign currencies, principally with British banks in sterling.[5]

The Federal Reserve Act of 1913, sections 13 and 14, encouraged the formal development of a structured and fluid secondary market for bankers' acceptances patterned after the existing and well-established European acceptance markets. The act created the U.S central bank and empowered it to rediscount acceptances meeting strict requirements. With respect to acceptances, the act had three specific objectives:

1. Provide liquidity relief to the U.S. banking industry through availability of a new source of funds provided by the secondary market.
2. Reduce U.S. corporate dependency on foreign currency loans which weakened the dollar.
3. Increase U.S. exports and increase the U.S. role in foreign trade through favorable financing terms.

Although the Federal Reserve Act allowed for domestic transactions (U.S. storage and shipment), the intent was to encourage international trade. From 1913 to the 1960s, acceptance financing was erratic, barely reaching $8 billion, while conventional loans reached $160 billion and commercial paper topped $40 billion in 1973. The tight money environment of the mid-70s saw banks eagerly looking for alternative sources of funds to ease their tight liquidity situation.

The industry turned to bankers' acceptance financing, which

---

[4]Ibid.
[5]Ibid.

provided liquidity relief. Although the regulations qualifying transactions for acceptance financing were, and are, stringent, the outstandings mushroomed, as indicated by the following chart.

The 1973–75 tight money period introduced corporate treasurers to the significant interest savings provided by acceptances compared to conventional loans. Further, bankers began actively marketing acceptances to the most creditworthy borrowers who had been financing with commercial paper. The rates are compa-

Chart II
Bankers' Acceptance Outstanding

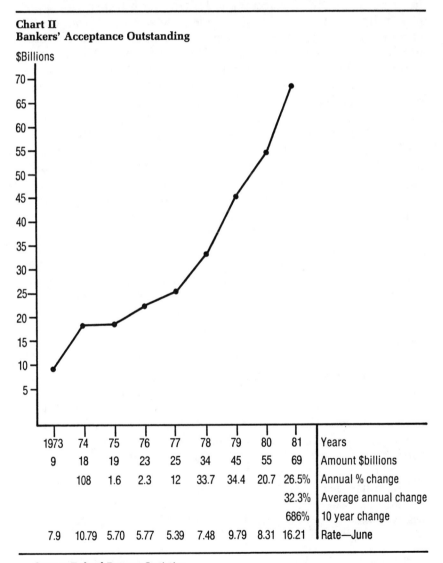

$Billions

Years	1973	74	75	76	77	78	79	80	81
Amount $billions	9	18	19	23	25	34	45	55	69
Annual % change		108	1.6	2.3	12	33.7	34.4	20.7	26.5%
Average annual change									32.3%
10 year change									686%
Rate—June	7.9	10.79	5.70	5.77	5.39	7.48	9.79	8.31	16.21

Source: Federal Reserve Statistics.

rable in numerous cases when all the associated costs for commercial paper are considered. The 686 percent growth in acceptances exceeded the 297 percent growth of commercial paper, Eurodollars at 462 percent, and commercial loans growth of 118 percent.

REGULATIONS

In order to qualify for acceptance financing a transaction must meet criteria established by the Federal Reserve Act, section 13, and related interpretations. Appendix 1 contains the act, which has been the source of considerable controversy. The primary reason for dispute stems from the fact that all but three of the interpretations were rendered between 1913 and 1933. In some cases the regulations are out of sync with modern law (Uniform Commercial Code) and current trade practices.

The 12 Federal Reserve districts enjoy some autonomy for reinterpreting the regulations. For transactions clearly falling out of the direct focus of the regulations, the reserve banks often refer decisions to the New York Federal Reserve for final review. In the event the final decision is contested, the petitioner may appeal to the board of governors of the Federal Reserve system. However, this is a lengthy process.

Some attempt has been made to clarify the ambiguity of dated regulations with modern law and trade practices. Attorney Henry Harfield has focused considerable attention on the topic.[6] It is our intention to approach the issue from the practitioners point of view. From extensive experience, we conclude that the regulations and modern practices focus on five fundamental principles.

1. *There must be an underlying trade transaction evidenced by a "contract" for international transactions, a warehouse receipt for domestic storage, and, until recently, a shipping bill of lading for domestic shipping transactions.* The bill-of-lading requirement was eliminated in 1982, and we presume that a borrower's certification that an underlying transaction exists will meet the spirit of the regulations.

There has been much confusion over the requirements for international and U.S. shipping and U.S. storage transactions. Many banks have required a bill of lading for international trans-

---

[6]Harfield, H. and Ward, W., eds., *Bank Credits and Acceptances*, 4th ed. (New York: Ronald Press, 1958).

actions, presumably on the mistaken belief that since U.S. shipping transactions require a bill of lading the same holds for international transactions. A purpose statement executed by the borrower, certifying that certain goods are or will be shipped internationally with an approximate value of X dollars, is sufficient. Albeit a bill of lading is evidence of the transaction, the regulations do not require this for international trade.

The interpretations specifically preclude funding general working capital with acceptance proceeds. But the acceptance may be drawn for a period covering the purchase, limited processing, shipment, and receivable period for goods. We conclude that the provision precluding the financing of working capital applies to supplementing general and nontrade related cash flow.

Although limited processing, adding value to the goods, is permitted, interpretations have precluded financing processing where the nature of the original product materially changes. Specifically, the shucking of peanuts does not materially change the nature of the peanut, while the conversion of the peanut to oil or peanut butter does.

2. *The goods must be readily marketable staples.* Section P 1375 of the regulations defines staples: "The term 'staples' includes manufactured goods as well as raw materials, provided the goods in question are non-perishable and have a wide ready market. They must be goods generally produced and well established in commerce, not an unusual or extraordinary commodity for which there is no ready market."[7] Section 1380 amplifies: "Member banks, as a matter of prudence, should not consider. ...any staple which is in its nature so perishable as not to be reasonably sure of maintaining its value as security at least for the life of the draft drawn against it."[8]

There has been considerable debate over the readily marketable aspect of a product, given certain characteristic changes. For example, a syndicate of banks financing a major coffee manufacturer claim that the finished ground coffee labeled with the manufacturer's package is not readily marketable. The banks have concluded that they may finance the importation of coffee beans and their processing up to the point of final packaging. However, they maintain that the product, once packaged, is no longer readily marketable. Our position is that the substance of the coffee bean has not materially changed, irrespective of the

---

[7]Published Interpretations of The Board of Governors of the Federal Reserve System (1981).

[8]Ibid.

packaging. The product basically remains the same and is a readily marketable staple under the strictest definition.

3. *Goods must move into the normal channels of trade.* This refers to the time normally involved in purchasing, processing, and selling the goods and precludes financing speculation. Section 1400 states, "A draft which is drawn to carry goods for speculative purposes or for an indefinite period of time without the purpose to sell, ship, or manufacture within a reasonable time is not eligible for acceptance."[9]

When questions surface surrounding the time factor, three general approaches are suggested to determine time or tenor of the acceptance:

a. The industry average product turnover time.
b. The borrower's average product turnover time.
c. A specific contracted time.

4. *The financing may not exceed 180 days.* Acceptances may not finance a transaction beyond 180 days. Therefore if a borrower has a specific transaction exceeding the limit, only the last 180 days may be financed with proceeds of a bankers' acceptance. This ensures the self-liquidating nature of the transaction and reinforces the prohibition against funding speculative and working capital transactions.

5. *Transaction proceeds must liquidate the acceptance at maturity.* This is a generally accepted procedure ensuring that an underlying and specific trade transaction exists and is self-liquidating in nature.

These principles form the general parameters for acceptance financing. The regulations and interpretations serve to reinforce and clarify the above fundamentals. Caution must be used when attempting to clarify the interpretations which are dated and often apply to one type of transaction; for example, domestic storage but not to other types, such as international trade.

The banking industry has a difficult time with the regulations within the framework of modern trade practices and the industry's built-in bureaucracies covering banking jurisdiction. Rarely is the banking officer permitted to make decisions regarding the Federal Reserve regulations. These problems are directed to the legal staff or outside counsel for interpretation—often a time-consuming and expensive effort even where clear precedent is

---

[9]Ibid.

established. "The current trend in regulating the use of acceptance financing is toward streamlining the procedures and encouraging expanded use of acceptances."

Penalties

Acceptances created to finance transactions meeting the preceding regulations are termed *eligible*. Specifically, the bank creating the acceptance may present the documents covering the transaction to the Federal Reserve as collateral for a loan in the event of a liquidity squeeze. If a transaction violates any one of the covenants, the transaction is termed *ineligible* and the bank may not secure a loan from the Federal Reserve with it. An ineligible acceptance bears a financial penalty for the bank that may be applied retroactively, and the bank may attempt to pass these penalties on to the borrower.

The penalties are known as reserves and are governed by Federal Reserve regulation D, section 2.4.1, which covers reserves on deposits and discounted ineligible bankers' acceptances. It is important to note that reserves are applied only when the creating bank discounts the ineligible acceptance in the secondary market. Ineligible acceptances held in the bank's portfolio are funded by deposits for which reserves are maintained at the time the deposit was made. Currently, the reserve rate is 3 percent but it may be changed by the Federal Reserve in its efforts to control money supply.

To properly price the acceptance, the banker must clearly understand if the underlying transaction meets eligibility requirements. If the transaction is not eligible, the appropriate reserve factor must be added to the total cost for the borrower's account. The borrower should be confident that the transaction is eligible, because banks rarely hold the borrower harmless for costs associated with borrowing, and this includes retroactive reserves. Therefore, to accurately compare borrowing alternatives, the company must know its implied and contingent costs. An alternative is for the banks to certify that the transaction meets eligibility criteria.

The basic obstacle for many corporate banking officers, concerning acceptances, is that they are academically and professionally balance sheet in their orientation. Their training has focused on the creditworthiness of the borrower. Without detracting from the importance of a sound balance sheet, acceptance financing is transactional in orientation, requiring a different focus.

MECHANICS

Bank selection is important when considering acceptance financing. Given the various regulations that must be met, the borrower should be confident in the banker's ability to properly structure the transaction while minimizing the administration of this financing alternative. Further, a creative and knowledgeable banker will be able to design alternative structures.

As banks pay various rates for deposits based on their own creditworthiness, they also pay different market discounts for acceptances. Therefore, in order to enjoy the best rates, the company should select the banks with the best credit ratings. The major money center banks usually enjoy the best rates, which may result in savings of .25–1 percent per annum for the borrower. This equates to a $2,500–$10,000 savings per $1 million of outstandings per year.

Although major banks enjoy recognition and access to the secondary market for liquidating acceptances, regional or local banks may create their own discount market. Local banks provide certificates of deposit for local investors. Similarly, they can include acceptances as an investment alternative.

A Tennessee bank established its regional secondary market in Nashville. When a corporate client requested funds under an acceptance facility, the bank telephoned select institutions, including corporations, universities, and government concerns, soliciting their discounting of the acceptance. This enabled the bank to compete with money center banks.

Another consideration for selecting a bank is the limit of acceptances the bank may create. Effective October 8, 1982, President Ronald Reagan signed the Export Trading Company Act, which included provisions amending the Federal Reserve Act's limits on outstanding eligible acceptances. Although formerly limited to 50 percent, a bank may now create aggregate outstanding eligible acceptances to 150 percent of its capital and surplus. With Federal Reserve approval, a national bank may create aggregate outstanding eligible acceptances up to 200 percent of capital and surplus. The former limit was 100 percent of capital and surplus under Section 13, sub. 5200, of the revised status of the Federal Reserve Act. Banks with formerly approved 100 percent limits must reapply for the new 200 percent limit approval. Approval must be granted by the board of governors of the Federal Reserve System.

The October 8, 1982 revision, limits the amount of domestic acceptances to 50 percent of the bank's aggregate limit, and a bank may not create unsecured acceptances for any one borrower exceeding 15 percent of that bank's capital and surplus. Acceptances exceeding the 15 percent limit must be fully secured throughout the life of the acceptance.

When selecting a bank the corporation should consider the discount rate charged the bank by the investment community, and the size of the bank. This will provide some insight into the availability of funds under an acceptance facility. Where the bank's size limits its ability to readily provide acceptance financing, a syndicate of banks may be considered.

With the demand for acceptance financing, even the largest money center banks reach their limits. The new regulations will effectively double the potential limits, but past growth history indicates that increasing demand may result in outstandings meeting the new limits. This is not a major issue, since acceptances are short-term and mature quickly, leaving room for additional acceptances on a first come–first served basis.

A bank syndication, where many banks provide acceptance lines of credit, will dilute the availability risk for the borrower. Agent banks exclude from their limits, acceptances sold to other banks through participation agreements. The amount sold to the participating bank is subtracted from the agent bank's limits and added to the outstandings of the participating bank.

On October 2, 1982, President Reagan signed House Resolution 8313, the Export Trade Act, which amended Section 207 of the Federal Reserve Act (12 USC 372) covering bankers' acceptances. The thrust of this amendment was to eliminate the title document previously required for domestic shipping transactions, increase aggregate bank limits covering acceptances, and provide for participating acceptances to correspondent banks.

Previously, participating acceptance credit was awkward since the total amount of the acceptance applied to the creating agent bank's acceptance limits. Pricing acceptances that were participated was difficult because of differing discount rates to banks. The new legislation eliminates that portion of an acceptance participated with a correspondent bank from the creating bank's acceptance limits. This will minimize the pricing confusion, since the creating bank's discount rate will cover the entire acceptance to include the portion participated.

This legislation allows a bank to create acceptances exceeding its 15 percent limit to any one customer by participating the excess to a correspondent bank. The evidence of participation is to be shown on the actual draft, which states the amount and participating bank.

It is premature to determine the accounting treatments for the participation. It would appear that the full asset and liability of the acceptance would appear on the creating bank's balance sheet, since its unconditional liability to the secondary market investor is evidenced on the acceptance.

It is suggested, given time zone differences and quickly changing rates, that the corporation execute a number of drafts for each bank, to be held by the bank until needed. The drafts are numbered and maintained in the bank's vaults. When drawings occur, the company advises the banks of the underlying transaction, and the banks date the drafts and stamp them "Accepted" for discounting in the secondary market. Simultaneously, the banks credit the borrower's account with the face amount of the draft less the discount rate and commission.

In order to maintain the competitive environment, it is advised that the borrower insist that quotes be submitted on an individual bid basis. The syndication process lends itself to stabilizing rates, which may be to the disadvantage of the borrower and to banks with less favorable discount rates.

The loan application prepared by the bank for internal credit approval is identical to the commercial loan package, since the actual credit analysis is the same. The application will indicate the acceptance option for the company. Most importantly, the application should include the officer's confidence in the eligibility of the transaction. This should be a statement identifying the transaction, the terms thereof, and any conditions differing from the conventional line.

The actual credit analysis is identical to the conventional loan analysis. However, since there is an underlying transaction, the risk factors are reduced and the rate should reflect this. Because there must be an underlying trade transaction, an additional source of repayment exists, aside from the borrower's creditworthiness. Where an acceptance is drawn to finance the export of goods under a confirmed, irrevocable letter of credit, the bank's exposure is transferred from the borrower to the opening correspondent bank. Since the risk has been transferred, given the definition of interest, the rate should be adjusted appropriately. (The section on letters of credit in this chapter amplifies this point.) It is noted that for prime credit names, any additional credit support most probably will not affect the rate, since those companies already enjoy most-favored rate status.

The loan agreement will differ slightly from the conventional loan document, citing the availability of acceptance financing and the term of the funding. Also, the company will execute a documentary acceptance agreement. Sometimes these agreements are quite extensive and often refer to the secured nature of the transaction. This may have negative implications for certain borrowers who will not or can not, by way of other agreements, provide security. A copy of a standard acceptance agreement is shown in Appendix Two.

Since October 8, 1982, no title document has been required for international or U.S. shipping transactions; therefore, there is no legal collateral or support for the word *Security* in these agreements.

For domestic storage transactions where a warehouse receipt is required, the secured nature is also in question. Section 1425 of the Federal Reserve Act allows for the release of the warehouse receipt to the borrower.

We conclude that the purpose of the receipt is not to secure the transaction throughout its life but to evidence the existence of the goods supporting the transaction.

When the bank will not take title without the Fed's requirement, when the bank immediately releases title documents to the

Warehouse Report

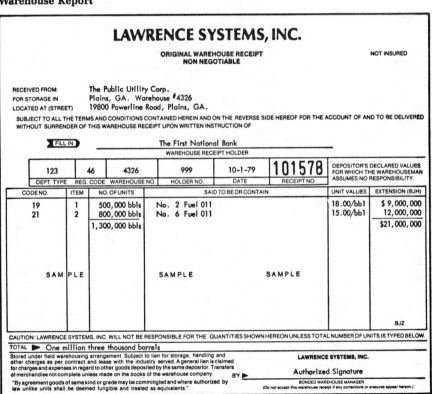

LAWRENCE SYSTEMS, INC.

FIELD WAREHOUSE STORAGE AGREEMENT

THIS AGREEMENT, made and entered into this _____ day of _____, 19_____,

by and between LAWRENCE SYSTEMS, INC., a California corporation, hereinafter called "Lawrence," having a mailing address

at _____,

and_____

having a mailing address at _____.

hereinafter called "Depositor,"

WITNESSETH:

Upon the terms and conditions hereinafter set forth, Depositor hereby employs Lawrence to establish and operate all field warehouses and provide all usual field warehouse services required by Depositor's business, and Lawrence hereby accepts said employment.

1. Depositor shall lease, or cause to be leased, to Lawrence, upon Lawrence's form of Field Warehouse Lease, adequate warehouse storage space for the warehousing of commodities. Said warehouse storage space shall be so located and constructed as to assure the proper storing and safety of warehoused commodities.

2. The following commodities will be warehoused:_____

3. Depositor shall pay to Lawrence for the services rendered hereunder and for the employees or agents required by Lawrence to conduct said field warehouse service the charges set forth in a supplemental billing agreement between Lawrence and Depositor, whether the services are rendered with respect to commodities of Depositor or with respect to commodities of third parties deposited at the request of Depositor.

4. Depositor will have Lawrence named as a loss payee, as its interest may appear, in all insurance policies carried by Depositor affecting all commodities in the custody or control of Lawrence and will cause its insurance carrier to waive all rights of subrogation against Lawrence under all insurance policies insuring in any way real or personal property of Depositor or in which it has any interest.

5. As security for all charges, costs, and expenses earned or incurred by Lawrence hereunder, Lawrence shall have a continuing lien on all commodities deposited.

6. Depositor shall furnish to Lawrence financial statements accurately and completely reflecting Depositor's financial condition whenever in the regular course of Depositor's business such statements are prepared. Depositor shall furnish to Lawrence annual statements (Balance Sheet, Statement of Income, including notes thereto, etc.) each year during the term hereof.

7. All commodities of like or unlike description wherever authorized by law, stored hereunder may be commingled and warehoused as one general lot of fungible goods, and the holder of a warehouse receipt shall be entitled to such portion of such general lot as the amount of the commodity represented by such receipt bears to the whole of such general lot of such commodity.

8. Lawrence shall be under no obligation to accept for storage any merchandise or commodities for which warehouse receipts are not to be issued. In the event Lawrence shall accept the same and make no charge for the storage thereof, such storage shall be as a convenience to Depositor and solely at Depositor's risk and Depositor hereby agrees to indemnify and hold harmless Lawrence against all damage, risk, claim and expense which Lawrence may incur or be subject to by reason of permitting such free storage, including claims made against said goods by third parties. Depositor agrees that it will not present for storage any goods unless the same are owned by Depositor free and clear of every lien, burden or charge, legal or equitable.

9. Depositor agrees to refer to Lawrence, at Lawrence's option, employees or agents reasonably satisfactory to Lawrence to act as field representatives in the Lawrence warehouse to assist in the operation thereof. Depositor agrees that all such representatives are to take instructions only from Lawrence in regard to the receipt, storage and delivery of goods for which Lawrence has issued its warehouse receipts or otherwise assumed liability. Lawrence agrees that Depositor may give instructions to such representatives provided such instructions in no way conflict with the instructions of Lawrence. Depositor shall indemnify and hold harmless Lawrence against any loss, damage, claim or liability arising directly or indirectly as the result of (i) the negligent or wrongful conduct of such representatives, unless acting in accordance with instructions from Lawrence, or (ii) any act or representation of any agent, employee or other person acting for or on behalf of Depositor.

10. Depositor hereby authorizes the holder of any warehouse receipt issued pursuant to its request to disclose to Lawrence any information in its possession relating to Depositor's financial condition.

11. This agreement shall continue in full force and effect for three (3) years from the date hereof, and thereafter for successive three (3) year terms unless either party gives to the other written notice of intention to terminate at least ninety (90) days prior to the expiration of the then current three (3) year term; provided, that no such notice of termination given by Depositor shall become effective unless all warehouse receipts, or other evidence of the storage of commodities, issued by Lawrence shall have been surrendered to Lawrence and cancelled and all charges of Lawrence shall have been paid prior to the expiration of the then current term; and provided further, that Lawrence shall have the right to cancel this agreement at any time upon giving ten (10) days written notice to Depositor if Depositor is in arrears in payment of charges or is interfering with the operation of any warehouse established pursuant to this agreement. At any time after a notice of termination has been delivered hereunder, Lawrence shall not be obligated to accept any additional commodities into said warehouses.

IN WITNESS WHEREOF, the parties hereto have caused this agreement to be duly executed the day and year first above written.

_____
(DEPOSITOR)

LAWRENCE SYSTEMS, INC.

By_____
TITLE

By_____
SENIOR VICE PRESIDENT

borrower, when no UCC-1 is filed, and when the bank does not perfect a lien on sale proceeds, the word *security* in the documentary acceptance agreement is without practical substance.

The negotiations and structure of the acceptance credit are similar to the conventional loan. The fundamental difference is the inclusion of the borrower's option to borrow under the prime line or acceptance line. Where borrowings occur under the acceptance facility, the bank must be satisfied as to the eligibility of the transaction.

Since bank examiners focus most of their attention on actual documentation, the banks self-regulate themselves regarding the specifics of the transaction. The bank should advise the borrower of the fundamental requirements, and the borrower should be aware of the criteria ensuring that no reserves costs will be passed on to the borrower. Although the Fed has no jurisdiction over corporations, penalties assessed the bank may be passed on to the customer.

This situation recently occurred with a major food processor, which buys raw agricultural products from international suppliers. The company contracts with U.S.-based brokers and dealers to enter the international market and purchase raw goods. The goods are shipped to the United States with title passing to the U.S. broker/dealer. Eventually, the borrower purchases the goods from the broker, and they are shipped to the buyer's processing plants.

Five major banks supply credit, including the availability of an acceptance facility, to the borrower. The five banks unanimously agree that the raw materials transaction qualifies for acceptance financing since the goods come from international suppliers. However, this structure is ineligible for acceptance financing, and the transaction is subject to reserves. Unless otherwise specified, the banks may pass these reserves on to the borrower, effectively increasing the borrower's costs.

Discussions with the Fed reveal that the importing U.S. broker-dealer may finance the goods with acceptances under the regulations covering international transactions. However, since the title passes from the foreign seller to the broker and not directly from the foreign supplier to the ultimate buyer, the U.S. buyer's transaction is not covered by international guidelines and is a domestic transaction. This transaction could have been structured to avoid reserves or possible Federal Reserve criticism.

When the company requires funds, it advises the bank of the transaction specifics and the date. The bank date-stamps the draft and affixes its acceptance qualifying it for discount in the secondary market. This process eliminates any timing problems and allows for immediate disbursement of funds to the borrower.

Although acceptances are at a fixed rate for periods of 30, 60, 90, 120, 150, or 180 days, the acceptance may be prepaid in the event the transaction liquidates itself before maturity of the acceptance. The commission, reflecting the bank's "endorsement" engaging its liability, is usually not refunded, but the discount covering the remaining period of the acceptance may be rebated at the prevailing rate.

A major distinction between acceptance financing and alternatives is that there must be an underlying trade transaction for banker's acceptances. In order to understand the role of acceptances we will explore the two domestic transactions and the four international transactions giving rise to acceptance financing. The life cycle of each structure is diagramed with a corresponding narrative.

Domestic Storage

The storage of readily marketable goods within the United States may be financed by eligible banker's acceptances. However, unlike the international transaction where evidence of sale is required, the storage transaction must be evidenced by a warehouse receipt or similar (title) document issued by an independent third party.[10]

The warehouse receipt must accompany the draft when presented to the bank and may be released to consummate sales.[11]

Acceptances drawn to finance storage transactions must be secured at the time of acceptance but for purpose of discount need not remain secured to the same extent, except where they exceed the 15 percent limitation on acceptances for any one customer.[12]

On May 10, 1978, the Board of Governors of the Federal Reserve issued interpretation no. R-0135, covering the procedures for properly structuring the warehousing arrangement. It condoned the use of a field warehouse for issuing warehouse receipts covering eligible bankers' acceptances where the field warehouse is specifically in the warehousing business, has financial substance, is bonded, and subscribes to proper possession and control requirements.

---

[10]MacPhee, W. "Bankers' Acceptance Finance," *The Journal of Commercial Bank Lending* (1978).

[11]Ibid.

[12]Ibid.

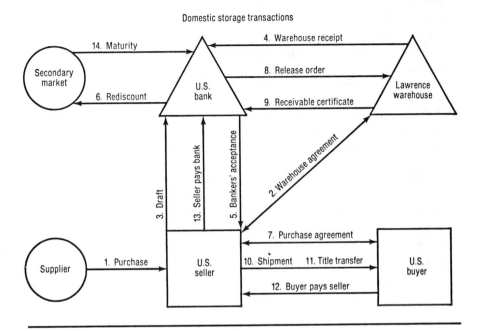

Domestic storage transactions

Domestic Storage/Transaction

Situation: U.S. company requires financing covering a domestic transaction: storage, shipment, and receivable time.

1. Seller procures goods from its supplier.
2. Seller enters into a warehouse agreement with Lawrence, which leases storage facilities from the seller.
3. Seller presents its draft to the bank after negotiating the credit terms and conditions.
4. Lawrence presents its warehouse receipt to the bank, evidencing the third-party control of stored goods as required by the Fed.
5. The bank discounts the draft (face value less interest rate) and credits proceeds to seller's account.
6. At the bank's option, it either rediscounts the acceptance in the secondary market or holds it in its loan portfolio.
7. Seller and buyer enter into a purchase agreement.
8. Bank releases goods to effect shipment.
9. Lawrence certifies the validity of the receivable.
10. Goods are shipped.
11. Buyer takes possession of goods.
12. Buyer pays seller.
13. Seller pays bank.
14. Investor presents draft at maturity and bank pays face value with proceeds of sale.

Domestic Shipping

On October 8, 1982, paragraph 7, Section 13 of the Federal Reserve Act was amended changing the requirements for U.S. shipping transactions. The bill of lading conveying title to the goods financed is no longer required. In lieu of the shipping document, many banks are requiring the borrower to issue a purpose statement certifying the value and shipment of the goods.

It is suspected that the reason for this amendment was to place regulations covering domestic shipments on an equal basis with regulations covering international shipment where a title document has not been required. It is surmised that this will significantly increase the use of domestic acceptance financing by softening the requirements. Further, these changes may encourage encroachment on domestic storage requirements since goods shipped to the buyer will be stored, undergo processing, and be resold. Since the amendment is new it is too early to know the final impact.

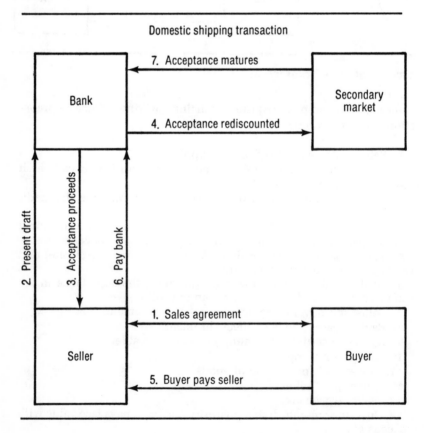

Domestic shipping transaction

Domestic Shipping Transaction

Situation: A U.S. company sells goods to a U.S. buyer, who requests the seller provide 30-day financing terms. The seller is willing to extend terms and refinances the receivable with its bank with an acceptance.

1. The buyer and seller agree on the terms and conditions of sale, and the goods are shipped.
2. The seller provides the bank with its draft and purpose statement certifying that goods have been shipped and identifying the value and nature of the product.
3. The bank discounts the draft and credits proceeds (face value less interest) to the seller's account.
4. At the bank's discretion, the accepted draft will be held in the bank's portfolio or rediscounted in the secondary market.
5. Thirty days later, the buyer pays the seller for the goods.
6. The seller pays the bank for the face value of the acceptance.
7. The investor presents the acceptance to the bank, which repurchases the acceptance.

International Transactions

In order to fully understand international trade, we will focus on the vehicles that facilitate these transactions and the associated risks. The following diagrams the four international transactions. Each structure is numerically diagramed, corresponding to the narrative that follows. It is important to note that acceptances may finance international transactions whether arising from L/C's or collections.

Pre-Export Financing

In this type of transaction, the U.S. exporter requires financing to marshall and process goods contracted for by a foreign buyer. The U.S. exporter presents evidence of the international sale, accompanied by its time draft, to the bank with the maturity of the draft coinciding with the expected payment date. Associated sales costs, such as insurance and freight, which are passed on to the buyer, may be included in the draft amount. The draft is then discounted with net proceeds credited to the customer's account. At maturity, the U.S. exporter pays the bank with sales proceeds.

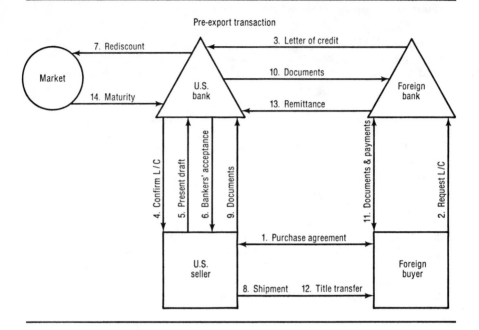

Pre-export transaction

Pre-Export Transaction

Situation: U.S. seller requires financing to deliver product to buyer.

1. Buyer and seller agreement covering terms and conditions of sale (open account, collection, or letter of credit).

2. Buyer (after negotiating credit requirements) requests its bank to open sight letter of credit in favor of U.S. seller.

3. Foreign bank opens sight letter of credit in favor of U.S. seller through its U.S. correspondent bank.

4. U.S. bank confirms letter of credit to U.S. seller.

5. Seller who requires financing to deliver product to buyer arranges with its bank to discount draft with maturity, coinciding with seller's anticipation of sale proceeds.

6. U.S. bank stamps draft "Accepted," making it the bank's obligation to an investor and discounts (face value less interest charge) acceptance crediting proceeds to seller's account.

7. U.S. bank, at its option, sells draft in secondary market.

8. U.S. seller ships goods to buyer and obtains necessary documents in compliance with letter of credit.

9. U.S. seller submits documents to U.S. bank for negotiation.

10. U.S. bank submits documents to foreign bank.

11. Foreign bank presents documents to foreign buyer and debits buyer's acount covering payment.

12. Foreign buyer takes possession of goods against presentation of bill of lading document to steamship company.

13. Foreign bank remits funds available under Letter of Credit to U.S. bank.

14. U.S. bank is presented acceptance at maturity (if it had been sold by bank in secondary market). U.S. bank pays holder of acceptance with proceeds of foreign bank remittance required under the letter of credit.

Post-Export Financing

The U.S. exporter may provide financing to an overseas buyer who needs time to further process and sell goods. The buyer will repay the U.S. exporter with the sale proceeds. This form of finance is unique in that it assumes the U.S. exporter will pass its interest charges on to the foreign buyer. These charges may be less costly than if the financing was done in the importer's country, thus making the importer's goods more price-competitive or increasing its return on sales.

Under post-export financing, the U.S. exporter draws a draft covering the expected shipping and receivable time. The draft, along with evidence of sale, is presented to the exporter's bank, which discounts the draft and credits the proceeds to the exporter's account. At maturity, sale proceeds are remitted by the foreign importer and applied to the acceptance. Both pre-export and post-export financing may be covered by the same draft.

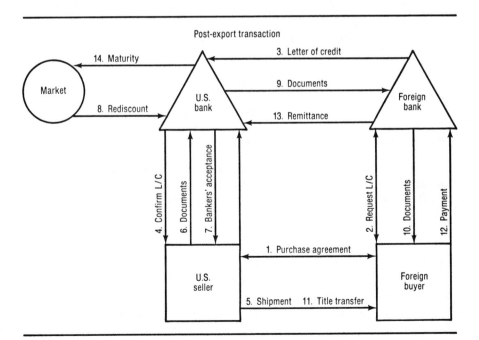

Post-export transaction

Post-Export Transaction

Situation: U.S. seller extends credit to foreign buyer, enabling buyer to sell goods with sales proceeds paying U.S. seller.

1. Buyer and seller reach agreement covering terms and conditions of sale (open account, collection, or letter of credit—L/C).

2. Foreign buyer, after negotiating credit requirements with its bank, requests bank to open usance letter of credit, requiring payment at a time after sight, in favor of U.S. seller, with the U.S. bank authorized to discount drafts.

3. Foreign bank opens usance letter of credit in favor of U.S. seller through its U.S. correspondent bank.

4. U.S. Bank confirms usance letter of credit to U.S. seller. (If L/C was advised but not confirmed, the U.S. seller's exposure is the foreign bank.)

5. U.S. seller ships goods to foreign buyer and obtains shipping documents required under L/C.

6. U.S. seller presents documents to bank acompanied by its time draft and requests U.S. bank to discount draft (face value less interest charge) Acceptance will have a maturity date that coincides with the usance time of L/C.

7. U.S. bank stamps draft "Accepted," making it the bank's obligation to an investor. Bank discounts draft and credits proceeds to seller's account.

8. U.S. bank, at its option, rediscounts draft in secondary market or maintains draft in its own investment portfolio.

9. U.S. bank forwards documents, complying with L/C, to foreign correspondent bank.

10. Foreign bank presents documents to buyer.

11. Foreign buyer takes possession of goods against its presentation of bill of lading document to steamship company.

12. At time specified in L/C, foreign bank debits buyer's account for amount of L/C.

13. Foreign bank remits proceeds to U.S. bank.

14. Investor presents acceptance at maturity to U.S. bank which pays face value with proceeds of L/C remitted by foreign bank in no. 13 above.

Impact: The foreign buyer enjoys the U.S. financing rate since buyer is essentially receiving inventory financing extended by the U.S. seller, which prudently would increase the sales price reflecting its cost of capital.

Pre-Import Financing

A U.S. importer may be required to advance funds to its overseas seller for the marshaling, processing, storage, and shipment of goods. In this case, the U.S. buyer extends credit to its foreign seller, which may now enjoy a cheaper cost of financing. U.S. financing charges may be less costly than foreign cost of funds, which would be passed on to the U.S. importer. The bank's exposure is its U.S. customer, while the U.S. importer's exposure is the foreign seller.

The U.S. buyer shows evidence that an order is placed and presents the draft to the bank. The draft is discounted with dollar proceeds converted to the appropriate foreign currency and remitted to the foreign seller. The seller obtains the goods and ships to the U.S. buyer. At maturity, the importer's account is debited with proceeds liquidating the acceptance.

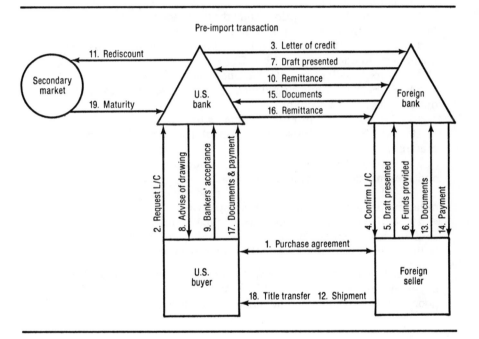

Pre-import transaction

Pre-Import Transaction

Situation: U.S. buyer extends credit to foreign seller, enabling seller to purchase and deliver product to U.S. buyer.

1. Buyer and seller reach agreement covering terms and conditions of sale (open account, collection, or letter of credit—L/C).
2. U.S. buyer (after negotiating credit requirements with bank) requests its bank to open "red clause" letter of credit in favor of foreign seller.

3. U.S. bank opens red clause L/C in favor of foreign seller through its foreign correspondent. The red clause L/C allows seller to draw against L/C prior to presentation of documents and is the exposure of the U.S. buyer.

4. Foreign bank confirms letter of credit to foreign seller.

5. Seller, which requires financing to purchase and deliver goods, draws its draft on foreign bank.

6. Foreign bank credits funds to foreign seller.

7. Foreign bank presents draft to U.S. bank.

8. U.S. bank advises U.S. buyer of drawing under L/C.

9. U.S. buyer presents its draft to U.S. bank.

10. U.S. bank stamps draft "Accepted," making it the bank's obligation, and discounts draft (face value less interest charge) and credits proceeds to foreign bank.

11. U.S. bank, at its option, sells draft in secondary market or holds draft in its own investment portfolio.

12. Foreign seller ships goods to U.S. buyer and obtains required documents in compliance with L/C.

13. Foreign seller presents documents to its bank.

14. Foreign bank credits balance of L/C (L/C amount less red clause drawing) to seller's account.

15. Foreign bank presents documents to U.S. bank.

16. U.S. bank reimburses foreign bank (L/C amount less red clause drawing).

17. U.S. bank debits U.S. buyer's account full value of L/C amount and presents documents to U.S. buyer.

18. U.S. buyer takes possession of goods against presentation of bill of lading document to steamship company.

19. U.S. bank is presented acceptance at maturity (if it had been sold in the secondary market). U.S. bank pays holder of acceptance with proceeds from debiting U.S. buyer's account (17) above.

Impact: This is working capital financing extended by the U.S. buyer to foreign seller. The U.S. buyer would reduce the cost of the goods by its cost of capital advanced to the foreign seller.

Post-Import Financing

The terms of trade covering importation of goods often require immediate payment by the U.S. buyer. Rather than pay for the goods immediately, the U.S. importer may present evidence of the purchase accompanied by its time draft. The bank discounts the draft with proceeds remitted to the foreign seller.

The tenor of the acceptance may cover importation, shipment to the U.S. plant, processing, storage, shipment to the ultimate buyer, and trade terms. The aggregate time must be anticipated to synchronize the maturity of the acceptance with the final liquidation of the transaction.

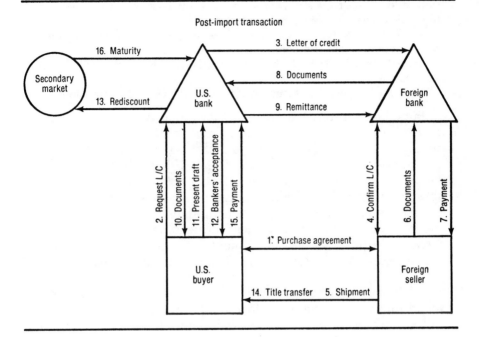

Post-import transaction

Post-Import Transaction

Situation: U.S. importer requires trade-payable financing, enabling it to sell goods with sale proceeds paying a foreign seller.

1. Buyer and seller reach agreement covering terms and conditions of sale (open account, collection, or letter of credit—L/C).
2. U.S. buyer, after negotiating credit requirements, requests its bank to open-sight L/C in favor of foreign seller.
3. U.S. bank opens L/C in favor of foreign seller through foreign bank.
4. Foreign bank confirms L/C to foreign seller.
5. Foreign seller ships goods to U.S. buyer.
6. Foreign seller obtains and presents documents to foreign bank.
7. Foreign bank negotiates documents and credits seller's account with L/C proceeds.
8. Foreign bank forwards documents to U.S. bank.
9. U.S. bank remits funds available under L/C to foreign bank.
10. U.S. bank presents documents to U.S. buyer for payment.
11. U.S. buyer, requiring time to sell goods, submits its draft to bank.
12. U.S. bank discounts draft (face value less interest charge).
13. U.S. bank stamps draft "Accepted," making it the bank's obliga-

tion, and at the bank's option sells the draft in secondary market or holds it in its own investment portfolio.

14. U.S. buyer takes possession of goods against release of shipping documents to steamship company.

15. At maturity, U.S. bank debits U.S. buyer's account face value of acceptance.

16. Investor presents acceptance to bank for face-value payment.

Fundamental to managing short-term borrowings is the company's role as banker in extending trade credit to the buyers of its goods. This role is identical to that of a commercial bank. For companies with international sales, the difficulty of credit analysis is compounded by foreign country risk, foreign bank risk, foreign buyer risk, and foreign currency exchange exposure. To appreciate short-term financing techniques in the international arena, we will explore the critical influencing factors. Although some of the points appear fundamental, they routinely elude major corporations—including well known multinationals.

1. *Foreign Exchange:* Dollar-denominated sales contracts avoid foreign currency risk since the U.S. seller is paid in U.S. dollars. When contracts call for payment to the U.S. seller in the currency of the foreign buyer, the risk of exchanging the currency to dollars is for the seller's account. Naturally, many factors influence the relationship of one currency to another. These factors may increase (revalue) or decrease (devalue) the value of one currency in relation to another.

If the dollar increases relative to the buyer's currency and payment is to be made in the foreign currency, there is no impact for the buyer, and the seller's cash from sales will decrease in proportion to the revalued dollar.

If the foreign buyer's currency increases against the seller's dollar, there is no impact or benefit for the buyer. The seller will realize more cash from the sales proportionate to the devaluation of the dollar. This occurs when the seller presents the foreign currency to the money exchangers and receives more dollars for the same amount of foreign currency.

If the contract is dollar-denominated, the U.S. seller has effectively hedged its position against any currency fluctuation. The risk of currency change will be for the foreign buyer who will gain or lose, depending on interim currency fluctuations. Naturally, given the vagaries of commodities, there may be substantial gains or losses for the exposed party which are tantamount to speculating in the futures market and should be avoided.

In the event a U.S. seller agrees to payment in a foreign currency, it may hedge against currency fluctuations by entering into a foreign currency contract with a major international bank or by hedging the currency in the futures market. To do so, the company contractually agrees to sell the foreign currency to the bank on a prescribed date corresponding to its expected receipt of the currency, and the bank quotes an exchange rate. There are two costs associated with this procedure: (a) the fee charged by the bank and (b) a basic charge reflected by the difference between the present exchange rate and the hedged rate. These costs may be absorbed by the U.S. seller, or the costs of the goods may be inflated to cover the hedge.

2. *Foreign government risk:* Although most countries subscribe to international trade law administered by the international court, a country's sovereignty prevails. Iran, where the government unilaterally nationalized the banks, refused to honor the trade laws. U.S. companies that had delivered goods on open-account terms or against an *advised* letter of credit (without U.S. bank guarantee) were not paid. In this case, U.S. corporations received judgment against Iran through the international court.

This court's power to liquidate the claims is predicated on the country's willingness to cooperate. In some cases, Iran's bank accounts with U.S. banks were attached, and U.S. banks attempted to offset defaults through attachment procedures.

Although the procedures for settling international trade disputes exists, actual collection is tedious and most expensive. Most importantly, it is completely avoidable when a *confirmed* letter of credit (U.S. bank guarantee) is used.

3. *Foreign bank risk:* Many U.S. sellers are comforted when shipping goods against receipt of a letter of credit. A letter of credit (L/C) is the bank's *promise* to pay the seller upon the seller's presentation of documents required under the letter of credit. Banks do not actually inspect the goods; they inspect the documents purporting to represent the goods. Appropriate documents may include shipping bill of lading (document of title), export licenses, import licenses, inspection certificates, and fumigation certificates for agriculture goods.

In cases where a U.S. seller ships goods to a foreign buyer against a foreign bank's letter of credit, the U.S. seller's risk is the future ability of the foreign bank to perform. If the foreign bank becomes insolvent after goods reach the foreign country but before the foreign bank pays the U.S seller, the U.S. seller may lose its goods. In this case, the L/C is administratively *advised* to the U.S. seller through a U.S. bank.

Where L/Cs are *advised*, the U.S. bank acts as a conduit, passing documents to the foreign opening bank and funds to the U.S.

seller. The U.S. bank does not engage its liability to the seller in the event the foreign bank does not pay. This is known as an *advised* letter of credit and the seller bears full foreign country bank risk.

4. *U.S. bank risk:* Where a U.S. bank confirms (engages its liability), a letter of credit there is a theoretical risk for the U.S. seller. This would surface if the confirming U.S. bank failed. Although certain bank liabilities are insured, such as deposits less than $100,000, the bank's performance under an L/C is not covered. Practically speaking, it is believed that the Federal Reserve Bank might intervene, since default might influence international trade.

International Trade Procedures

There are two fundamental trade procedures with different risks for the U.S. seller: collections and letters of credit.

Collections. The U.S. bank acts as a conduit for delivering documents covering goods to the foreign bank, and the buyer transfers payment to the seller through the U.S. banking system. Collection procedures do not obligate the U.S. or foreign bank to pay the U.S. seller. Bank payment is based upon receipt of the buyer's payment.

1. Documents against payment: The title and required documents are sent to the buyer through the U.S. and foreign banks simultaneously with the shipment of goods. The foreign bank will not release the goods until it receives payment from the buyer, then it transfers these funds to the U.S. seller via the U.S. bank.

Exposure: The primary risk is that the foreign buyer may not pay for the goods, resulting in storage costs, reshipping costs, and possible interim market decline in the value of the goods. Since the title for the goods remains with the seller, it will not lose the product. Other possible exposures include foreign government and bank risk. The procedure is identical to C.O.D. transactions.

2. Documents against acceptance: Again, the title and required documents are sent to the buyer through banking channels. In this case, the title and goods are released to the buyer for a specified period of time. The buyer's liability is evidenced by its execution of a time draft, which is an order to pay a specific amount on a certain date to the seller.

Exposure: Since there is no bank obligation and the goods are released, the seller has full risk. The difference between this procedure and selling on open account is the degree of risk. In this case, the seller has the draft evidencing the debt and may pursue legal action through the international courts.

Letters of Credit. This is a legal document engaging the bank's obligation to pay the seller (beneficiary) upon presentation of documents conforming to the L/C, irrespective of the buyer's (account party's) ability or intent to pay. The purpose is to transfer the credit risk from the buyer to the bank.

1. *Advised letter of credit:* A U.S. bank *advises* (without obligation) a U.S. seller that a foreign bank (opening bank) will pay the seller upon presentation of documents conforming with the L/C to the foreign bank via the U.S. bank. In this case the U.S. bank is merely a conduit and does not engage its liability. (See Appendix Six.)

Exposure: The primary exposure is the fidelity and capability of the foreign bank to pay the seller. Other possible exposures include the foreign country which may impose sanctions precluding the opening bank from performing, as was the case with Iran.

2. *Confirmed letters of credit:* A U.S. bank *confirms* (engages its obligation) to pay the U.S. seller upon presentation of documents conforming to the L/C irrespective of the foreign government's, foreign bank's, or foreign buyer's ability or intent to pay.

Exposure: Since all foreign exposure is eliminated, the only risk is the United States confirming bank's ability to pay the seller. Because the U.S. government does not guarantee a U.S. bank's solvency to pay under letters of credit, it is the seller's responsibility to determine the bank's creditworthiness. There are 14,000 banks in the United States, and determining risk is impossible. It is suggested that major banking institutions most familiar with letters of credit be used for international transactions.

The major difference between the advised and confirmed letters of credit was amplified by the Iranian situation. U.S. sellers that shipped goods against *advised* L/Cs lost their goods pending costly and time-consuming litigation. U.S. sellers that shipped goods against L/Cs *confirmed* by U.S. banks were paid, and the risk was transferred to the U.S. banks, which pursued litigation when the Iranian banks failed to pay.

We conclude that the primary difference between the procedures is risk exposure. The less the risk, the more the cost. Since the costs are usually for the buyer, the seller must be mindful of the real risks in order to be competitive. It is fair to assume that a U.S. seller should be relatively comfortable with an advised L/C opened by a recognized bank in a major country. To insist on a confirmed L/C from a buyer in England when the L/C is opened by Barclays Bank, ranked number 6 (assets) in the world, is unnecessary. A list of the 100 largest world banks appears in Appendix Seven.

CHARACTERISTICS

A bankers' acceptance is a fixed-rate and fixed-term instrument available for financing underlying and self-liquidating transactions. The rate is established by the secondary market, which includes a variety of money market short-term investments available to investors. This includes treasury bills and commercial paper. Since acceptance rates are more immediately responsive to economic phenomena than the administratively established prime, moves in the prime rate are generally preceded by similar moves by acceptances. The bank's cost of funds is calculated over a historical commercial paper rate. Since commercial paper competes with acceptances, the move in the prime logically follows similar trends of the acceptance rate.

The acceptance rate is quoted in 30-day increments up to 180 days. The standard face amount, or par value, is $500,000, for ease of marketing to the secondary market. Acceptances may be less than $500,000, but banks prefer drafts in $500,000 denominations. A $10 million transaction requires 20 drafts at $500,000 each. Occasionally, a draft exceeding $500,000 for a period other than a 30-day increment will be accepted. This usually requires the direct placement of the acceptance by the bank to a private party.

For acceptances under $500,000, the bank packages the individual acceptances into lots of $500,000. Since the investor's immediate recourse is to the creating bank, the concept of packaging acceptances from different borrowers is incidental relative to investor risk.

When financing with acceptances, the borrower should review the general rate trend and time of financing. If the trend shows rates increasing, it is logical that the borrower will fix the current rate for the longest period. If rates are falling, the borrower will fix rates for a shorter period. It must be noted that the Federal Reserve will not permit the rollover (refinancing) of acceptances in order to speculate on rate changes. For this reason, we recommend that borrowers avail themselves of variable prime-related financing and acceptance financing and not rely on one source of funds. This provides optimal flexibility: when rates are stable, acceptances will be the least costly; when rates are increasing, acceptances will lock in current rates for the short-term; and when rates are declining, the variable prime rate will move downward without locking the borrower into higher fixed-term acceptance rates.

The borrowing strategy focuses on three variables: rate changes, time, and velocity. In order to accurately manage borrowings, the treasurer would have to know, in advance, the amount and velocity of change. These influencing factors affecting a commodity are impossible to forecast accurately. Therefore a best-guess effort focusing on regression, probability, and plotting models is the approach to be taken. Once the general trend is determined, the borrower's strategy is designed to minimize the cost. A company borrowing strictly under an acceptance line will hold costs down in a rising rate environment and possibly incur larger borrowing costs in a declining rate climate. However, given the rate differential between acceptance borrowings and prime, which may be as much as 3 percent, the borrower must make certain assumptions in order to determine which is the best alternative.

When rates are rising there is no ambiguity, and the company borrows under the lower fixed-rate, fixed-term acceptance facility. The dilemma occurs when rates are declining. It is then that the treasurer must use the crystal ball approach to make assumptions regarding when and how much the rates will decline.

This process begins by identifying the existing rate differential and determining the probability of the weighted average prime rate dropping below the fixed acceptance rate. Since the prime rate will probably be higher than the acceptance rate at any given time, the weighted average prime will have to drop to some point below the acceptance rate, compensating for the time it took for the prime to equal the acceptance rate. The actual rate below the acceptance cost is a function of the rate differential and the velocity of the falling prime rate.

By changing the time or rate differential, various probabilities are generated. The larger the rate differential, the less the probability that the weighted average prime will fall below the fixed acceptance. Conversely, the less the rate differential, the higher the probability that the weighted average prime will drop below the previously fixed acceptance rate. The longer the financing period, the greater the chances of a falling prime dropping below the fixed-rate acceptance.

The blended probabilities will determine which alternative to select. Changing either variable will affect the probability of the weighted average prime falling below the fixed acceptance rate.

Historically, when the cost of a commodity has been disproportionate with supply and demand, volatile changes have occurred. In the silver market in 1980, for example, the price per ounce dropped quickly from $50 to $10 after being manipulated to an artificially high price. The same holds true for the commodity of money. If interest rates are out of sync with supply and demand, we expect volatile moves. Therefore the probability is higher for the floating prime rate to drop below the acceptance rate when rates are disproportionately high compared to when rates are moderate or low. An example will identify the impact of the three variables.

Situation: A corporation's rate differential is 3 percent in favor of the acceptance rate compared to prime. The treasurer is reviewing a 30-day financing requirement and rates are high but beginning to decline. The treasurer's conclusion:

1. If rates are disproportionately high, the probability increases for a volatile prime drop.

2. Since the rate differential is high, the probability is low that the prime will drop below the acceptance rate.

3. Since the finance period is short, the probability of prime dropping below the acceptance rate is low.

The rate differential and time variables indicate a low probability that the floating prime will drop below the fixed acceptance. However, the general high-rate environment indicates a high probability for volatile swings in the rates. The degree to which one variable offsets another is difficult to assess. Our experience indicates that the most influential variable is the rate differential, then time, followed by the general rate environment.

We conclude that it is erroneous to assume that the most attractive short-term borrowing alternative in a declining rate environment is necessarily the floating prime loan. Although the floating aspect is attractive when rates are declining, this is heavily influenced by the rate differential, time, and the velocity relative to supply-and-demand considerations. Regression analysis and simulation modeling programs are the basis for determining the influencing properties of the three variables for any given time against which sound borrowing decisions are made.

This analysis is based strictly on short-term (under 180-day) rates. Over time, the prime rate will drop below the fixed acceptance rate in a declining rate environment. But to ride the rate downward with prime, simply because it is floating, is an arbitrary decision without foundation. An alternative strategy is to roll over the acceptances as the rate drops, thereby enjoying the downward trend. As stated, under certain circumstances, this might be considered an ineligible acceptance; however, we will see that the marginal cost increase for reserves will be less than prime-related borrowings.

The pricing variable for acceptances differs from conventional loans. The primary source of funds for the conventional loan is deposits with varying terms of maturity and rates depending on the creditworthiness of the bank. The secondary investment community provides the funds for bankers' acceptances. This rate, the discount, is quoted for periods up to 180 days and in 30-day increments.

The discount rate is based on competitive rates for other money market offerings. The primary reasons this rate is less than prime are that (1) eligible acceptances do not bear reserve costs; (2) the administrative costs for banks are minimal; and (3) the risk for the investor is theoretically less since the acceptance is self-liquidating and the responsibility is that of the accepting bank and of the borrower issuing the draft. The acceptance is referred to as *two-name paper* since the investor has recourse to the bank accepting the draft and the borrower which issued the draft. An investor has three sources of liquidation: the creating bank, the borrower, and sale of the goods financed.

The discount rate differs depending on the market's perception of the creating banks' creditworthiness. The prime money center banks usually command the most favorable rates. The market adds 15–35 basis points to second- or third-tier banks, and, naturally, this cost is passed to the borrower. In the event a bank's performance drops, the market will show this with higher rates, reflecting market perception of risk. This risk-adjustment factor was recently applied to a major money center bank whose performance slipped because of its involvement with the now defunct Penn Square Bank of Oklahoma. The money center bank had enjoyed the most favorable rates provided by the secondary market. However, loan losses reduced its performance and the market adjusted the rate upward by 1 percent, a significant penalty. When this increase is passed on to the borrower, the 1% penalty converts into additional interest expense of $10,000 per million dollars of debt per year.

The market will also adjust its rate for ineligible acceptances, which no longer qualify as collateral for Federal Reserve loans. This adjustment ranges from 20 to 35 basis points. Any market adjustment is passed to the borrower.

This adjustment does not appear to be justified from a credit point of view, since the investor's recourse is to the creating bank, irrespective of eligibility. We speculate that this adjustment makes the acceptances more attractive to investors who otherwise prefer eligible acceptances.

The bank adds its commission fee for engaging its obligation, evidenced by its stamp of "Accepted" on the draft. Until 1976, this commission was standard at 1.5 percent per annum. This standard was eliminated when banks eagerly expanded their use of acceptances in order to enjoy liquidity relief during periods of tight money. Presently, commissions range from approximately .25 percent to 2 percent, depending on the nature of the transaction and the borrower's credit standing.

Many banks arbitrarily apply the commissions without a formal rationale. Generally, if a company is rated by Moody's or Standard & Poor's, the rating may be the basis for setting the commission. For discounted drafts which are less than $500,000 each, the bank will add an adjustment reflecting added marketing costs.

Acceptance Commission Table

Company Rating	Commission
A–1	½%
A–2	¾
A–3	1
B	1–1¼

When a company is not rated, a credit scoring approach may be used (see Figure 3–1). The company is scored against credit criteria which are weighted according to the importance of the category. The final score is converted to a corresponding acceptance commission. This procedure provides continuity and substantiates the commission for the customer. Since banks quote acceptance rates on an all-in basis (discount plus commission), it is difficult to immediately know the commission. To determine the commission, the company may call the bank's bond department and ask for the prevailing acceptance discount covering the financing period. By subtracting the bond department's rate from the corporation's all-in rate, the treasurer can determine the commission.

Although the scoring attempts to relate the rate to risk, other considerations may be important. As shown by the international

FIGURE 3–1
Credit Scoring

BORROWER CLASSIFICATION WORKSHEET

Date _____

Company Name _____ SIC _____ DUNS _____

Parent Name _____ % Owned _____ DUNS _____

I. *Years of Existence*
Number of years in present form and business _____

Score:	25 or more = 10	10 to 14 = 5
	20 to 24 = 8	5 to 9 = 3
	15 to 19 = 6	3 to 4 = 1

Score: _____

II. *Years of Consecutive Profitability*
Number of years, starting with most recent period and working back, or unbroken positive net income _____

Score:	20 or more consecutive years	= 10
	15 consecutive and 19 years out of last 20	= 9
	15 or more consecutive years	= 8
	10 consecutive and 18 years out of last 20	= 7
	10 or more consecutive years	= 6
	5 consecutive and 17 years out of last 20	= 5
	5 or more consecutive years	= 4
	19 out of last 20 years	= 3
	17 out of last 20 years	= 2

Interim profitability score: _____

Profitability Adjustment
Subtract points if net income in any of the last five years declined more than 20 percent from the level of the previous year. Work out only for years of decline of 20 percent or more (.20 or greater).

Year of Decline	Net Income Prior Year		Net Income Current		Net Income Prior Year			Decline Factor		Adjust- ment
Most recent _____	–	_____	/	_____	=	_____	×	10	=	_____
1st prior _____	–	_____	/	_____	=	_____	×	5	=	_____
2nd prior _____	–	_____	/	_____	=	_____	×	3.3	=	_____
3rd prior _____	–	_____	/	_____	=	_____	×	2.5	=	_____
4th prior _____	–	_____	/	_____	=	_____	×	1	=	_____

Total adjustment: _____

If adjustment is greater than interim profitability score, enter zero, otherwise subtract adjustment from interim profitability score.

Final profitability score: _____

FIGURE 3–1 *(concluded)*

III. *Dividend Score*
Number of consecutive years of unbroken dividend payments starting with most recent period and working back.

Score: 20 or more = 5   10 or more = 2
        15 or more = 3   5 or more = 1

Score: _____

IV. *Total Debt-to-Equity Ratio*   Most recent
Score: .25 or less = 10   .86 to 1.00   = 1
        .26 to .33 = 9   1.01 to 1.20 = 0
        .34 to .40 = 8   1.21 to 1.40 = (− 1)
        .41 to .50 = 7   1.41 to 1.60 = (− 2)
        .51 to .60 = 5   1.61 to 1.80 = (− 3)
        .61 to .70 = 4   1.81 to 2.00 = (− 4)
        .70 to .85 = 2   2.01 to 2.50 = (− 6)
                              2.51 to 3.00 = (− 8)
                              3.01 to higher = (− 10)

Score: _____

V. *Current Ratio*   Most recent
Score: 4 or higher = 5   .90 to .99   = (− 1)
        3 to 3.99   = 4   .80 to .89   = (− 3)
        2.50 to 2.99 = 3   .70 to .79   = (− 5)
        2.00 to 2.49 = 2   .50 to .69   = (− 8)
        1.50 to 1.99 = 1   .49 or lower = (− 10)
        1.00 to 1.49 = 0

Score: _____

VI. *Debt Coverage Ratio*
Most recent year's ratio _____ × .5 = _____
1st prior year's ratio   _____ × .33 = _____
2nd prior year's ratio   _____ × .17 = _____
                                    Total _____

Score: 7.5 times or higher = 5   1.25 to 1.49 times = (− 1)
        5.0 to 7.4 times   = 4   1.00 to 1.24 times = (− 2)
        3.0 to 4.9 times   = 3   .50 to .99 times = (− 3)
        2.0 to 2.9 times   = 2   .00 to .49 times = (− 4)
        1.75 to 1.99 times = 1   Less than 0.00   = (− 5)
        1.50 to 1.74 times = 0

Score: _____
Total score: _____

Letter Rating
  AA = 30 or higher   C = 0 to 9.9
  A = 20 to 29.9   D = OLEM or a negative score
  B = 10 to 19.9   F = Classified

Letter rating: _____

If the letter rating does not accurately reflect the creditworthiness of the borrower, what rating should apply and why?

trade-flow charts, the borrower's credit is not an issue when the acceptance is financing a post-export transaction against a confirmed letter of credit. In this case the creating bank's source of repayment is the international correspondent opening bank. Therefore the U.S. bank's risk is the creditworthiness of the opening bank, and the commission should reflect this fact.

If the borrower's credit scoring resulted in a commission of 1½ percent but the opening bank's rating is equivalent to A-1, then the commission for the transaction should be ½ percent, according to the rating table.

A discount interest adjustment is added to acceptances. This reflects the borrower's opportunity cost for paying interest prior to usage compared to conventional loans where interest is paid in arrears. To properly compare the total costs, this calculation must be performed. The formula for the interest discount adjustment is:

$$\frac{(R + C) \times CD \text{ Rate} \times \text{Days}}{360}$$

where:

R = Market discount
C = Bank's commission
CD = The prevailing certificate of deposit rate corresponding to the financing period.
Days = Financing period

A company with a 10 percent discount rate and 1 percent commission will receive an all-in rate quote of 11 percent. Assuming the financing is for 90 days and the CD rate is 8 percent, the discount adjustment is calculated as follows:

$$\frac{11\% \times .08 \times 90}{360} = .22$$

To calculate the decimal equivalent of the reserves for ineligible acceptances, the formula is:

$$\frac{\text{Discount rate} + \text{Commission}}{1.0 - \text{Reserve}} - (\text{Discount rate} + \text{Commission})$$

Given a 10 percent discount, a 1 percent commission and a 3 percent reserve factor, the calculation is:

$$\frac{10 + 1}{1.0 - .3} - (10 + 1)$$

or

$$\frac{11}{.97} - 11 = .34$$

A common pitfall for a bank is failure to add the reserve factor when calculating ineligible acceptances maintained in the bank's portfolio. The assumption is that reserves are not required since the acceptance is not rediscounted in the secondary market. However, reserves are maintained by the bank on deposits used to fund the ineligible acceptance. The appropriate reserve factor should be added, ensuring proper bank return.

We have explored all the factors influencing the acceptance rate. Below is a comparison of the three options available to the corporation as of November 18, 1982, for eligible acceptances, ineligible acceptances, and conventional loans.

90–Day Cost Analysis B-Rated Company (November 18, 1982)

	Eligible Acceptance	Ineligible Acceptance	Prime Advance
Discount	9.00%	9.00%	
Prime			12%
Commission	1.00	1.00	
Balance/spread			1
Discount adjustment	.22	.22	
Market adjustment		.30	
Reserve factor		.31	
Total	10.22%	10.83%	13%

Assuming a $1 million transaction, the corporate borrower would save 2.78 percent financing with eligible acceptances compared to prime advances, or $6,950 for 90 days. On an annualized basis, this would be a $27,800 savings. The table clearly shows that the ineligible acceptance, with its reserve requirements and market adjustment, would save the company 2.18 percent, or $22,103 annually, compared to conventional loans.

If the financing covered a domestic storage transaction, we would add approximately 25–50 basis points for the warehouse receipt. This would reduce the difference between acceptances and advances, but the benefits would remain in favor of bankers' acceptances. After this adjustment, the saving is 2.28 percent, or $23,116 annualized, in favor of bankers' acceptances.

With few exceptions the acceptance rates have been less than prime as the following table shows. Historically, bankers' acceptances have been less costly than other short-term alternatives, with the possible exception of A-1 commercial paper.

Table 3–1 identifies the component rates of the four primary options available. It is important to compare rates for the same period since different rates are quoted for different terms. When performing rate comparisons, 30-day acceptance rates should not be compared with 90-day commercial paper. This comparison would result in an unfair advantage for acceptances as a result of the shorter financing period. The rate spread may increase by as much as 50 basis points between 30-day and 180-day finance periods for the same funding instruments.

In order to compete with the comparatively low-cost commercial paper, banks aggressively marketed bankers' acceptances. In 1980 they introduced a subprime rate for the most creditworthy companies. This is often tied to the certificate of deposit rate and is referred to as *matched funding*. The rate closely tracks acceptance rates and is most attractive, compared to prime. Like acceptances, the bank adds a commission to the CD rate and quotes an all-in rate to the company.

Although acceptances are often more attractive than other short-term alternatives, the major disadvantage is meeting the qualifications established by the Federal Reserve. Further, if a warehouse receipt is required, the administrative burden may increase. Commercial paper and Eurodollars have minimal requirements and are used to finance general working capital without covering a specific underlying or self-liquidating transaction. Therefore, the trade-off for using acceptances is cost versus flexibility.

It is noted that most corporate borrowers do not have access to the commercial paper market or subprime lending. In these cases, acceptances are the most attractive alternative, as there are numerous benefits in acceptance financing for the bank, borrowers, and investors.

Bank Benefits

1. Acceptance financing is most efficient, since the demand for funds is presented to the bank, which has immediate access to the supply of funds when needed. For conventional loans, the bank has the supply (deposits) and then must identify the demand.

2. Acceptance provides liquidity relief through the secondary market. This allows the bank to meet loan demands without relying on profits or deposits.

3. The bank earns fee income from acceptances, since its actual cash deposits do not fund the transaction.

TABLE 3–1
Rate Comparison, B-Rated Company (*90 Days, June 1973–1982*)

	90-Day Rate	Bank Commission	Bank Balances	Discount Adjustment	Market Adjustment	Dealer Commission	Total Rate
1973							
Prime	7.75	0	1.16	0	0	0	8.91
Acceptances	7.90	.75	0	.19	0	0	8.84
Commercial paper	8.00	0	.80	.19	0	.13	9.12
Eurodollars	8.81	.75	0	0	0	0	9.56
1974							
Prime	11.75	0	1.76	0	0	0	13.51
Acceptances	10.79	.75	0	.32	0	0	11.86
Commercial paper	11.18	0	1.12	0	0	.13	12.43
Eurodollars	12.04	.75	0	0	0	0	12.79
1975							
Prime	7.00	0	1.05	0	0	0	8.05
Acceptances	5.70	.75	0	.09	0	0	6.54
Commercial paper	5.67	0	.57	.09	0	.13	6.46
Eurodollars	6.10	.75	0	0	0	0	6.85
1976							
Prime	7.25	0	1.09	0	0	0	8.34
Acceptances	5.77	.75	0	.09	0	0	6.52
Commercial paper	5.58	0	.56	.09	0	.13	6.36
Eurodollars	6.22	.75	0	0	0	0	6.97

1977							
Prime	7.00	0	1.05	0	0	0	8.05
Acceptances	5.39	.75	0	.08	0	0	6.22
Commercial paper	5.42	0	.54	.08	0	.13	6.17
Eurodollars	5.78	.75	0	0	0	0	6.53
1978							
Prime	9.00	0	1.35	0	0	0	10.35
Acceptances	7.48	.75	0	.12	0	0	8.23
Commercial paper	7.75	0	.78	.12	0	.13	8.75
Eurodollars	8.33	.75	0	0	0	0	9.08
1979							
Prime	11.50	0	1.72	0	0	0	13.22
Acceptances	9.79	.75	0	.25	0	0	10.79
Commercial paper	9.77	0	.98	.25	0	.13	11.13
Eurodollars	10.52	.75	0	0	0	0	11.27
1980							
Prime	10.04	0	1.51	0	0	0	11.55
Acceptances	8.31	.75	0	.21	0	0	9.27
Commercial paper	8.27	0	.82	.21	0	.13	9.43
Eurodollars	9.41	.75	0	0	0	0	10.16
1981							
Prime	17.87	0	2.68	0	0	0	20.55
Acceptances	16.21	.75	0	.40	0	0	17.36
Commercial paper	16.24	0	1.62	.40	0	.13	18.39
Eurodollars	18.00	.75	0	0	0	0	18.75

4. The spread or rate differential between the acceptance rate and prime may be considerable, so the bank may be able to increase its return on assets and return on equity while providing lower financing costs to the borrower.

5. With the rate advantage of acceptances over prime, the bank may use acceptances as a business development tool when pursuing new opportunities.

6. In the face of competition, the bank may provide favorable acceptance rates to retain a corporate relationship.

7. The bankers' acceptance is an investment alternative for the bank, which may hold it in its portfolio as a loan or discount it in the secondary market, at its option.

8. The bank's credit exposure is reduced with acceptance financing, since there is an identified, underlying, and self-liquidating trade transaction. This becomes the bank's primary source of repayment, and the customer's credit standing is the secondary source of repayment.

9. If the acceptance is "secured" throughout its life, the bank may provide financing exceeding the 15 percent capital plus surplus limit.

Bank Obstacles

Many banks provide bonuses based on loan volume to branch managers. Since acceptances are often booked in the international divisions of major banks, the manager's bonus will not include acceptance earnings. This has caused resistance to acceptances at the branch level and has resulted in business lost to other banks.

Some banks attempt to resolve this problem through establishing a profit allocation system. In this case, the branch earns the majority of the profits since it is responsibile for the business development and assumes the credit risk, while the international division receives a percentage for the administration of acceptances. This is performed by actually transferring profits. Also, paper profits are allocated and referred to as *shadow profits* for profit-center performance analysis.

When a bank has an excess liquidity position, it understandably prefers to loan its money inventory. At such a time it is not to the bank's advantage to provide acceptances while allowing excess cash to be idle, against which it is paying interest to depositors. Occasionally a bank will add exorbitant commissions in order to encourage the company to borrow under a subprime or prime line. This ensures that the bank is using existing funds.

Corporate Benefits

1. Acceptances reduce interest expense, since they are less costly than prime borrowings.

2. Using acceptances may increase cash flow, since compensating balances are usually not associated with bankers' acceptances.

3. Acceptance financing provides the borrower with a reliable alternative source of funds during periods of tight money.

4. During periods of rising rates, acceptances' fixed rates will provide added cost savings.

Corporate Obstacles

The primary disadvantage in acceptance financing is the fixed-term/rate aspect during a declining rate environment. This also holds true for other matched funding or fixed-rate alternatives, such as commercial paper and Eurodollars. As described earlier in this chapter, the treasurer must weigh the influences of the rate differential, financing time, and general rate environment to determine if the acceptance or floating prime rate will be the best option.

Since acceptances must fund an underlying transaction, proceeds may not finance general working capital. Where the warehouse receipt is required for domestic storage transactions, the borrower will incur added administration.

The third obstacle to acceptance financing is that it is for short periods not exceeding 180 days.

Investor Benefits

1. Acceptances may offer a high return on investor equity.

2. Acceptances offer a high degree of safety, since the investor has recourse to the creating bank, the borrower, and the underlying transaction. An investor has never lost money in bankers' acceptance.

Investor Obstacles

The primary obstacle, when acceptances are compared to other bank investments under $100,000, is the lack of FDIC insurance. The Federal Deposit insurance corporation guarantees bank deposits up to $100,000 but does not cover acceptances. This obstacle is offset by the historically sound performance of acceptances, with no defaults since their introduction in the United

States in 1913. For investments exceeding $100,000, the FDIC guarantee is not an issue when making investment comparisons.

A second obstacle is that the investment is short-term under 180 days. Therefore, high rates may not be locked in for extended periods.

Documents

In addition to the loan agreement, corporate resolution to borrow, and drafts, acceptance financing requires other documents. A documentary acceptance agreement will be executed. If the transaction is to be fully secured, then a security agreement, UCC-1, warehouse agreement, and warehouse receipt are required. Examples of each are provided in the Appendix.

SUMMARY

At this juncture we have focused on two of the five borrowing alternatives, conventional loans and acceptances. We conclude that the corporate borrower should avail itself of floating prime and acceptances. This maximizes flexibility and increases control over interest expense. Since acceptances are usually less costly, compared to prime, the corporation may save substantially by financing certain transactions (primarily international trade) with acceptances. These savings can reach $20,000 to 30,000 per million dollars borrowed per year. When the transaction does not meet the criteria, or when rates are expected to drop, the floating prime borrowings will meet the financing requirements.

APPENDIX ONE

PUBLISHED INTERPRETATIONS

OF THE

BOARD OF GOVERNORS

OF THE

FEDERAL RESERVE SYSTEM

———

COMPILED UNDER THE DIRECTION OF THE BOARD
IN THE BOARD'S LEGAL DIVISION

As of June 30, 1980

DISCOUNTS AND ADVANCES

D. BANKERS ACCEPTANCES

(1) Creation

(a) GENERALLY

¶ 1050.   **Effect of Federal Reserve Act upon powers of State member banks.**—State member banks are not restricted by section 13 as to the kinds of acceptances which they may make, but are restricted as to the amounts of such acceptances. *Digest of* 1923 BULLETIN 316.

NOTE.—As to amount limitations, see ¶1650 et seq.

¶ 1051.   **Inapplicability of amount limitations to "ineligible acceptances".**—Since 1923, the Board has been of the view that "the acceptance power of State member banks is not necessarily confined to the provisions of section 13 [of the Federal Reserve Act], inasmuch as the laws of many States confer broader acceptance powers upon their State banks, and certain State member banks may, therefore, legally make acceptances of kinds which are not eligible for rediscount, but which may be eligible for purchase by Federal reserve banks under section 14." 1923 F. R. BULLETIN 316, 317.

In 1963, the Comptroller of the Currency ruled that "[n]ational banks are not limited in the character of acceptances which they may make in financing credit transactions, and bankers' acceptances may be used for such purpose, since the making of acceptances is an essential part of banking authorized by 12 U.S.C. 24." *Comptroller's Manual* 7.7420. Therefore, national banks are authorized by the Comptroller to make acceptances under 12 U.S.C. § 24, although the acceptances are not of the type described in section 13 of the Federal Reserve Act.

A review of the legislative history surrounding the enactment of the acceptance provisions of section 13 reveals that Congress believed in 1913 that it was granting to national banks a power which they would not otherwise possess and had not previously possessed. See remarks of Congressmen Phelan, Helvering, Saunders and Glass, 51 *Cong. Rec.* 4676, 4798, 4885, and 5064 (September 10, 12, 13 and 17 of 1913). Nevertheless, the Courts have long recognized the evolutionary nature of banking and of the scope of the "incidental powers" clause of 12 U.S.C. § 24. See *Merchants Bank* v. *State Bank*, 77 U.S. 604 (1870) (upholding the power of a national bank to certify a check under the "incidental powers" clause of 12 U.S.C. § 24).

It now appears that, based on the Board's 1923 ruling and the Comptroller's 1963 ruling, both State member banks and national banks may make acceptances which are not of the type described in section 13 of the Federal Reserve Act. Yet, this appears to be a development that Congress did not contemplate when it drafted the acceptance provisions of section 13.

The question is presented whether the amount limitations of section 13 should apply to acceptances made by a member bank that are not of the type described in section 13. (The amount limitations are of two kinds: (a) a limitation on the amount that may be accepted *for any one customer*, and (b) a limitation on the *aggregate* amount of acceptances that a member bank may make.) In interpreting any Federal statutory provision, the primary guide is the intent of Congress, yet, as noted earlier, Congress did not contemplate in 1913 the development of so-called "ineligible acceptances." (Although there is some indication that Congress did contemplate State member banks' making acceptances of a

FEDERAL RESERVE BANKS

type not described in section 13 [remarks of Congressman Glass, 51 *Cong. Rec.* 5064], the primary focus of Congressional attention was on the acceptance powers of national banks.) In the absence of an indication of Congressional intent, we are left to reach an interpretation that is in harmony with the language of the statutory provisions and with the purposes of the Federal Reserve Act.

Section 13 authorizes acceptances of two types. The seventh paragraph of section 13 (12 U.S.C. § 372) authorizes certain acceptances that arise out of specific transactions in goods. (These acceptances are sometimes referred to as "commercial acceptances.") The twelfth paragraph of section 13 authorizes member banks to make acceptances "for the purpose of furnishing dollar exchange as required by the usages of trade" in foreign transactions. (Such acceptances are referred to as "dollar exchange acceptances.") In the twelfth paragraph, there is a 10 per cent limit on the amount of dollar exchange acceptances that may be accepted for any one customer (unless adequately secured) and a limitation on the aggregate amount of dollar exchange acceptances that a member bank may make. (The twelfth paragraph, in imposing these limitations, refers to the acceptance of "such drafts or bills of exchange referred to [in] this paragraph.") Similarly, the seventh paragraph imposes on commercial acceptances a parallel 10 per cent per-customer limitation, and limitations on the aggregate amount of commercial acceptances. (In the case of the aggregate limitations, the seventh paragraph states that "no bank shall accept *such bills* to an amount" in excess of the aggregate limit; the reference to "such bills" makes clear that the limitation is only in respect of drafts or bills of exchange of the specific type described in the seventh paragraph.)

Based on the language and parallel structure of the seventh and twelfth paragraphs of section 13, and in the absence of a statement of Congressional intent in the legislative history, the Board concludes that the per-customer and aggregate limitations of the twelfth paragraph apply only to acceptances of the type described in that paragraph (dollar exchange acceptances), and the per-customer and aggregate limitations of the seventh paragraph (12 U.S.C. § 372) apply only to acceptances of the type described in that paragraph. 1973 BULLETIN 450; 12 CFR 250.163.

NOTE.—As to amount limitations, see ¶ 1650 et seq.

¶ 1055. **Acceptance must be made by person upon whom drawn.**—A draft drawn upon a land company but accepted by a bank is eligible neither as a banker's acceptance within the meaning of the Board's regulations, nor as a trade acceptance, since an acceptance must be accepted by the person upon whom it is drawn. *Digest of* 1916 BULLETIN 112.

¶ 1060. **Indorsement.**—Acceptances in blank need not bear the indorsement of the last party owning the acceptances. It is preferable, however, that all acceptances bear the indorsement of the prior holder. *Digest of* 1918 BULLETIN 744.

(b) RENEWALS

¶ 1075. **Compliance with requirements for original acceptance.**—Warehouse receipts or bills of lading securing original drafts are released upon the acceptance of the original drafts. A national bank may not properly accept a renewal of a draft drawn by the purchaser of goods and secured at the time of original acceptance by a bill of lading or warehouse receipt, unless the renewal acceptance

DISCOUNTS AND ADVANCES

complies with the terms of the law and the rulings and regulations of the Board applicable to the original acceptance. While a national bank may agree in advance to accept drafts aggregating certain amounts for a period of more than six months, each individual draft must comply with the provisions of the law relating to the acceptance of the original draft. *Digest of* 1920 BULLETIN 66.

¶ 1080. **Ineligibility where period of original transaction has elapsed.**—A renewal draft can not be eligible if at the time of its acceptance the period required for the conclusion of the transaction out of which the original draft was drawn shall have elapsed. Where it is impracticable at the time the original draft is drawn to determine the conditions which will exist at the time the renewal draft is to be drawn, the question of eligibility of such renewal drafts will depend upon the stage of the transaction that may have been reached when such renewal drafts are drawn. *Digest of* 1919 BULLETIN 858.

¶ 1085. **Agreement of member bank to accept renewal draft.**—A member bank can not accept an original draft unless it is drawn in compliance with the terms of section 13. Consequently, it can not agree unconditionally to accept a renewal draft, but can agree to accept only in the event that the renewal draft is eligible for acceptance under the terms of the law. *Digest of* 1921 BULLETIN 963, 964.

¶ 1090. **Agreement to make renewals after remote period of time.**—A borrower proposes to draw drafts against readily marketable staples, which are under contract for sale and delivery at a remote period of time, in order to carry the goods pending delivery, such drafts to be 90-day drafts secured by warehouse receipts covering the goods to be sold, subject to renewal for 90 days. A draft secured by a warehouse receipt should not be accepted subject to an agreement by the accepting bank to make renewals, when it is contemplated that a period of six months is sufficient to cover all reasonable contingencies in the orderly marketing of the staples, which, by hypothesis, must be readily marketable. If a borrower needs funds for a period in excess of six months, he should obtain funds upon his direct note. *Digest of* 1920 BULLETIN 277.

(2) *Acceptances Involving Importation or Exportation of Goods*

(a) IN GENERAL

¶ 1100. **General principles.**—In order to comply with the Board's Regulations, as applied to dealers purchasing the same class of goods, both for export and domestic sale, there must be provision (a) that the dealer has a contract for the exportation of goods in a specified amount within a specified and reasonable time; (b) that the total amount of drafts under the credit opened shall not exceed the aggregate amount of export transactions contracted for; (c) that the proceeds of the drafts will be used to consummate the export transactions referred to; that shipping documents covering the goods will be furnished in due course and that the proceeds of the sale of the goods will be applied in liquidation of the credit.

The provision in Regulation A, Series of 1920, with regard to furnishing "exchange arising out of the transaction being financed by the credit," is an

FEDERAL RESERVE BANKS

alternative to furnishing documents only in import transactions. *Digest of* 1921 BULLETIN 70.

NOTE.—The Board's Regulations no longer demand strict compliance with these requirements, but merely substantial compliance with the basic principles involved.

(b) ACTUAL TRANSACTION NECESSARY

¶ 1110. **Necessity for actual contract of sale.**—A clean draft drawn by an exporter in Chile upon a member bank for the purpose of providing funds with which to purchase beans, peas, etc., from farmers in Chile, is not eligible for acceptance unless the Chilean exporter is under contract to ship such beans, peas, etc., to some other country and the member bank has a guarantee to this effect. In order that a draft may be said to grow out of a transaction involving the importation or exportation of goods, there must exist some actual contract of sale and it must appear that the drafts in question are drawn in advance of the actual shipment of the goods under the contract of sale. The mere fact that the exporter intends to sell these goods in a foreign country is not sufficient. *Digest of* 1917 BULLETIN 378.

¶ 1115. **Acceptance must be for person with contract to export or import.**— A draft drawn by the seller of packing-house products sold to a purchaser under contract to export such products to Europe is ineligible when the acceptance is made at the instance of the seller, since the seller has no contract to export and the transaction involved is completed when the sale to the purchaser is made. A different situation, however, would result if the draft were accepted at the instance of the purchaser of the goods, the purchaser having a contract to export the goods. *Digest of* 1918 BULLETIN 435; 1915 BULLETIN 276.

NOTE.—This ruling was modified, to some extent, by ¶1195.

[*The Next Page is Page 71.*]

DISCOUNTS AND ADVANCES

¶ 1125. **Drafts drawn by foreign exporter-manufacturer under agreement to manufacture and ship products into this country.**—A South American products company, desiring funds to manufacture quebracho extract and meat products and sell them in the United States, agreed with a domestic banking firm to consign to the firm such merchandise when manufactured and when shipping facilities should become available, the banking firm to procure the acceptance of drafts drawn by the products company on a member bank and give the proceeds to the products company. The agreement further provided that the merchandise will be produced and consigned to the banking firm in time to meet the maturity of the drafts and that the merchandise shall all have been sold at the time of arrival for immediate delivery. Such drafts are ineligible for discount, since they can not be said to grow out of transactions involving the importation or exportation of goods within the proper meaning of section 13 of the Federal Reserve Act. *Digest of* 1918 BULLETIN 976.

¶ 1130. **Acceptances to extend credits on open accounts to foreign purchasers.**—An American exporter is compelled to sell goods abroad on open account; he proposes to draw drafts on a member bank against such open account, exhibiting duplicate invoice and duplicate documents showing shipments actually made during the past week, such drafts to be for 90 days and subject to privilege of one or two renewals if necessary. Drafts of this nature are ineligible for discount, for the Act does not authorize member banks to accept drafts for the purpose of enabling domestic concerns to extend credits on open account to foreign purchasers. *Digest of* 1919 BULLETIN 254.

NOTE.—This ruling was modified, to some extent, by ¶1195.

(c) "GOODS" DEFINED

¶ 1150. **Coin as "goods".**—A bill of exchange drawn to finance the shipment of gold coin from this country to Europe or to Canada, is eligible for purchase by a Federal Reserve Bank, since gold coin is "goods" within the meaning of section 13, and consequently such acceptances may be said to be based upon or involving the exportation of goods. *Digest of* 1917 BULLETIN 29.

¶ 1155. **Bullion as "goods".**—A banker's acceptance covering the shipment of gold bars to Peru is eligible for purchase by a Federal Reserve Bank, since gold bars may properly be considered as goods, and hence the acceptance may be said to be based upon or involving the exportation of goods. *Digest of* 1917 BULLETIN 29.

¶ 1160. **Identification of specific goods.**—It is not necessary that the specific goods be identified at the time of acceptance if there is a contract calling for the import or export of goods. *Digest of* 1915 BULLETIN 405.

FEDERAL RESERVE BANKS

(d) RELATION TO DATE AND PERIOD OF SHIPMENT

¶ 1175. **Consummation of sale of goods immaterial.**—A national bank may properly accept a draft drawn for the purpose of importing goods, whether or not the sale of the goods under consideration has actually been consummated at the time of the acceptance of the draft, provided the bank is assured that the proceeds of the draft will ultimately be used to finance a transaction involving the importation of goods. It is immaterial whether or not the goods have actually been sold at the time of acceptance. It is not necessary, therefore, that they be identified at that time. The accepting bank, however, must be reasonably sure that the draft is drawn for the purpose of financing a transaction involving the importation or exportation of the goods and that its proceeds will be used for that purpose. *Digest of* 1917 BULLETIN 527.

¶ 1180. **Transfer of title prior to actual shipment.**—A draft drawn for the purpose of financing the sale of goods to a purchaser abroad, the goods to be delivered aboard the ship and paid for within a reasonable time thereafter, is eligible for acceptance, even though the title to the goods is transferred to the purchaser before foreign shipment actually begins. *Digest of* 1917 BULLETIN 878.

¶ 1185. **Eligibility of acceptance where goods have not been actually shipped.**—An American importer receives advice from a foreign seller that he has shipped goods for export to this country; the advice is accompanied by a bill for the goods and arrives before the bill of lading; the American importer draws a draft upon his bank, although at that time the goods sold are still unshipped or lying in a foreign port, or afloat, or in this country. Where there has been an actual sale of goods for export from a foreign country, a draft drawn for the purpose of financing the purchase of such goods is eligible for acceptance, whether or not the bill of lading is attached to the draft and whether or not the goods have been actually shipped. *Digest of* 1920 BULLETIN 162.

¶ 1190. **Effect of delay in shipment.**—Drafts drawn upon a national bank in settlement of advances for cotton being accumulated by cotton buyers are eligible for rediscount if the draft is based upon a transaction involving the importation or exportation of goods. The mere fact that there is a temporary delay in the actual shipment of goods is immaterial. *Digest of* 1916 BULLETIN 458.

¶ 1195. **Acceptance after completion of shipment.**—Bankers' acceptances may properly be considered as growing out of transactions involving the importation or exportation of goods when drawn for the purpose of financing the sale and distribution on usual credit terms of imported or exported goods into the channels of trade, whether or not the bills are accepted after the physical importation or exportation has been completed. Under no circumstances, however, should there be outstanding at any time more than one acceptance against the same goods. Previous conflicting rulings reversed. *Digest of* 1927 BULLETIN 860.

NOTE.—This ruling superseded, to some extent, ¶¶1115, 1130.

¶ 1200. **Refinancing of foreign dealers in distributing American goods.**—An American manufacturer ships automobiles to a dealer abroad who resells the cars to customers on a deferred-payment plan, taking in payment instalment notes or acceptances and retaining title to the cars until the last instalment is

DISCOUNTS AND ADVANCES

paid. A foreign banking institution organized in this country makes advances to the foreign dealer against such notes or acceptances and, in order to refinance itself, such institution desires that the retail paper arising in this manner shall be considered a proper basis for an acceptance credit to be issued by member banks. Such a plan contemplates the financing of the sale of goods by retailers to consumers and involves material departures from the customary use of bankers' acceptance credits as approved by the Board. Accordingly, the Board does not approve the use of bankers' acceptances in refinancing advances made to retail dealers in foreign countries against instalment paper taken by such dealers in the retail distribution of American goods abroad. *Digest of* 1929 BULLETIN 294.

(e) SECURITY

¶ 1225. **Where dealer is engaged in both foreign and domestic transactions.—** A dealer engaged in both foreign and domestic transactions, having drawn drafts accepted by a member bank in an export transaction should be given the option, with the consent of the accepting bank, to secure such drafts in the manner required of those drawn in domestic transactions, if he wishes to use the proceeds derived from the sale of the goods exported for purposes other than the payment of such acceptances. *Digest of* 1918 BULLETIN 438.

¶ 1230. **Documentary drafts on a foreign buyer.—**A draft drawn upon a national bank secured by a documentary draft drawn by the same drawer upon a foreign buyer, which latter draft is secured by shipping documents, is eligible for acceptance by a national bank. *Digest of* 1920 BULLETIN 610.

(3) *Acceptances Against Domestic Shipments*

(a) PURPOSE OF TRANSACTION

¶ 1250. **Draft must be drawn to finance shipment, not merely as loan.—**A draft drawn by the purchaser of goods against a national bank is not eligible for acceptance under section 13 of the Federal Reserve Act merely because it is secured by a bill of lading covering the goods bought. The seller shipped goods and mailed the bill of lading to the purchaser, who, on its arrival, drew on his member bank, attaching the bill of lading to the draft as security. Such a draft is not eligible for acceptance, for in substance the transaction is merely a straight loan to the drawer secured by a bill of lading and does not come within the spirit of section 13. The provisions of this section contemplate some actual connection between the acceptance of the draft and the transaction involving the sale and shipment of the goods; that is, the draft should be drawn to finance the shipment. *Digest of* 1917 BULLETIN 380.

¶ 1255. **Acceptances to provide working capital.—**A member bank issues a letter of credit at the instance of a tanner in favor of a packer, authorizing the packer to draw drafts against hides shipped by him to the tanner. The tanner is to process the hides and market them for an agreed commission, remitting the balance of the proceeds to the packer. The drafts are drawn for a period in excess of the time required to ship the hides and have sufficient maturity to cover part, at least, of the time required for the tanning process. Although the bank's customer is not the purchaser of the goods shipped, but only the consignee thereof, the drafts appear to be drawn for the purpose of furnishing him with additional

FEDERAL RESERVE BANKS

working capital during the period required for manufacturing or processing the goods and should not, therefore, be regarded favorably by Federal Reserve Banks. *Digest of* 1921 BULLETIN 1312.

NOTE.—To same effect, see 1920 BULLETIN 1301. However, these interpretations were superseded, to the extent of any inconsistency, by ¶1325.

(b) ATTACHMENT OF SHIPPING DOCUMENTS

¶ 1275. **Definition of shipping documents.**—The term "shipping documents" includes an order bill of lading or a straight bill of lading, whichever is issued by the carrier in the particular case, but does not include freight receipts or mere copies of original bills of lading. The protection afforded by a straight bill is not absolute, but the provisions of the regulations require only that the accepting bank be furnished with the best security which has been issued by the carrier in the transaction. *Digest of* 1921 BULLETIN 191.

¶ 1280. **Express company receipt.**—A gold refiner proposes to finance a purchase of gold by drawing on a national bank, which is asked to accept against an express company receipt covering the shipment of the gold. Such a receipt is not a shipping document conveying or securing title as required by law and the draft is, therefore, ineligible for acceptance. *Digest of* 1923 BULLETIN 158.

¶ 1285. **Necessity.**—The acceptance of a draft by a member bank against an acceptance agreement which purports to assign to the bank certain collateral security, but which does not specifically mention any security as assigned, is an ordinary accommodation acceptance, and is not authorized by law. Such a draft is not eligible for acceptance since shipping documents are not attached and since it can not be said to be secured by a warehouse receipt or similar document covering readily marketable staples. *Digest of* 1918 BULLETIN 311.

¶ 1290. **Attachment at time of acceptance.**—Where drafts are to be accepted before the bills of lading covering the shipments have been issued, such a draft is ineligible for acceptance, since a draft drawn upon a national bank covering domestic shipment of goods is not eligible for acceptance by such bank under the provisions of section 13 unless shipping documents are attached at the time of acceptance. *Digest of* 1919 BULLETIN 471.

¶ 1295. **Physical attachment unnecessary.**—The provision of section 13 which authorizes any member bank to accept drafts based upon the domestic shipment of goods, provided shipping documents are "attached," should not be construed so as to require that the documents be physically fastened to the draft. It is sufficient if the accepting bank has possession of the documents at the time of acceptance. *Digest of* 1917 BULLETIN 765.

¶ 1300. **Custody of documents by agent of accepting bank held sufficient.**—Shipping documents may be said to be "attached at the time of acceptance" within the meaning of section 13, where such shipping documents at the time of acceptance are delivered to an agent of the accepting bank at a place other than the location of the bank, since possession of the agent is possession of the principal in the eyes of the law. *Digest of* 1918 BULLETIN 971, 972.

DISCOUNTS AND ADVANCES

¶ 1305. **Documents must convey security title.**—Under the provisions of section 13, which authorize any member bank to accept drafts based upon domestic shipment of goods, provided shipping documents conveying or securing title are attached, such documents must be made out or indorsed so as to convey or secure title to the accepting bank. *Digest of* 1918 BULLETIN 198.

¶ 1310. **Release of shipping documents upon acceptance of draft.**—The accepting bank need not retain the bill of lading during the life of the acceptance, providing shipping documents are attached at the time of acceptance. *Digest of* 1918 BULLETIN 634.

¶ 1315. **Acceptance not eligible merely because secured by shipping documents.**—A tobacco manufacturer buys tobacco for the purpose of manufacturing for export. The process of manufacture from time of purchase to the time of sale requires from 9 to 13 months. The manufacturer draws 90-day drafts on his bank subject to renewals of 90 days each. Warehouse receipts or bills of lading will be attached to the draft at the time it is presented for acceptance, but thereafter such warehouse receipts or bills of lading will be released. As there is no existing contract providing for the export of tobacco, such drafts are not eligible for acceptance as drafts growing out of an export transaction. Nor would it seem that a draft secured by a bill of lading covering tobacco shipped to the manufacturer will be eligible for acceptance, since a draft drawn by the purchaser of goods is not eligible for acceptance merely because it is secured by a bill of lading covering the goods bought. In such a case the draft would be eligible only if the proceeds of the draft are to be applied by the drawer—that is, the buyer—to the payment of the goods covered by the bill of lading. If the proceeds are to be used to finance the manufacture and sale of tobacco as a finished product, such drafts will be ineligible for acceptance. *Digest of* 1920 BULLETIN 66.

(c) MATURITY

¶ 1325. **Consistency with customary credit time.**—A seller of certain staples draws a sight draft on the purchaser in New York with bill of lading attached and sends such draft with bill of lading attached to a member bank in New York designated by the purchaser. The latter then draws a 90-day bill on such bank which is accepted by the bank, the bank having at the time in its possession the bill of lading covering the staples in process of shipment. The acceptance is discounted by the purchaser and the proceeds used to pay the sight draft and to obtain the release of the bill of lading. It does not require 90 days for the completion of the shipment of goods, only a relatively short time being necessary for this purpose. In such circumstances, a draft drawn by the purchaser is eligible for acceptance by the member bank when it has a maturity consistent with the usual and customary credit time prevailing in the particular business, provided that all other relevant requirements of the law and of the Board's regulations are complied with. The fact that the accepting bank has possession of the bill of lading at the time of the acceptance of the draft is believed to be a substantial compliance with the requirement of the law that shipping documents conveying or securing title be attached at the time of the acceptance. *Digest of* 1929 BULLETIN 811.

FEDERAL RESERVE BANKS

¶ **1330. Acceptances to finance fattening and reselling cattle.**—A farmer purchases cattle with the intention of fattening them for a customary period of about three months and then reselling them. To procure funds with which to carry the cattle pending resale, he draws drafts on his bank, secured by bills of lading covering the shipment of the cattle to him. It is anticipated that the cattle will be resold during the life of the acceptances, and that the proceeds of the sale will be used to liquidate them. Such drafts are eligible for acceptance, provided the maturity is not in excess of the period of credit which is usual and reasonably necessary to finance transactions of this character, and when discounted and indorsed by a member bank other than the accepting bank, are eligible for rediscount, if otherwise in conformity with the law and regulations. *Digest of* 1921 BULLETIN 815.

¶ **1335. Acceptances to finance sale of oil.**—An oil producing company contracted to sell oil to an oil distributing company which in turn contracted to sell the oil to a railroad company. The producing company shipped the oil direct to the railroad company and the distributing company agreed immediately to pay the producing company. In order to finance the sale the distributing company drew drafts against its bank secured by shipping documents covering the oil. Such drafts are eligible for acceptance by a national bank when accompanied by shipping documents and, as the drafts are drawn to cover both the shipment and sale of the oil, they may be for a period which is usual and necessary in transactions of this character. *Digest of* 1921 BULLETIN 308.

¶ **1340. Acceptances to finance shipment and resale of cotton.**—A cotton broker draws on a member bank to finance the shipment of cotton, which has been purchased by him and is under contract of resale to a mill. The draft is accompanied by an order railroad bill of lading conveying and securing title to the cotton, and is accepted by the member bank. Under such circumstances, the acceptance may have a maturity covering both the period required for the actual shipment of the cotton and also any reasonable and usual period of credit extended to the mill under the contract of sale, not exceeding six months in all. *Digest of* 1922 BULLETIN 52.

¶ **1345. Maturity when draft is drawn to finance shipment alone.**—A member bank may properly accept drafts drawn against the shipment of goods from a corporation to its agent or branch, even though no sale of the goods is involved in the transaction. Where a draft is drawn against the shipment of goods in a transaction which does not involve a sale of these goods, that is, where the acceptance of the draft is for the purpose of financing a shipment alone, the maturity of the draft should approximate the duration of the transit of the goods. Where, however, a draft is drawn against the shipment of goods in a transaction involving the sale of those goods as well, the draft may properly be drawn and accepted for the purpose of financing not merely the shipment, but also the sale of the goods, and its maturity need not be limited by the period required for shipment, although it can not, of course, exceed six months. *Digest of* 1917 BULLETIN 690.

DISCOUNTS AND ADVANCES

(4) *Acceptances against Storage of Staples*

(a) READILY MARKETABLE STAPLES

¶ **1375. Meaning of term "staples".**—The term "staples" includes manufactured goods as well as raw materials, provided the goods in question are nonperishable and have a wide ready market. They must be goods generally produced and well established in commerce, not an unusual or extraordinary commodity for which there is no ready market. Therefore cotton yarns and flour are "staples" of the kinds intended. *Digest of* 1916 BULLETIN 523.

¶ **1380. Nonperishable requirement.**—Member banks, as a matter of prudence, should not consider as eligible any staple which is in its nature so perishable as not to be reasonably sure of maintaining its value as security at least for the life of the draft drawn against it. *Digest of* 1919 BULLETIN 652.

¶ **1385. Particular instances.**—The following have been held to constitute readily marketable staples:

    Cattle. 1918 BULLETIN 309.
    Coal. 1923 BULLETIN 1194.
    Cotton. 1917 BULLETIN 30.
    Cottonseed. 1925 BULLETIN 737.
    Cotton yarns. 1916 BULLETIN 523.
    Flour. 1916 BULLETIN 523.
    Potatoes. 1917 BULLETIN 614.
    Sugar in bond. 1918 BULLETIN 520.
    Wool. 1918 BULLETIN 636.

The following have been held *not* to constitute readily marketable staples:

    Automobiles or automobile tires. 1920 BULLETIN 65.
    Automobile parts. 1921 BULLETIN 699.

(b) PURPOSE OF TRANSACTION

¶ **1400. Not eligible if drawn to carry goods for speculative purposes.**—A draft secured by a warehouse receipt should not be considered eligible for acceptance unless the goods covered by the warehouse receipt are being held in storage pending a reasonably immediate sale, shipment, or distribution into the process of manufacture. A draft which is drawn to carry goods for speculative purposes or for an indefinite period of time without the purpose to sell, ship, or manufacture within a reasonable time is not eligible for acceptance. Such a draft would be merely a cloak to evade the restrictions of section 5200, Revised Statutes. *Digest of* 1919 BULLETIN 858.

¶ **1405. Not eligible if drawn to furnish working capital.**—A cotton broker contracts to sell cotton to a mill, either at a definite price or at the current market price at the time delivery is ultimately taken. Pending consummation of the transaction, the cotton is stored with a mill, which issues a warehouse receipt therefor. Irrespective of whether such receipt would constitute proper security to support an acceptance drawn by the cotton broker, it appears that the real purpose of the proposed acceptance credit is to furnish the mill with working capital rather than to finance the sale of the cotton from broker to mill, or the temporary storage thereof pending sale, and consequently such an acceptance would be improper. *Digest of* 1922 BULLETIN 52.

FEDERAL RESERVE BANKS

(c) WAREHOUSE RECEIPTS AND OTHER SECURITY

¶ **1425. Necessity for security after acceptance.**—Acceptances drawn to finance storage transactions must be secured at the time of acceptance, but for the purpose of discount need not remain secured to the same extent, except where they exceed the 10 per cent limitation on acceptances for any one customer. There is no requirement in the law that acceptances within this limitation remain secured after acceptance, but as a matter of policy, and to prevent abuse of the acceptance privilege, the Board has seen fit to provide by regulation that Federal Reserve Banks which have discounted such acceptances should require some form of security in addition to the customers' general credit, such as a trust receipt or an agreement of the kind described in Regulation A. So far as concerns the power of a member bank to accept, however, the Board's regulations contain no requirement that acceptances within the 10 per cent limitation remain secured. *Digest of* 1923 BULLETIN 316.

¶ **1430. Insurance by warehouseman independent of borrower.**—Where a corporation which issues warehouse receipts is formed as a subterfuge for the purpose of evading this requirement, such facts should be taken into consideration in passing upon the eligibility of drafts secured by such warehouse receipts. If the borrower exercises control over the corporation issuing the warehouse receipt so as to give him control over the goods in storage, the organization of the corporation is a subterfuge. In order that the warehouse receipts may be sufficient the corporation issuing such receipts must be organized in good faith as an independent corporation. *Digest of* 1918 BULLETIN 31.

¶ **1435. Borrower must not have access to premises or control over goods.**—Certain canned goods and other materials not necessary for immediate purposes are set aside and placed in storage on part of the premises owned by the owner of the goods, but leased to a lessee who issues warehouse receipts covering the goods in storage. If the premises in question are actually turned over to the lessee under a bona fide lease, the lessee being independent of the borrower and having entire custody and control of the goods, the member bank may accept drafts drawn against warehouse receipts issued by the lessee, but it must be understood that the borrower shall not have access to the premises and shall exercise no control over the goods stored. *Digest of* 1918 BULLETIN 634.

¶ **1440. Warehouseman as employee of borrowing company.**—Where a separate corporation has been created and the receipts are issued by that corporation and not by the borrowers, such receipts are a proper basis for an acceptance. As the corporations have practically the same officers, the manager of the warehousing company should not be an employee of the borrowing company. *Digest of* 1918 BULLETIN 862.

¶ **1445. Goods held by persons employed by owner.**—The Board has been asked to review an Interpretation it issued in 1933 concerning the eligibility for rediscount by a Federal Reserve Bank of bankers' acceptances issued against field warehouse receipts where the custodian of the goods is a present or former employee of the borrower. [¶ 1445 Published Interpretations, 1933 BULLETIN

(6-78)

DISCOUNTS AND ADVANCES

188] The Board determined at that time that the acceptances were not eligible because:

> such receipts do not comply with the requirement of section 13 of the Federal Reserve Act that a banker's acceptance be "secured at the time of acceptance by a warehouse receipt or other such document *conveying or securing title* covering readily marketable staples," nor with the requirement of section XI of the Board's Regulation A that it be "secured at the time of acceptance by a warehouse, terminal, or other similar receipt, conveying security title to such staples, *issued by a party independent of the customer."*

The requirement that the receipt be "issued by a party independent of the customer" was deleted from Regulation A in 1973, and thus the primary issue for the Board's consideration is whether a field warehouse receipt is a document "securing title" to readily marketable staples.

While bankers' acceptances secured by field warehouse receipts are rarely offered for rediscount or as collateral for an advance, the issue of "eligibility" is still significant. If an ineligible acceptance is discounted and then sold by a member bank, the proceeds are deemed to be "deposits" under section 204.1(f) of Regulation D and are subject to reserve requirements.

In reviewing this matter, the Board has taken into consideration the changes that have occurred in commercial law and practice since 1933. Modern commercial law, embodied in the Uniform Commercial Code, refers to "perfecting security interests" rather than "securing title" to goods. The Board believes that if, under State law, the issuance of a field warehouse receipt provides the lender with a perfected security interest in the goods, the receipt should be regarded as a document "securing title" to goods for the purposes of § 13 of the Federal Reserve Act. It should be noted, however, that the mere existence of a perfected security interest alone is not sufficient; the Act requires that the acceptance be secured by a warehouse receipt or its equivalent.

Under the U.C.C., evidence of an agreement between the secured party and the debtor must exist before a security interest can attach [U.C.C. § 9-202]. This agreement may be evidenced by: (1) a written security agreement signed by the debtor, or (2) the collateral being placed in the possession of the secured party or his agent [U.C.C. § 9-203]. Generally, a security interest is perfected by the filing of a financing statement [U.C.C. § 9-302]. However, if the collateral is in the possession of a bailee, then perfection can be achieved by: (1) having warehouse receipts issued in the name of the secured party: (2) notifying the bailee of the secured party's interest: or (3) having a financing statement filed. [U.C.C. § 9-304(3)].

If the field warehousing operation is properly conducted, a security interest in the goods is perfected when a warehouse receipt is issued in the name of the secured party (the lending bank). Therefore, warehouse receipts issued pursuant to a bona fide field warehousing operation satisfy the legal requirements of section 13 of the Federal Reserve Act. Moreover, in a properly conducted field warehousing operation, the warehouse manager will be trained, bonded, supervised, and audited by the field warehousing company. This procedure tends to insure that he will not be impermissibly controlled by his former (or sometimes present) employer, the borrower, even though he may look to the borrower for reemployment at some future time. A prudent lender will, of course, carefully review the field warehousing operation to ensure that stated procedures are satisfactory and that they are

FEDERAL RESERVE BANKS

actually being followed. The lender may also wish to review the field warehousing operation to ensure that stated procedures are satisfactory and, that they are actually being followed. The lender may also wish to review the field warehousing company's fidelity bonds and legal liability insurance policies to ensure that they provide satisfactory protection to the lender.

If the warehousing operation is not conducted properly, however, and the manager remains under the control of the borrower, the security interest may be lost. Consequently, the lender may wish to require a written security agreement and the filing of a financing statement to ensure that the lender will have a perfected security interest even if it is later determined that the field warehousing operation was not properly conducted. It should be noted, however, that the Federal Reserve Act clearly requires that the bankers' acceptance be secured by a warehouse receipt in order to satisfy the requirements of eligibility, and a written security agreement and filed financing statement, while desirable, cannot serve as a substitute for a warehouse receipt.

This Interpretation is based on facts that have been presented in regard to field warehousing operations conducted by established, professional field warehouse companies, and it does not necessarily apply to all field warehousing operations. Thus ¶ 1430 and ¶ 1440 of the Published Interpretations [1918 BULLETIN 31 and 1918 BULLETIN 862] maintain their validity with regard to corporations formed for the purpose of conducting limited field warehousing operations. Furthermore, the prohibition contained in ¶ 1435 Published Interpretations [1918 BULLETIN 634] that "the borrower shall not have access to the premises and shall exercise no control over the goods stored" retains its validity, except that access for inspection purposes is still permitted under ¶ 1450 [1926 BULLETIN 666]. The purpose for the acceptance transaction must be proper and cannot be for speculation [¶ 1400, 1919 BULLETIN 858] or for the purpose of furnishing working capitol [¶ 1405, 1922 BULLETIN 52].

This interpretation supersedes only the previous ¶ 1445 of the Published Interpretations [1933 BULLETIN 188], and is not intended to affect any other Board Interpretation regarding field warehousing [1978 BULLETIN 486; 12 CFR 201.110].

¶ **1450.   Access by borrower for purpose of inspection.**—Bankers' acceptances secured by cottonseed stored in a warehouse owned by the owner of the cottonseed but leased to an independent public warehouse corporation under bona fide lease, the corporation assuming exclusive control and management of such warehouse and operating it as a public warehouse bonded and licensed under the United States Warehouse Act, may be eligible for rediscount at a Federal Reserve Bank, although the owners of the cottonseed are permitted access to the seed in storage at proper and reasonable times for the purpose only of inspecting the condition of the seed, providing that on all such occasions the consent of the independent warehouse corporation is first secured and that the owner of the seed or his representative is accompanied by a proper representative of the warehouse corporation. It is also necessary that the cottonseed be stored under such conditions as to protect it adequately from deterioration. *Digest of* 1926 BULLETIN 666.

[*Next Page is 80.4.*]   (6-78)

DISCOUNTS AND ADVANCES

¶ **1455. Control of warehouse by accepting bank.**—The borrower proposes to set aside readily marketable goods and materials in a warehouse controlled by a separate corporation engaged solely in the warehouse business, the entire stock of which is owned by the borrower. It is proposed that the accepting bank have an agent on the premises who shall have access to the goods. It is not sufficient that the accepting bank merely have "access." If, however, its representative is given control of the warehouse so that the acceptor has a right to remove the goods and place them in storage elsewhere at the expense of the warehouse corporation, acceptances issued against such warehouse receipts are eligible. *Digest of* 1918 BULLETIN 862.

¶ **1460. Warehouse receipts covering agricultural products of cooperative marketing associations.**—Producers of agricultural commodities form a cooperative marketing association and convey to it the commodities when produced for the purpose of resale. Pending sale the commodities are stored in warehouses independent of the association. Drafts drawn by the association and secured by negotiable warehouse receipts are eligible for acceptance and rediscount, if otherwise in conformity with the law and regulations. If it is known that a six months' credit is required, it is improper to draw two 90-day acceptances. *Digest of* 1921 BULLETIN 963.

NOTE.—Such acceptances may now be eligible for discount with maturities up to six months.

¶ **1465. Warehouse receipt covering sugar in bond.**—Member banks may legally accept drafts drawn against warehouse receipts covering sugar in bond under transit entry where the receipt issued by the collector is in negotiable form, and where the sugar cannot be withdrawn for domestic sale or consumption without special permission of the Treasury Department. *Digest of* 1918 BULLETIN 520.

¶ **1470. Receipt issued by custodian of building.**—An acceptance drawn against wool stored in buildings under the control of a custodian entirely independent of the borrower is eligible for rediscount, since the custodian's receipt or certificate may be treated as a warehouse receipt within section 13. *Digest of* 1918 BULLETIN 636.

¶ **1475. Chattel mortgage.**—A chattel mortgage is not a document similar to a warehouse receipt, since the borrower retains possession of the goods and conveys to the bank only the legal title. Federal Reserve Banks should consider ineligible for discount bills secured by chattel mortgages, whether accepted by member or nonmember banks. *Digest of* 1918 BULLETIN 309, 437, 871.

¶ **1480. Warehouse receipts as collateral for bank loans generally.**—General discussion of acceptability and importance of warehouse receipts as collateral security for bank loans, especially as regards receipts of warehousemen licensed under the United States Warehouse Act. *Digest of* 1921 BULLETIN 1314.

(5) Dollar Exchange Acceptances

FEDERAL RESERVE BANKS

¶ **1500. Eligibility as dependent upon "usages of trade".**—The eligibility for acceptance of drafts drawn for the purpose of furnishing dollar exchange depends upon "the usages of trade in the respective countries, dependencies, or insular possessions." In other words, the purpose in view in making such acceptances is that of "furnishing dollar exchange as required by the usages of trade." On the other hand, where it is customary to make remittance in payment of foreign debts by checks rather than by three-month bankers' drafts, it cannot be said that bankers' acceptances are required by the usages of trade. The Board therefore refused to issue permits to accept drafts drawn in England or France, for between those countries and the United States it has been customary to make remittance by check or cable transfers. *Digest of* 1916 BULLETIN 665.

The Board has designated the following as countries whose usages of trade require the furnishing of dollar exchange, so that member banks may accept drafts drawn upon them by banks or bankers in such countries: Australia, New Zealand, and other Australasian dependencies; Argentina, Bolivia, Brazil, British Guiana, British Honduras, Chile, Colombia, Costa Rica, Cuba, Dutch East Indies, Dutch Guiana, Ecuador, French Guiana, French West Indies, Guatemala, Honduras, Nicaragua, Panama, Paraguay, Peru, Puerto Rico, Salvador, Dominican Republic, Trinidad, Uruguay, and Venezuela. *Digest of* 1916 BULLETIN 665; 1918 BULLETIN 938; 1920 BULLETIN 1175; 1921 BULLETIN 188; 1922 BULLETIN 50 and 680.

¶ **1505. Effect of permission of Board.**—Where the Board has granted permission to a member bank to accept drafts drawn upon it for the purpose of furnishing dollar exchange with respect to any country, the member bank is entitled to exercise similar accepting powers with respect to all countries that have been or hereafter may be designated by the Board as countries whose usages of trade require the furnishing of dollar exchange. *Digest of* 1918 BULLETIN 1119; 1922 BULLETIN 680.

DISCOUNTS AND ADVANCES

¶ **1510. Sufficiency of applications for permission.**—A national bank must show that the usages of trade in the country in which the drafts are drawn are such as to require the drawing of drafts of this character. Applications will not be granted if it appears that the drafts are to be drawn merely because dollar exchange is at a premium in the country where the drafts are to be drawn. *Digest of* 1920 BULLETIN 835.

¶ **1515. Limitation upon amount.**—The limitation imposed upon the amount of drafts which a member bank may accept for the purpose of furnishing dollar exchange is separate and distinct from and not included in the limits imposed by section 13 upon the amount of drafts or bills of exchange drawn against the shipment of goods or against warehouse receipts covering readily marketable staples which a member bank may accept. *Digest of* 1917 BULLETIN 528.

NOTE.—As to limitations upon amount of bankers' acceptances, see ¶1650 et seq.

(6) *Letters of Credit and Acceptance Credits*

¶ **1550. Commercial letters of credit.**—An exhaustive and detailed discussion of commercial letters of credit in their legal and practical aspects. *Digest of* 1921 BULLETIN 158, 410, 681, 926.

¶ **1555. Syndicate acceptance credits.**—General considerations with regard to prerequisites of eligibility under syndicate acceptance credits set forth in substance as follows: (1) Acceptance credits should rarely extend more than one year and never more than two years, (2) participating banks should not purchase their own acceptances, and sales thereof should be made at rates current at the time of sale, (3) underlying transactions should be commercial and the acceptances must be eligible under the Board's rules and regulations, and (4) Federal Reserve Banks should be consulted as to all large acceptance transactions. *Digest of* 1918 BULLETIN 257.

¶ **1560. Authority of national banks to guarantee letters of credit and acceptances and to appoint correspondent bank as agent to issue letters of credit and acceptances.**—(1) A national bank has no authority to guarantee or act as surety upon a letter of credit or to indorse an acceptance for accommodation; such acts are *ultra vires.*

(2) A national bank may purchase an acceptance and immediately resell it with its indorsement, since the power to indorse is incidental to the power to negotiate.

(3) National banks may continue to carry on the business now being handled by guaranteeing letters of credit with only slight modification, viz., the interior national bank may appoint the large city bank as its agent to issue a letter of credit and accept drafts drawn thereunder, the letter to be issued in the name of the city bank, but in fact the city bank to act as an agent of an undisclosed principal, namely, the interior bank, in issuing the letter of credit and accepting the drafts drawn thereunder. The interior bank may agree unconditionally to reimburse its agent as such for any moneys paid out, or to put the agent in funds to meet the maturing acceptances. *Digest of* 1921 BULLETIN 547.

¶ **1565. Acceptances under guarantee of national bank as subject to limitations upon acceptance powers.**—Drafts accepted by a foreign correspondent at the request and under the guarantee of a national bank in the United States

FEDERAL RESERVE BANKS

should be reported as a direct liability of such national bank and should be treated as subject to the limitations imposed by the Federal Reserve Act on the acceptance power of national banks. *Digest of* 1918 BULLETIN 311.

¶ 1570.   **Commercial letter of credit not subject to limitation on aggregate amount of acceptances.**—Section 13 prescribes a limitation on the aggregate amount of acceptances which a member bank may have outstanding at any one time. This limitation does not, however, apply to a commercial letter of credit as such, which is only an agreement to make acceptances, but only to the acceptances when and as made thereunder. Consequently the amount of a letter of credit may be in excess of the 50 or 100 per cent limitation, provided that drafts to be drawn thereunder shall not be accepted and remain outstanding at any one time, when, added to other outstanding acceptances of the member bank, they exceed such limitation. Member banks should, however, exercise prudence in issuing a letter of credit under which acceptances in excess of the limitation may result. *Digest of* 1921 BULLETIN 816.

NOTE.—As to limitations upon amount of acceptances, see ¶1650 et seq.

(7) *Rediscount by Federal Reserve Banks*

¶ 1600.   **Authority generally.**—(1) A Federal Reserve bank is not authorized by the Board's regulations or otherwise to purchase or discount an acceptance made by a member bank which the member bank had no authority to make, but a Federal Reserve bank may, under Regulation B, purchase acceptances made by other institutions than member banks and may also purchase acceptances made by State member banks under acceptance powers not conferred by section 13. Federal Reserve banks may also, under section 14, purchase acceptances which under section 13, they are not authorized to discount.

(2) Federal Reserve banks are authorized to purchase in the open market all classes of acceptances which are made eligible for rediscount under section 13, and may also purchase certain additional classes of acceptances not eligible for rediscount. These additional classes of acceptances are specified in Regulation B. [*Digest of* 1923 BULLETIN 316.]

¶ 1605.   **Forms of certificates evidencing eligibility of bankers' acceptances.**— Approved forms of certificates evidencing the eligibility for discount of bankers' acceptances (a) arising out of domestic shipments; (b) arising out of import and export transactions; and (c) arising out of warehouse secured credit. *Digest of* 1928 BULLETIN 517.

¶ 1610.   **Rediscount of acceptances against goods on consignment and unsold.** —A draft drawn to finance the exportation of goods shipped by an American exporter on consignment to his agent in a foreign country may be eligible for rediscount or purchase, when the goods exported have not been sold, provided that the goods are actually shipped for export and that shipping documents covering the goods are attached at the time the draft is presented for acceptance. Before such acceptances are accepted for rediscount or purchase, however, the Federal Reserve Bank should be reasonably sure that the goods will be sold before the maturity of the acceptances, as the use of acceptances is proper only where it is anticipated at the time the acceptances are drawn that they will be liquidated out of the proceeds derived from the sale of the goods. *Digest of* 1921 BULLETIN 419.

(3-65)

DISCOUNTS AND ADVANCES

¶ **1615.   Rediscounts of renewal acceptances.**—A Federal Reserve Bank, while not authorized to agree in advance to discount renewals, may do so if at the time the renewal is made the renewal may be said to grow out of the import or export of goods.   This would be the case if the import or export transactions had not been liquidated at the maturity of the original acceptance.   *Digest of* 1915 BULLETIN 126.

NOTE.—The same principles would apply to renewal acceptances growing out of domestic shipment or proper storage of goods.   As to bankers' acceptances growing out of the import or export of goods see ¶1110 et seq.   As to acceptance of renewal drafts generally, see ¶1075 et seq.

(8) *Amount Limitations*

NOTE.—As to the inapplicability of amount limitations to ineligible acceptances see ¶ 1051.

(a) TO ONE BORROWER

¶ **1650.   When bank holds "actual security".**—The 10 per cent limitation of section 13 contemplates that the accepting bank may properly rely upon the general credit of the customer in acceptance transactions up to 10 per cent of its capital and surplus, but that for any acceptance liability in excess of that amount incurred for the same customer it must hold some actual security. Consequently a member bank may accept for any one customer in excess of 10 per cent of its capital and surplus, provided it is secured, by attached documents or by some other actual security growing out of the same transaction, as to all acceptances in excess of the 10 per cent limitation.   *Digest of* 1919 BULLETIN 364.

¶ **1655.   Trust receipts as actual security.**—If an acceptance is secured by shipping documents, which are surrendered by the acceptor for a trust receipt, which permits the purchaser of the goods to retain control of the goods, the accepting bank can not be said to be secured "by some other actual security" as provided in section 13.   A trust receipt, however, which does not permit the purchaser to procure control of the goods, may properly be said to be actual security within the meaning of the act.   *Digest of* 1917 BULLETIN 881.

NOTE.—See also 1917 BULLETIN 286.

¶ **1660.   Control of customer over goods rendering trust receipt ineffective.**— A bank accepts drafts drawn to finance a domestic shipment of goods secured by bills of lading. At the completion of the shipment the goods are to be warehoused, and during the interval between the surrender of the bills of lading, in order to obtain the goods from the railroad, and the issuance of warehouse receipts, the customer proposes to secure the bank by giving it a trust receipt, which provides that the customer receives the bills of lading in trust and as agent for the bank and for the sole purpose of diverting the cars carrying the goods to the warehouse.   Attached to the trust receipt will be copies of the customer's instructions to the railroad to divert the cars to the warehouse and of his instruction to the warehouse to send the receipts, when issued, to the bank. Such a trust receipt does not constitute such actual security as is required for outstanding acceptances of one customer in excess of 10 per cent of the accepting bank's capital and surplus, since the customer will have control over the goods in spite of the terms of the trust receipt. The bills of lading might, however, be delivered to one of the bank's employees or an independent third party as agent for the bank, who could arrange for the transfer of the goods to the warehouse and give the bank the warehouse receipts, and by this method retain the bank's control over the goods, thus satisfying the legal and regulatory requirements. *Digest of* 1921 BULLETIN 1313.

FEDERAL RESERVE BANKS

¶ 1665. **Trade acceptances as actual security.**—Where a member bank has accepted a draft drawn by an American exporter for the purpose of financing the exportation of goods, such draft being secured by a trade acceptance and bill of lading, the trade acceptance, on acceptance by the drawee, constitutes "actual security" within the provisions of section 13, although the shipping documents are subsequently released. *Digest of* 1920 BULLETIN 1065.

¶ 1670. **Substitution of security in domestic transaction.**—A member bank may accept either in a domestic or foreign transaction for any one person in excess of 10 per cent of its capital and surplus, provided the draft is secured throughout its life. A member bank can not accept in a domestic transaction unless secured at the time of acceptance, but may release the security subsequently upon the execution of a trust receipt or an agreement that the proceeds of the sale of the goods will be deposited with the accepting bank and not used for other purposes. *Digest of* 1919 BULLETIN 143.

NOTE.—It would seem that the last sentence in the above ruling refers to drafts within the 10 per cent limitation, since drafts in excess of 10 per cent must, as stated, remain actually secured.

¶ 1675. **Substitution of new drafts secured by bills of lading.**—A corporation ships goods consigned to its own agent. It draws a time draft on its bank with bills of lading attached. The bank accepts, the acceptances being in excess of 10 per cent of the bank's capital and surplus. The bill of lading may be released by the bank to the agent, i.e., the consignee, provided that the agent substitutes therefor other drafts secured by bills of lading covering the same goods, which are being shipped by the agent to various dealers, since the new drafts, secured by bills of lading covering the same goods, constitute actual security growing out of the same transaction within the meaning of section 13. *Digest of* 1919 BULLETIN 468.

(b) AGGREGATE AMOUNT

¶ 1700. **Bank's own acceptances not included.**—Where a member bank purchases its own acceptances before maturity, such acceptances need not be included in the aggregate of acceptances prescribed by section 13, since the purchase of such an acceptance cancels the obligation of the bank. If a member bank subsequently disposes of its acceptance either by sale or by hypothecation, thus renewing its obligation to pay it at maturity, the acceptance should be included in the amount outstanding. *Digest of* 1916 BULLETIN 397.

¶ 1705. **Permission to accept up to 100 per cent of capital and surplus.**—Where a bank has been granted permission to accept in an amount not exceeding in the aggregate 100 per cent of its paid-up capital and surplus, it is not necessary for such bank to obtain additional authority from the Board each time it increases its surplus. *Digest of* 1919 BULLETIN 143.

¶ 1710. **Acceptances in domestic transactions.**—The Federal Reserve Board can not authorize a member bank to accept drafts drawn against it in domestic transactions in excess of 50 per cent of the accepting bank's capital and surplus. It may authorize a member bank to accept drafts up to 100 per cent, including both domestic and foreign drafts, but the domestic drafts are subject to the 50 per cent limitation noted above. This 50 per cent limit, however, does not apply to drafts drawn on and accepted by an individual other than the bank, and discounted by the bank. *Digest of* 1918 BULLETIN 1119.

[*The Next Page is Page 89.*]

APPENDIX TWO

ACCEPTANCE AGREEMENT

To: SECURITY PACIFIC NATIONAL BANK
Los Angeles, California

In consideration of your acceptance of our drafts drawn on you at _____ { sight / date

in the aggregate amount of $_____ , to be outstanding at any one time, we hereby agree that we will pay to you in lawful money of the United States or its equivalent not later than one day before the maturity of said acceptance amounts equivalent to such acceptances respectively. We hereby authorize you to charge our account for such amounts. If you do not charge our account or our account has insufficient amounts to repay the acceptances, said acceptances or any amounts due thereunder not so paid shall thereafter bear like interest as the principal and should any of said acceptances not be so paid then

said acceptances shall thereafter bear interest at the rate of _____ % per annum, which interest we agree to pay.

The above drafts are drawn against _____

for which negotiable warehouse receipts of independent public warehouse companies, negotiable order bills of lading, endorsed in blank and/or other actual security and/or documents growing out of this transaction in extent and form acceptable to you in which we have good and free title, are herewith deposited with you, as collateral security for our obligation to meet and pay each and all of said drafts, as herein and therein provided, and all other drafts which may hereafter be accepted by you, as well as for the payment of any and every debt or liability of every nature of the undersigned to you, and we agree that we will maintain at all times with you similar receipts, bills of lading and/or other collateral representing the above mentioned merchandise with a margin on the following basis: The amount of acceptances hereunder is to be for _____% of the market value, on the date of the acceptances respectively, of the said merchandise covered by said warehouse receipts and/or bills of lading and/or other documents. It is understood that this margin is to be kept at all times so that if said merchandise should decline in value during said period of acceptance, additional deposits of warehouse receipts, bills of lading and/or other documents or collateral satisfactory to you will be immediately made to restore the original percentage, or that we will pay you on account of all acceptances hereunder a cash sum equivalent to such depreciation. We further agree to furnish on demand such additional collateral as you may require from time to time.

We guarantee the genuineness, validity and correctness of all documents of title or other instruments which have been or which will be deposited with you as security for our drafts on you, including all figures, marks and numbers contained therein, and we further guarantee that you shall not be held responsible for the value, quantity, quality, or character, condition, delivery or existence of the goods represented by such documents, and we hereby agree to indemnify you from any loss occasioned thereby.

We hereby agree that on our failure promptly to meet or pay any of our said drafts, or upon our failure promptly to comply with any other of the terms of this agreement, or of any of said drafts, or in the event of our suspension of business, failure or assignment for the benefit of creditors, or the filing of a petition in bankruptcy against us or by us all of our obligations and liabilities to you, including all of our said drafts, shall immediately and without notice to or demand upon us accrue and mature and become due and payable, in which case interest or discount thereon shall be charged or adjusted to the date of such accelerated maturity, at the rate which said obligations bear; and in any of such events we authorize you to sell all or any of said merchandise and/or other collateral or security at public or private sale without demand upon us, without advertisement and without notice to us, such demand, advertisement and notice being hereby expressly waived, and at such sale you may become the purchaser thereof either in whole or in part, crediting the proceeds thereof against our said obligations and rendering any surplus to us, we to remain liable for any deficiency, which deficiency we agree to promptly pay to you without notice to or demand upon us.

It is further agreed, that any surplus arising from the sale of said collaterals, beyond the amount due hereon, shall be applicable upon any claim in your favor arising directly or by assignment against the undersigned at the time of said sale, whether the same be then due or not due.

At any such sale the purchaser thereof shall acquire the property so sold free from any right or equity of redemption, of the undersigned, such right and equity being hereby expressly waived and released.

Insurance in companies and form satisfactory to you and in amounts equaling the full insurable value of the commodities represented by said receipts and/or bills of lading and/or other documents, and such others as we may furnish as additional collateral or security hereunder, shall at all times be affected by us, with loss, if any, payable to you, such insurance certificate, and/or policies to be deposited with you and held and used by you as additional collateral.

We further agree to indemnify and save you harmless from any loss, costs, damage, liability, and expense including attorneys fees, which you may suffer or incur by reason of the failure of the undersigned to perform any of the obligations arising under this agreement or under said drafts or any of same.

This agreement shall be deemed to be a contract made under the laws of the State of California and this agreement shall be governed by and construed in accordance with the laws of the State of California.

It is also understood and agreed that said drafts are to be discounted by SECURITY PACIFIC NATIONAL BANK at _____ .

It is further understood that this arrangement is to remain in force until_____
_____

Dated: _____   _____

050543 4x85° 16V

APPENDIX THREE

This FINANCING STATEMENT is presented for filing pursuant to the California Uniform Commercial Code.

1. DEBTOR (LAST NAME FIRST—IF AN INDIVIDUAL)

1A. SOCIAL SECURITY OR FEDERAL TAX NO

MAILING ADDRESS

1C. CITY, STATE

1D. ZIP CODE

2. ADDITIONAL DEBTOR (IF ANY) (LAST NAME FIRST—IF AN INDIVIDUAL)

2A. SOCIAL SECURITY OR FEDERAL TAX NO

2B. MAILING ADDRESS

2C. CITY, STATE

2D. ZIP CODE

3. DEBTOR'S TRADE NAMES OR STYLES (IF ANY)

3A. FEDERAL TAX NUMBER

4. SECURED PARTY
NAME
MAILING ADDRESS
CITY   STATE   ZIP CODE

4A. SOCIAL SECURITY NO FEDERAL TAX NO OR BANK TRANSIT AND A B A NO

5. ASSIGNEE OF SECURED PARTY (IF ANY)
NAME
MAILING ADDRESS
CITY   STATE   ZIP CODE

5A. SOCIAL SECURITY NO FEDERAL TAX NO OR BANK TRANSIT AND A B A NO

6. This FINANCING STATEMENT covers the following types or items of property (include description of real property on which located and owner of record when required by instruction 4).

7. CHECK IF APPLICABLE [X]   7A. [ ] PRODUCTS OF COLLATERAL ARE ALSO COVERED

7B. DEBTOR(S) SIGNATURE NOT REQUIRED IN ACCORDANCE WITH INSTRUCTION 5(a) ITEM: [ ](1) [ ](2) [ ](3) [ ](4)

8. CHECK IF APPLICABLE [X]   [ ] DEBTOR IS A "TRANSMITTING UTILITY" IN ACCORDANCE WITH UCC § 9105 (1) (n)

9. DATE:
► SIGNATURE(S) OF DEBTOR(S)
TYPE OR PRINT NAME(S) OF DEBTOR(S)
► SIGNATURE(S) OF SECURED PARTY(IES)
TYPE OR PRINT NAME(S) OF SECURED PARTY(IES)

CODE 1 2 3 4 5 6 7 8 9 0

10. THIS SPACE FOR USE OF FILING OFFICER (DATE, TIME, FILE NUMBER AND FILING OFFICER)

11. Return copy to:
NAME
ADDRESS
CITY
STATE
ZIP CODE

* (1) FILING OFFICER COPY

FORM UCC-1—FILING FEE $3.00 Approved by the Secretary of State

APPENDIX FOUR

NATIONAL BANK _____ OFFICE

SECURITY AGREEMENT _____ CALIFORNIA

TRANSACTION	COLLATERAL
ACCEPTANCES	INSTRUMENTS
ADVANCES	DOCUMENTS
LOANS	

The undersigned Debtor hereby agrees with Crocker National Bank (herein called Bank) as follows:

1. SECURITY INTEREST. A security interest pursuant to the Uniform Commercial Code is hereby created and provided for Bank in and attaches to the property (herein called Collateral) described at Paragraph 2 below to secure payment and performance of the indebtedness and obligations (herein called Debtor s Obligations) described at Paragraph 3 below.

2. COLLATERAL. All: (a) Instruments (drafts, bills of exchange, etc.) and Documents (bills of lading, warehouse receipts, etc.) of Debtor heretofore, now, or hereafter (1) delivered to or howsoever received by Bank and whether by or from Debtor or any other and whether for collection, security or otherwise for the account of Debtor, or (2) released by Bank to Debtor hereunder or pursuant to any collateral acknowledgment or receipt, supplement hereto, request or other agreement of Debtor (herein called Collateral Release), or (3) identified by copies or other, written evidence thereof delivered by Debtor to Bank. (b) Goods, including inventory, and other property of Debtor howsoever relating to, or covered or represented by, or described, specified or referred to in, such Instruments, Documents, Collateral Releases, copies or other evidence, and all Goods, including Inventory, and other property which have been, are now or may be shipped, stored, purchased, acquired or financed in connection with any Acceptance, Advance or Loan by Bank for or to Debtor: (c) Accounts, Chattel Paper and Contract Rights, and all replacements, substitutions, exchanges, additions, accessions, products, rights and dividends relating to Collateral, and all returned Goods, whether as Inventory or otherwise, delivery of which gave rise to such an Account or Chattel Paper; (d) other security, property and money of Debtor whensoever and howsoever in the possession, custody or control of Bank (including in transit to or for the account of Bank) or in or to which Bank now has or hereafter acquires a security interest; (e) unearned premiums and proceeds of policies now and hereafter insuring Collateral; and (f) Proceeds of Collateral.

3. DEBTOR'S OBLIGATIONS. As used herein "Debtor's Obligations" means all debts, obligations and liabilities, now or hereafter existing, of Debtor or any of them to Bank, whether absolute or contingent, secured or unsecured, due or not due, liquidated or unliquidated, joint or several, and howsoever incurred or evidenced, including without limitation all Acceptances, Advances and Loans, and all commissions, freight, storage, insurance, duties, brokerage, attorneys' fees and other charges, costs and expense paid or incurred by Bank howsoever for or in connection with the Collateral or the performance or enforcement of any obligation of Debtor or the exercising of any right, power or remedy hereunder. Debtor jointly and severally, if more than one, hereby promises to pay to Bank, or order, at its Office above, upon demand (unless otherwise agreed in writing) and in lawful money of the United States (when appropriate at the rate of exchange in effect in San Francisco or Los Angeles, California, when paid), all of said debts, obligations and liabilities with interest thereon until paid and commission on each Acceptance at the rates agreed or specified by Bank from time to time.

4. OTHER PROVISIONS. This Agreement: (a) includes the provisions on the reverse hereof and such provisions are a part of this Agreement; (b) is made under and shall be governed by the laws of the State of California in all respects and including matters of construction, validity and performance; (c) is binding upon the respective heirs, successors and assigns of Debtor: and (d) cannot be withdrawn or canceled, and no term or provision hereof may be waived altered, modified or amended, except in writing duly signed by an authorized officer of Bank.

Date _____   _____

_____   _____

_____

APPENDIX FIVE

CORPORATE RESOLUTION TO BORROW

RESOLVED, that this corporation, ...
borrow from BANK OF AMERICA NATIONAL TRUST AND SAVINGS ASSOCIATION, a national banking association, hereinafter referred to as "Bank," from time to time, such sum or sums of money as, in the judgement of the officer or officers hereinafter authorized, this corporation may require; provided that the aggregate amount of such borrowing, pursuant to this resolution, shall

not at any one time exceed the sum of ....

.... Dollars ($ ....),
in addition to such amount as may be otherwise authorized:

   RESOLVED FURTHER, that

   ....   the ....

   or ....   the ....

   and ....   the ....

   or ....   the ....

of this corporation (the officer or officers, or officers acting in combination, authorized to act pursuant hereto being hereinafter designated as "authorized officers"), be and they are hereby authorized, directed and empowered, in the name of this corporation, to execute and deliver to Bank, and Bank is requested to accept, the note or notes, advance account agreements, acceptance agreements or other instruments evidencing the indebtedness of this corporation for the monies so borrowed, or to be borrowed, with interest thereon, and said authorized officers are authorized from time to time to execute renewals or extensions of said note or notes, advance account agreements, acceptance agreements or other instruments.
   RESOLVED FURTHER, that said authorized officers be and they are hereby authorized, directed and empowered, as security for any note or notes or any other indebtedness of this corporation to Bank, whether arising pursuant to this resolution or otherwise, to grant a security interest in, transfer, or otherwise hypothecate to Bank, or deed in trust for its benefit, any property belonging to or under the control of this corporation, and to execute and deliver to Bank any and all loan or credit agreements, grants, transfers, security agreements, deeds of trust and other hypothecation agreements, which said instruments and note or notes and other instruments referred to in the preceeding paragraph may contain such provisions, covenants, recitals and agreements as Bank may require and said authorized officers may approve, and the execution thereof by said authorized officers shall be conclusive evidence of such approval.
   FURTHER RESOLVED, that said authorized officers may, and they are hereby authorized, directed and empowered, in addition to the authorized borrowing set forth above (a) to discount with or sell to Bank, security agreements, leases, bailment agreements, notes, acceptances, drafts, receivables and evidences of indebtedness payable to this corporation, upon such terms as may be agreed upon by them and Bank, and to endorse in the name of this corporation said notes, acceptances, drafts, receivables, and evidences of indebtedness so discounted, and to guarantee the payment of the same to Bank and (b) to apply for and obtain from Bank letters of credit and in connection therewith to execute security agreements, applications, guaranties, indemnities and other financial undertakings.
   RESOLVED FURTHER, that Bank is authorized to act upon this resolution until written notice of its revocation is delivered to Bank, and that the authority hereby granted shall apply with equal force and effect to the successors in office of the officers herein named.

   I, ..., Secretary

of .... , a corporation, incorporated

under the laws of the State of..., do hereby certify that the foregoing is a full, true and correct copy of a resolution of the Board of Directors of said corporation, duly and regularly adopted by the Board of Directors of said corpora-

tion in all respects as required by law, and by the by-laws of said corporation, on the..., day

of ...., 19..........., at which meeting a majority of the Board of Directors of said corporation was present and voted in favor of said resolution.
   I further certify that said resolution is still in full force and effect and has not been amended or revoked, and that the specimen signatures appearing below are the signatures of the officers authorized to sign for this corporation by vitue of this resolution.
   IN WITNESS WHEREOF, I have hereunto set my hand as such Secretary, and affixed the corporate seal of said corporation,

this .... day of ...., 19...........

   AUTHORIZED SIGNATURES:

....
            (Signature)   (Signature)   SECRETARY OF
                                            Affix
....
            (Signature)   A CORPORATION
                                      corporate seal
....   here
            (Signature)

....
            (Signature)

APPENDIX SIX

DOCUMENTARY CREDIT — IRREVOCABLE	Credit Number	
ISSUING BANK	Issuing bank 663819 -IM	Advising bank 82143-8 EX
		ACCOUNTEE
Barclay's Bank London	London Computer Systems Ltd.	

BENEFICIARY	**AMOUNT**
Graphic Engineering Inc. Santa Clara, California 96814	One Million Eight Hundred Thousand U.S. dollars, $1,800,000.00
	Date **EXPIRY** December 31, 1982

We confirm this irrevocable letter of credit and 30 day ᵁsance drafts may be drawn on us when accompanied by the following documents:

1. Commercial invoice in duplicate

2. U.S. export certificate in duplicate

3. U.S. fumigation certificate

4. Packing list signed by Messrs. Smith and Co. certificating inspection

5. Insurance to the order of Barclay's Bank Ltd.

6. Bill of lading in duplicate co-signed to London Computer Systems Ltd. and marked "Prepaid" covering thirty six graphic display boards

Partial shipments permitted and transhipments prohibited. All bank charges for account of applicant.

The original letter of credit must be presented to the negotiating bank together with the documents.

The amount of each draft must be endorsed on the reverse of this credit by the negotiating bank.

NOTE: Documents must conform strictly with the terms of the Credit. If you are unable to comply with its terms please communicate with your customer promptly with a view to having the condition changed. NOTE CAREFULLY THE DESCRIPTION OF THE MERCHANDISE MENTIONED IN THE CREDIT AS IT MUST BE DESCRIBED IN EXACTLY THAT FORM IN YOUR DOCUMENTS.

ADVISING BANK'S NOTIFICATION

☐ This letter is solely an advice of credit established by the issuing bank and conveys no engagement by us.

☐ We confirm this Credit and thereby undertake that all drafts drawn and presented as above specified will be duly honored by us.

CONTINENTAL BANK INTERNATIONAL

SAMPLE

Authorized signature

WHITE: BENEFICIARY COPY   PINK: FILE COPY   GREEN: CORRESPONDENT COPY

APPENDIX SEVEN

100 LARGEST WORLD BANKS IN TOTAL ASSETS

Bank	Assets ($ billions)	Rank	Country
Algemene Bank	49	33	Netherlands
Amsterdam/Rotterdam	44	40	Netherlands
Banco Commerciale	38	50	Italy
Banco Nationale Lavoro	43	41	Italy
Banco Central Madrid	19	90	Spain
Banco Di Napoli	18	97	Italy
Banco Di Roma	27	67	Italy
Banco Do Brasil	65	18	Brazil
Banco Español Credito	34	55	Spain
Bancomer	18	98	Mexico
Bank of America	113	1	United States
Bankers Trust Company	32	57	United States
Bank Fuer Gemeinwirtschaft	25	71	Germany
Bank Hapoalim	18	95	Israel
Bank Leumi Le-Israel	21	85	Israel
Bank Melli	20	85	Iran
Bank of Montreal	47	35	Canada
Bank of New South Wales	19	91	Australia
Bank of Nova Scotia	41	45	Canada
Bank of Tokyo, Ltd.	56	23	Japan
Bank of Yokoyama, Ltd.	19	92	Japan
Banque Brexelles Lambert	23	75	Belgium
Banque de I'lndochine et de Sues	24	73	France
Banque de Paris et des pays Bas	19	89	France
Banque Nationale de Paris	107	2	France
Barclays Bank International Ltd.	57	22	United Kingdom
Barclays Bank PLC	93	6	United Kingdom
Bayerische Hypoltheken-und Wechsel-Bank	39	49	Germany
Bayerische Landesbank Girozentrale	39	48	Germany
Bayerische Vereinsbank	43	42	Germany
Canadian Imperial Bank of Commerciel	50	31	Canada
Chase Manhattan Bank Na	73	15	United States
Chemical Bank	41	44	United States
Citibank Na	98	4	United States
Commerzbank	45	37	Germany
Commonwealth Banking Corp.	21	82	Australia
Continental Illinois National Bank & Trust Company	42	43	United States
Credit Agrecole Mutuel	98	3	France
Creditansalt-Bankverein	18	99	Austria
Credit Lyonnais	94	5	France
Credit Italiano	29	60	Italy
Credito Suisse	41	47	Switzerland
Crocker National Bank	21	83	United States
Dai-Ichi Kangyo Bank, Ltd.	88	8	France
Daiwa Bank, Ltd.	36	52	Japan
Deutsche Bank	85	9	Germany
Deutsche Genossenschofts Bank	28	63	Germany
Dresdner Bank	58	19	Germany

Appendix Seven *(concluded)*

Bank	Assets ($ billions)	Rank	Country
First Interstate Bank of California	19	94	United States
First National Bank	31	58	United States
Fuji Bank, Ltd.	76	13	`Japan
Groupe Des Banques Populaires	22	77	France
Hessische Landesbank-Girozentrale	23	74	Germany
Hokkaido Takushoku Bank, Ltd.	19	93	Japan
Hong Kong and Shanghai Banking Corporation	52	29	Hong Kong
Industrial Bank of Japan, Ltd.	58	20	Japan
International Westminster Bank PLC	26	70	United Kingdom
Istituto Bancario San Paolodi Torino	28	62	Germany
Kredietbank International Group	20	88	Belgium
Kyowa Bank Ltd.	46	36	Japan
Lloyds Bank International Ltd.	21	81	United Kingdom
Lloyds Bank PLC	52	26	United Kingdom
Long-Term Credit Bank of Japan Ltd.	46	36	Japan
Manufacturers Hanover Trust Company	51	30	United States
Midland Bank PLC	78	12	United Kingdom
Mitsubishi Bank Ltd.	76	14	Japan
Mitsubishi Trust & Banking Co., Ltd.	41	46	Japan
Mitsui Bank, Ltd.	54	25	Japan
Mitsui Trust & Banking Co., Ltd.	36	54	Japan
Monte dei Paschi di Siena	28	66	Italy
Morgan Guaranty Trust Company	50	32	United States
National Westminster Bank	82	10	United Kingdom
Nederlandsche Middenstandsbank	22	76	Netherlands
Nippon Credit Bank, Ltd.	28	64	Japan
Norddeutsche Landesbank Girozentral	22	79	Germany
Norinchukin Bank	57	21	Japan
Rabobank Nederland	44	38	Netherlands
Rafidain Bank	18	100	Iraq
Royal Bank of Canada	66	17	Canada
Saitama Bank Ltd.	24	72	Japan
Sanwa Bank Ltd.	67	16	Japan
Security Pacific National Bank	28	65	United States
Shoko Chukin Bank	27	68	Japan
Skandinaviska Enskilda Banker	22	78	Sweden
Societe Generale	88	7	France
Societe Generale de Banque	29	61	Belgium
Standard Chartered Bank PLC	37	51	United Kingdom
State Bank of India	20	86	India
Sumitomo Bank Ltd.	79	11	Japan
Sumitomo Trust & Banking Co., Ltd.	36	53	Japan
Svenska Handelsbanken	18	96	Sweden
Swiss Bank Corporation	49	34	Switzerland
Taiyo Kobe Bank, Ltd.	44	39	Japan
Tokai Bank Ltd.	52	27	Japan
Toronto Dominion Bank	32	56	Canada
Toyo Trust & Banking Co., Ltd.	21	80	Japan
Union Bank of Switzerland	52	28	Switzerland
Wells Fargo Bank Na	20	87	United States
Westdeutsche Landesbank Gerozentrale	55	24	Germany
Yasuda Trust & Banking Co., Ltd.	27	69	Japan

CHAPTER FOUR

COMMERCIAL

PAPER

Commercial paper is a generic term describing short-term, unsecured promissory notes issued through dealers by the most creditworthy industrial, utility, financial corporations, and cooperatives. These obligations are sold to major institutional investors, such as universities, pension funds, insurance companies, and other corporations.

The legal instrument is a note which is issued by a bank's paying agent to the issuer's commercial paper dealer. The dealer underwrites the commercial paper issue by providing immediate funds to the borrower and then markets the paper to secondary market investors. If the dealer is unable to market all the paper, it will retain the notes in its own investment portfolio. At maturity, the note holders present the paper to the paying agent bank, which redeems it with payment proceeds from the corporate issuer. Unlike bankers' acceptances, there need not be an underlying self-liquidating transaction, and outstanding commercial paper may be redeemed with proceeds of new issues. However, these notes are not automatically rolled over.

Like acceptances, commercial paper is fixed-rate and fixed-term and discounted, with the borrower (issuer) receiving the face, or par, value less the prevailing rate. At maturity, the borrower pays the full face value to the investor via the paying bank. Unlike acceptances, the bank does not engage its responsi-

BLANK COMMERCIAL PAPER NOTE

COMPANY

No. (No. here)

$ _____

Date _____

For value received COMPANY will pay bearer on _____

the sum of _____ _____ Dollars

at the office of FIRST NATIONAL BANK. Bank Plaza, New York, New York

Not valid for any purpose until countersigned by an authorized signature

Company

FIRST NATIONAL BANK. Issuing Agent

By _____
Official Signature

By _____
Official Signature

By _____
Authorized Signature

bility to repurchase the note but merely acts as a conduit, transferring the notes and payment between the issuer and investor.

These notes are usually issued for $1 million minimums for 30-day increments up to 270 days. Although issued to the public, the notes are exempt from registration with the Securities and Exchange Commission (SEC) under section 3(a)(3) of the 1933 Securities Act if the following criteria are met: (1) Notes may not exceed 270 days; (2) note proceeds must finance working capital and current transactions; and (3) note proceeds may not be intended for investment or speculation, although the company may invest in short-term opportunities pending final allocation to working capital requirements.

In order to access this attractive and flexible source of funds, the issuer must petition one of the four independent rating agencies for a commercial paper rating. The ratings differ, but fundamentally the agency thoroughly analyzes the issuer's historical creditworthiness and the general industry trend. Most issuers must have sufficient lines of credit committed by commercial banks for the purpose of redeeming the notes in the event the borrower defaults. These are referred to as back-up lines. These data are assessed and form the basis for the rating issued by the agency. There are four agencies that perform the rating function and apply rate gradients based on their analysis:

1. *Moody's* has two basic categories: prime and not rated. Prime ratings are graded P-1, P-2, or P-3, depending on the company's creditworthiness. The lower the number, the higher the creditworthiness.

2. *Standard & Poor's* has four rating categories: A, B, C, and D, with each category further defined by the numbers 1, 2, or 3. Like Moody's, the lower the number, the higher the creditworthiness, A-1 being the best rating.

3. *Fitch* provides four ratings: F-1, F-2, F-3 and F-4. F-4 is "Not recommended."

4. *Duff and Phelps* offer three ratings: D-1, D-2, and D-3. D-1 is the best rating.

The following flowchart identifies the commercial paper life cycle. The numbers correspond with the narrative.

1. The company requests the rating agency to issue a commercial paper rating. The better the rate, the lower the discount, or interest cost.

2. The agency analyzes the company, the industry, and other contingencies possibly impacting the company's creditworthiness and issues its rating.

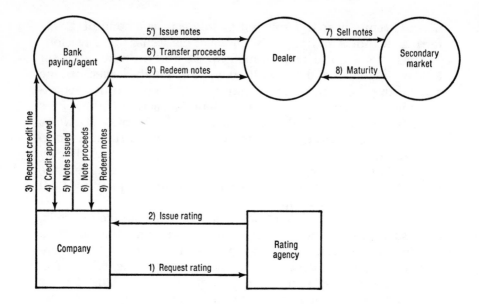

3. The corporation arranges for bank backup credit lines supporting outstanding commercial paper.

4. The bank performs its credit analysis and issues the credit commitment.

5. The company provides the agent paying bank with pre-printed notes, which are issued to the dealer.

6. The dealer pays the bank and underwrites the issue. The bank credits proceeds to the issuer's account.

7. The dealer markets the issue to investors, who pay the dealer.

8. At maturity, the dealer redeems the notes from investors.

9. At maturity, the bank debits the issuer's account and redeems the notes from the dealer.

Although the process appears extensive, the actual issue of paper and receipt of funds occurs within the same day. The procedures are well established and most efficient.

HISTORY

The commercial paper market, as it operates today, has been in existence for over a century, with the basic legal guidelines established with the Securities Act of 1933. However, the concept of one corporation issuing its note to an institutional investor has its roots well before the banking system.

At the outset, a firm would issue its note to an investor who was comfortable with the borrower's creditworthiness. The borrower would use the loan proceeds to supplement working capital and sell its goods. When customers bought the goods, the borrower repurchased the note from the investor. This process probably worked well within the local market where borrowers and investors were familiar with each other. However, as business expanded outside the local region, the borrower/lender familiarity declined.

Trading houses developed and provided a dealer underwriting function of purchasing the issuer's notes and remarketing them to prospective investors. We suspect that the dealer engaged its liability to redeem the paper at the early stages of development.

Although today's dealers are not obligated to guarantee commercial paper, for all practical purposes, the dealer will not market paper it would not hold in its own portfolio. Dealers underwrite the issue at the outset after performing their own thorough and independent analysis. Also, dealers will repurchase the notes from investors before maturity. Although these notes are not guaranteed and are unsecured, the analysis performed by the rating agencies, dealers, and banks providing backup lines is most thorough, and any default would not reflect well on the integrity of the market or the various participants.

Until 1967, the volume of commercial paper was relatively low, with total issues at $15 billion. Presently, the total outstandings exceed $160 billion. The following chart shows the dramatic increase.

The past decade has shown a remarkable growth rate of 297 percent, from $41 billion to $165 billion for commercial paper. According to reports published by the rating agencies, approximately 1,400 corporations and cooperatives have ratings. The basic breakdown is:

252 Public utilities.

507 Industrials.

172 Bank holding companies.

318 Finance companies.

172 Foreign firms.

Of the $165 billion in total outstandings, approximately 50 percent is placed by dealers and 50 percent is directly placed by the issuers. In these cases, the issuer's volume warrants the additional staff to handle the transactions. This expense offsets the

CHART III
Commercial Paper Outstanding

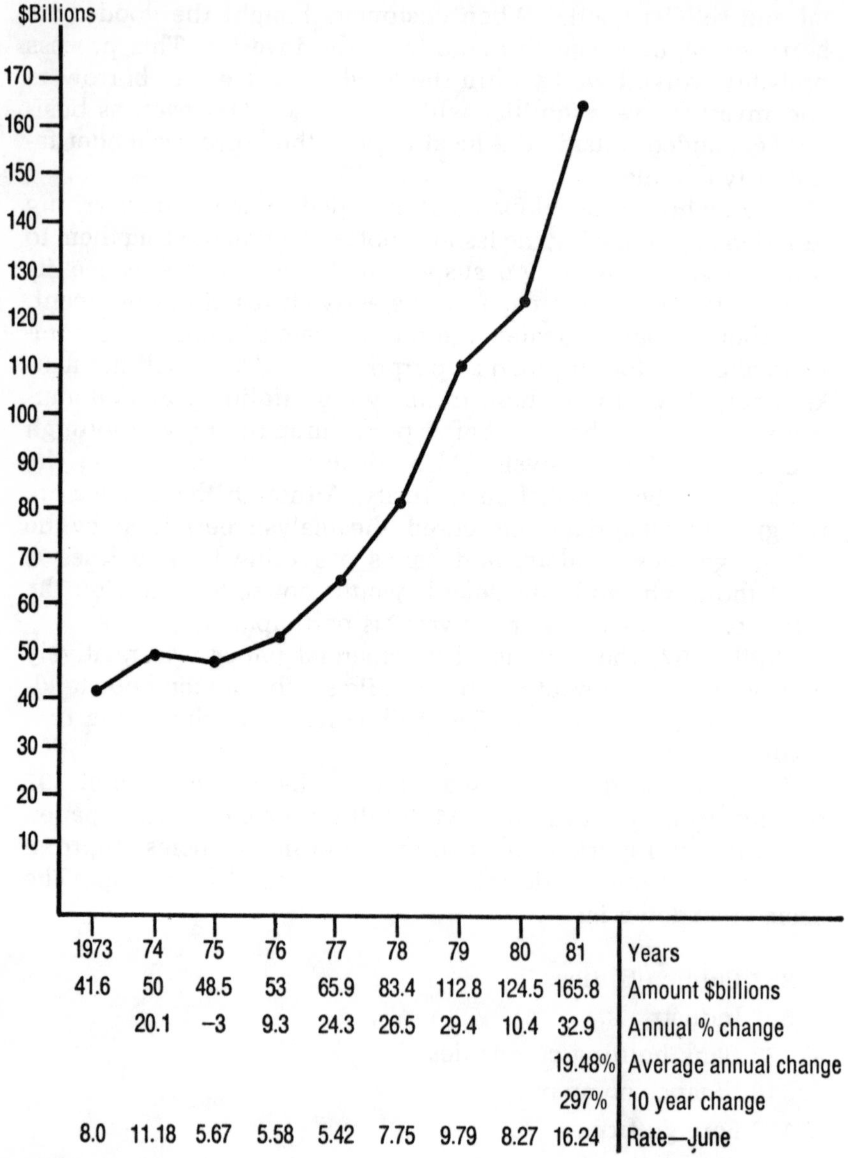

$Billions

Years	1973	74	75	76	77	78	79	80	81
Amount $billions	41.6	50	48.5	53	65.9	83.4	112.8	124.5	165.8
Annual % change		20.1	−3	9.3	24.3	26.5	29.4	10.4	32.9
Average annual change									19.48%
10 year change									297%
Rate—June	8.0	11.18	5.67	5.58	5.42	7.75	9.79	8.27	16.24

Source: Federal Reserve statistics.

dealer's commission of approximately ⅛ of 1 percent, or .125. Examples of major companies that directly place paper are:

General Motors Acceptance Corporation.

Bank America Corporation (holding company).

CIT Financial Corporation.

CITICORP (holding company).

Chase Manhattan Corporation (holding company).

Ford Motor Credit Corporation.

J. C. Penney Financial Corporation.

Sears Roebuck Financial Corporation.

Westinghouse Credit Corporation.

Although 50 percent of the commercial paper-dollar outstandings are issued by a select few major corporations, the majority of the actual issues are placed by six primary dealers. The following table shows the total number of issues according to the rating gradients for the six major commercial paper dealers as of July 31, 1982.[1]

Dealer Market Corporate Issues

(A, P, F) Rating	Becker	Goldman Sachs	Lehman Bros.	Merril Lynch	Salomon Bros.	First Boston
1	210	225	110	99	126	85
2	47	54	42	36	23	15
3	5	1	2	1	1	
L/C	22	40	34	25	6	17
Total	284	320	188	161	156	117

The notation L/C refers to letter of credit. In these cases, companies which are privately held and do not provide public financial disclosures issue commercial paper directly supported by a bank's undertaking. This undertaking is a form of guarantee evidenced by a bank's standby letter of credit, which acts as a performance bond. Insurance companies also issue such bonds supporting commercial paper.

A standby letter of credit, opened by a major bank, is attached to the issue and the dealer is the beneficiary. In the event the issuer defaults, the dealer draws under the letter of credit and pays investors. The bank in turn must pursue the issuer for re-

[1]Courtesy of A. G. Becker.

payment. In essence, the issuer's creditworthiness is supported by the bank's credit standing. The rating agencies assess the credit of the bank opening the letter of credit and apply the bank's commercial paper rate to the issue. The primary obstacle to this procedure is that it proportionately reduces the amount of commercial paper the bank's holding company may issue before affecting the bank's rating.

Banks perform an extensive credit analysis of commercial paper issuers, since the possibility exists that drawings against the L/C may occur to refinance maturing paper issues. The banks charge a fee for the standby L/C based on their assessment of the borrower. The fee ranges between 1/4 and 3/4 percent.

The lines of credit supporting commercial paper are to be held in abeyance and not applied to other working capital requirements. The annual CPA audit includes information detailing the amount of outstandings under the credit lines. This information is also requested by dealers and rating agencies. Although these credit lines are not intended to be used, the corporation pays for the commitment with fees or compensating balances. The fees range between $\frac{1}{8}$ percent and $\frac{1}{2}$ percent. Balances on the commitment range from 3 percent to 7 percent. The amount is predicated on the bank's perception of the borrower's creditworthiness. To accurately compare commercial paper costs with alternatives, the balances or fees must be added to the discount rate along with the dealer's commission.

MECHANICS

The following steps are required to establish a commercial paper program.

1. Select a commercial paper dealer to assist in structuring the program.

2. Obtain a board of directors' resolution authorizing the program.

3. Obtain counsel's opinion ensuring that the paper will be exempt from SEC registration.

4. Review cash flow and bank lines ensuring adequate coverage.

5. Apply for rating from one or more of the four agencies.

6. Select an issuing and paying agent bank.

7. Print and deliver notes to agent.

Selection of a dealer. Although the dealer's role appears uniform and standardized, attention devoted to commercial paper varies. A dealer, who should have a well-established record for successful placement of issues, will assist in presenting the company's financial picture to the rating agency. Areas for discussion when selecting a dealer should include the following:[2]

1. Determine cost to the borrower of alternative sources of funds.
2. Determine the dealer's understanding of the rating process and willingness to assist in obtaining the rating.
3. Assess the dealer's reputation in the market.
4. Determine the level of asset and managerial commitment to commercial paper.
5. Review the quality and frequency of counseling provided by the dealer regarding money rate trends.
6. Assess the dealer's ability and willingness to tap the market on short notice and for unusual maturities.
7. Determine the dealer's scope and knowledge of the market, the industry, and the company.

Board of directors' resolution. The dealer and rating agency require a copy of the issuer's board of directors' resolution authorizing the issuance of commercial paper (see Appendix One).

Opinion of counsel. The issuer must obtain an opinion from counsel who is familiar with securities law, certifying that the sale of notes, including consideration of the use of proceeds, will be exempt from registration under the 1933 act and that the notes will be valid, legal, and binding obligations of the issuer. Both the dealer and the rating agency will require this opinion (see Appendix Two).

Bank credit lines. As stated, commercial paper issuers are usually required to maintain unused lines of credit sufficient to cover outstanding paper issues.

Commercial paper ratings. It is recommended that the prospective issuer apply to two rating agencies for its paper rating, ensuring the highest marketability for its notes. Dealers familiar with the procedures can assist in the process. The application for a commercial paper rating is sent directly to the agency (see Appendix Three). Information regarding the issuer should be forwarded, including Security and Exchange 10K report filings, historical financial statements, intended use of proceeds, and re-

---

[2]Ibid.

view of bank credit lines. The agency will assess the prospect's creditworthiness, focusing on cash flow, liquidity ratio, and capitalization relative to future growth. Also, the agency will take into consideration (a) the prospects for the industry, (b) the issuer's position within the industry, (c) the philosophy and strength of management, and (d) the issuer's regulatory environment and other nonquantifiable and contingent factors affecting the probable performance and redemption of issued paper.[3]

This is followed by a meeting between the agency and issuer to discuss the pending rating. If the issuer feels the proposed rating does not accurately reflect the credit standing, it may terminate the process. With the exception of Moody's, agencies will not make declined ratings public. Moody's claims to reserve the right to make such ratings public.

Issuing/Paying agent. In order to implement a commercial paper program it is necessary to appoint an agent to issue and redeem the notes. This function is typically performed by New York money center banks.

Once the rating is issued and all documents properly executed, the company may commence issuing commercial paper. The process begins with the issuer depositing presigned notes with the paying agent. Like presigned acceptance drafts, the purpose is to provide administrative flexibility and immediate issue at the borrower's request. A cash flow analysis will·assist the dealer and borrower in anticipating cash needs.

When funds are needed, the borrower telephones or telexes the request to the issuing/paying agent and the dealer. This should be followed by a written confirmation. The issuing/paying agent enters the date and amount to the presigned notes and delivers them to the dealer. If this occurs before noon EST, the dealer will immediately credit funds to the borrower's account with the issuing/paying agent bank. These funds are referred to as Fed Funds, since they are immediately available through the New York Federal Reserve and there is no overnight transfer time or float. The amount deposited to the issuer's account is the face value of the note less the interest rate. Like acceptances, this is referred to as a discounted note.

The dealer undertakes to unconditionally purchase the notes and therefore underwrites the paper issue. The dealer then markets or rediscounts the paper in the secondary investment market. The market is vast in terms of investors and dollars, but the system for marketing the notes is fast and efficient. When the

---

[3]Ibid.

notes are discounted, the dealer either holds them in behalf of the investor or delivers notes against receipt of the investor's payment. Since the notes are discounted, the investor pays the dealer the face value less the rate. The dealer's average commission, ⅛ of 1 percent, is subtracted before the notes are sold.

At maturity the issuer instructs the issuing/paying agent to transfer Fed funds to the dealer, which redeems the notes from investors. The notes are repurchased for the face value. As stated, commercial paper may not be rolled over, but often the repurchase funds come from newly issued commercial paper.

In the event the investor wishes to sell the note to the dealer before maturity, most dealers will repurchase the paper at an adjusted rate. The investor receives the face value less a small fee.

CHARACTERISTICS

Commercial paper is a fixed-rate, fixed-term, unsecured, and discounted note. The rate is the prevailing discount rate established by the secondary investment market and is quoted in 30-day increments up to 270 days. The longer the period, the higher the rate. The notes are usually issued in multiples of $1 million. Odd lots, relative to the term and amount, may be issued; but placement is selective and requires more time, since the notes do not conform to the standards established for administrative efficiency.

Since the rate and tenor of commercial paper is fixed when issued, the borrower must assess rate trends to assist in determining the financing period. Unlike acceptances, the borrower is not required to have a specific, underlying transaction which influences the borrowing time. Trend analysis is critical to avoid locking in rates which later may prove to be excessive. All matched funding, where the rate and term are fixed, bears a rate risk compared to the floating prime borrowing offered by commercial banks.

It must be remembered that matched funding for the borrower is an interest rate hedge and assumes rates will not fall. We are reminded that money is a commodity whose price, the interest rate, is influenced by innumerable variables, not all of which are known at a given time. Therefore trend analysis and simulation computer modeling are necessary in order to determine rate fluctuation probabilities against which funding decisions are made. One method for minimizing the rate exposure is through the futures market, although this will not prevent the fluctuation of borrowing alternatives during the funding period.

This relatively new application enables borrowers to take

offsetting positions, minimizing the volatile rate or commodity movements. Where the borrower loses on the actual rate drops, compared to a floating rate, it will compensate with gains earned in the futures market.

A hedge reduces rate risk while sacrificing possible rate declines for the borrower. The borrower must realize three facts before intentionally taking a position: (a) The borrower is taking a speculative position when borrowing and not offsetting with a hedge; (b) does the borrower wish to speculate? and (c) what are the rate trends?

When the rate trends appear to be rising, the fixed-rate borrowings are obviously an advantage, since the rate is stable compared to floating prime rates that rise. However, when rates are declining, the borrower must carefully assess the rate differential, velocity of decline, and time involved.

Rate differential. The borrower first identifies the rate differential between the all-in commercial paper rate and the floating prime rate. This may be as high as 3 percent in favor of commercial paper. Holding other variables constant, the higher the rate differential, the lower the probability of the weighted average floating prime falling below the fixed-rate paper.

Since the paper will probably be lower than prime when the financing decision is made, the prime will have to float below the paper rate to the point offsetting the time it took the prime to equal the paper rate. Therefore, the *weighted average* floating prime is projected to determine the probability.

Financing time. The second variable to consider is the financing time. The longer the time, the greater the probability that the weighted average floating prime will drop below the fixed-rate paper in a declining rate environment. Conversely, the shorter the period, the less the probability.

Velocity. The third issue is the velocity of the rate change. When the price of a commodity is disproportionate with supply and demand, the probability of volatile price moves increases. Therefore, when rates are low or moderate, the velocity of change is likely to be less compared to disproportionately high rates. An example will further the point. If a company is considering a 30-day paper issue with a rate differential of 3 percent, and prime is 20 percent, what can we conclude?

1. The 3 percent rate differential is high; therefore the probability is low that the weighted average floating prime will fall below the paper rate.

2. The 30-day finance period is short; therefore the probability of the weighted average prime falling below the fixed paper rate is low.

3. The general rate environment is disproportionate to commodity supply and demand considerations, therefore the probability is high that the weighted average prime will fall before the fixed rate paper.

In this case, two of the variables are low and one is high. It is difficult to assess the offsetting influences of the three variables. Our experience shows that the order of influence is usually rate differential, time, and velocity. Extremes in any variable will change the degree of influence.

Unlike acceptances, commercial paper, matched funding from commercial banks, and Eurodollars may be refinanced without consideration of a specific underlying transaction. The borrower has the option of issuing 30-day commercial paper and refinancing it every 30 days as rates drop. Therefore, the time variable influence is lowered, reducing the probability that the weighted average floating prime will drop to some point below the fixed-rate paper.

The *pricing* components for commercial paper are the discount rate, risk adjustment, bank balance factor, dealer commission, and discounted interest adjustment. This is the all-in cost.

The *discount rate* is a function of money supply and demand and of alternative money market investments. The rates are quoted on a 30-day incremental basis up to 270 days.

The *risk adjustment* is a factor added, reflecting the market's risk perception of the issuer. Most notably, this adjustment relates to the paper's rating. Prime names command the best rates, while less attractive names pay a risk penalty. The difference between an A-1 rated and an A-2 rated company may be 25–35 basis points.

Bank balances or equivalent fees are maintained with the bank in consideration of the backup lines. This may be evidenced by a formal agreement or an understanding. The primary difference relates to the CPA-audited financial statements. IF there is an unwritten understanding, the balances will not be reported in the annual report. Prime name companies prefer to maintain balances based on an understanding with the banks.

The fees range between ⅛ and ¼ percent of the commitment, and balances range from 5 to 10 percent of the committed amount. A company with $30 million in commercial paper backup lines will pay fees of $37,500 to $75,000 or maintain balances of $1.5 million to $3 million, depending on its credit standing.

The balance equivalent of fees is calculated, based on the corporations' opportunity cost for maintaining interest-free balances. The actual cost can be either the expected rate of return for alternative investments, the internal rate of return on assets, or the prevailing CD rate. The bank, on the other hand, applies an internal melded, or the intra-bank transfer cost, to these balances. This rate usually differs slightly from the CD rate, since the bank has various sources of funds, which are averaged and weighted.

The generally accepted opportunity cost factor is the prevailing CD rate when calculating the fee equivalent. The following formula is applied.

$$\frac{\text{Commitment} \times \text{Balances required} \times \text{CD Rate} \times \text{365 Days}}{360}$$

or

$$\frac{\$30,000,000 \times 5\% \times 8\% \times 365}{360} = \$121,666$$

The fee equivalent for 5 percent balances maintained against a $30 million commitment with an 8 percent CD rate for one year is $121,666, or .405 percent (121,666 ÷ 30,000,000). The important point is that the balance requirement should approximate the fee equivalent.

It is noted that the balances were calculated on a year's basis. Since the balances or fees are paid for the full year, maximum return for the balances or fees is based on full-time utilization by the company. This is not an issue for the bank, since it will utilize the balances irrespective of the company's commercial paper issues.

We refer to the cash flow fundamentals which will determine the borrowing requirements and, therefore, the return on balances. If the borrowings are less than 100 percent, the balance factor is proportionately increased. Specifically, if the balance requirement is 5 percent but the commercial paper is utilized only 50 percent, the true balance equivalent is 10 percent. The formula is

$$\frac{100\%}{\% \text{ Utilization}} \times \text{Balance required}$$

or

$$\frac{100\%}{50\%} \times 5\% = 10\% \text{ Actual balances}$$

The same formula is applied to fees. The less the utilization, the higher the actual fee equivalent.

$$\frac{100\%}{\%\ \text{Utilization}} \times .405\% = \text{Fees}$$

or

$$\frac{100\%}{50\%} \times .405\% = .810 \text{ Fees, or } \$243,332$$

The *dealer commission* is usually ⅛ of 1 percent, except for Salomon Brothers, which charges ⅒ of 1 percent. This fee covers the administrative expenses for placing the paper and provides a slight return for the dealers' underwriting risk.

The *discounted interest adjustment* reflects the borrower's opportunity cost for paying interest prior to usage compared to conventional loans, where interest is paid in arrears. This adjustment also applies to bankers' acceptances, and the following calculation reveals that .20 must be added to the rate, assuming an 8 percent CD rate.

$$\frac{\text{All-in-rate} \times \text{90-day CD rate} \times \text{Days}}{360}$$

$$\frac{10\% \times 8\% \times 90}{360} = .20$$

The reader should realize that the true cost of borrowing in the commercial paper market exceeds the posted rates in *The Wall Street Journal*. These rates are investor-offered rates and not the total borrowing cost. The true all-in cost must be calculated in order to make valid rate comparisons, and the comparisons must be for the same time periods. It is inappropriate to compare 30-day paper with 90-day acceptances because the period rates differ.

With this insight into the various rate components, we will now compare the true all-in cost for the borrower of prime-related loans, eligible bankers' acceptances, and commercial paper. The rates are on a 90-day basis and apply to a B-rated company.

Certain adjustments will be made reflecting the perceived risk. The calculations are based on rates quoted by money center banks and dealers on November 19, 1982.

There is no question that the acceptance and commercial paper rates are considerably less than prime and would save the borrower approximately $27,000 per million dollars of outstandings per year. The acceptance and commercial paper rates differ by .03 in favor of commercial paper. Slight changes in either rate could offset this difference. The two areas for price manipulation are under the bank's influence. The bank negotiations determine

90-Day Rate Comparison *(B-rated company)*

		Alternatives	
Rate Components	*Prime*	*Bankers' Acceptances*	*Commercial Paper*
Base/discount rate	12.0	9.00	9.00
Risk adjustment	0.0	0.00	.25
Bank commission	0.0	1.00	0.00
Dealer commission	0.0	0.00	.12
Bank balances/spread	1.0	0.00	.60
Discount interest adjustment		.20	.20
Total all-in cost	13.00%	10.20	10.17

the commission for acceptances and the balances for commercial paper. As indicated, the acceptance and commercial paper base rates are close because they compete in the same secondary market with relatively comparable underlying risks.

Assuming a .03 rate differential in favor of commercial paper over acceptances, the borrower must be able to meet regulatory criteria in order to avoid reserve costs for ineligible acceptances. At the prevailing rate, the reserves for ineligible acceptances are 3 percent, which further reduces the attractiveness of acceptances. Furthermore, if a warehouse receipt is required, additional fees of approximately .20 to .35 percent will be added.

The 1,400 companies that currently qualify to issue commercial paper enjoy favorable rates compared to prime borrowings, and flexibility compared to acceptance financing. For noncommercial paper issuers, the rate advantage for acceptances clearly offsets the added administration compared to prime borrowings.

Table 4–1 provides a 10-year history and comparison of commercial paper, bankers' acceptances, and prime.

APPLICATION AND REGULATIONS

With the exception of the 270-day time limit, bank backup line credit limits, and the usual inability to apply commercial paper proceeds to long-term assets, there are no serious limitations for commercial paper. There need not be an underlying transaction and paper proceeds supplement working capital. The primary limits relate to the 15 percent contingent credit a bank may extend. Therefore, since acceptances, secured throughout their life, may exceed the 15 percent limit, they may enjoy an advantage over commercial paper. However, corporations having access to the commercial paper market will use multiple bank lines

TABLE 4–1
Rate Comparison, B-Rated Company (90 Days, June 1973–1982)

	90-Day Rate	Bank Commission	Bank Balances	Discount Adjustment	Market Adjustment	Dealer Commission	Total Rate
1973							
Prime	7.75	0	1.16	0	0	0	8.91
Acceptances	7.90	.75	0	.19	0	0	8.84
Commercial paper	8.00	0	.80	.19	0	.13	9.12
Eurodollars	8.81	.75	0	0	0	0	9.56
1974							
Prime	11.75	0	1.76	0	0	0	13.51
Acceptances	10.79	.75	0	.32	0	0	11.86
Commercial paper	11.18	0	1.12	0	0	.13	12.43
Eurodollars	12.04	.75	0	0	0	0	12.79
1975							
Prime	7.00	0	1.05	0	0	0	8.05
Acceptances	5.70	.75	0	.09	0	0	6.54
Commercial paper	5.67	0	.57	.09	0	.13	6.46
Eurodollars	6.10	.75	0	0	0	0	6.85
1976							
Prime	7.25	0	1.09	0	0	0	8.34
Acceptances	5.77	.75	0	.09	0	0	6.52
Commercial paper	5.58	0	.56	.09	0	.13	6.36
Eurodollars	6.22	.75	0	0	0	0	6.97

TABLE 4-1 (concluded)

	90-Day Rate	Bank Commis-sion	Bank Balances	Discount Adjust-ment	Market Adjust-ment	Dealer Commis-sion	Total Rate
1977							
Prime	7.00	0	1.05	0	0	0	8.05
Acceptances	5.39	.75	0	.08	0	0	6.22
Commercial paper	5.42	0	.54	.08	0	.13	6.17
Eurodollars	5.78	.75	0	0	0	0	6.53
1978							
Prime	9.00	0	1.35	0	0	0	10.35
Acceptances	7.48	.75	0	.12	0	0	8.23
Commercial paper	7.75	0	.78	.12	0	.13	8.75
Eurodollars	8.33	.75	0	0	0	0	9.08
1979							
Prime	11.50	0	1.72	0	0	0	13.22
Acceptances	9.79	.75	0	.25	0	0	10.79
Commercial paper	9.77	0	.98	.25	0	.13	11.13
Eurodollars	10.52	.75	0	0	.0	0	11.27
1980							
Prime	10.04	0	1.51	0	0	0	11.55
Acceptances	8.31	.75	0	.21	0	0	9.27
Commercial paper	8.27	0	.82	.21	0	.13	9.43
Eurodollars	9.41	.75	0	0	0	0	10.16
1981							
Prime	17.87	0	2.68	0	0	0	20.55
Acceptances	16.21	.75	0	.40	0	0	17.36
Commercial paper	16.24	0	1.62	.40	0	.13	18.39
Eurodollars	18.00	.75	0	0	0	0	18.75

supporting their paper, as opposed to allowing a bank to file UCCs and perfect their security through warehouse arrangements.

The primary disadvantage of commercial paper is the fixed rate in a declining rate environment. This obstacle is partially overcome by the 30-day refinancing periods, which allow the company to incrementally lower its rates as market rates decline.

There are numerous benefits for corporations, banks, and investors available from commercial paper.

Bank benefits

Banks earn income from balances or fees without impairing liquidity or assets. Since no assets are used, merely the bank's name, the return on assets is infinitesimal. Further, bank lines enable the bank to earn some return while providing the company with alternative sources of funds.

Bank obstacles

1. During periods of excess cash, banks would prefer to loan existing deposits.

2. Banks' profits are reduced, since they earn less from balances or fees compared to prime lending.

Corporate benefits

1. Commercial paper considerably reduces borrowing costs.

2. Paper provides an alternative source of funds.

3. Paper widely advertises the company's name for other possible security issues.

4. The fixed-rate nature of commercial paper reduces the absolute cost of money in a rising rate environment.

Corporate obstacles

The primary obstacle is the fixed-rate nature of commercial paper in a declining rate environment.

APPENDIX ONE*

BOARD OF DIRECTORS' RESOLUTION

I, __(Name of Officer)__ , HEREBY CERTIFY that I am the duly elected and qualifed Secretary of __(Name of Company)__ , a corporation chartered and existing under the laws of _(State of Incorporation)_ , and that at a duly constituted meeting of the Board of Directors of said Company, held at its principal office in __(Location)__ on __(Date)__ , at which said meeting a quorum was present, there were adopted the following resolutions:

RESOLVED, that the President or any Vice President of this Company be and each of them is hereby authorized and empowered, for and on behalf of this Company, to negotiate with A. G. Becker Incorporated to provide for, and to agree upon, the unsecured borrowing of any amount or amounts of money not to exceed an aggregate of $_____ at any one time outstanding, at an interest rate or rates to be agreed upon by the said Officers at the time of each such borrowing and the President or any Vice President and the Treasurer or any Assistant Treasurer of this Company be and they are hereby authorized and empowered to execute and deliver to said bank, banks, banking institutions, commercial paper dealers or other financing agencies in connection with such borrowing, a joint bank loan agreement, promissory notes or commercial paper, or any other instrument or instruments necessary to said borrowing for an amount not to exceed an aggregate of $_____ at any one time outstanding, such obligations to mature not later than 270 days from date of issue, to bear interest at the rate or rates theretofore determined, to be in such form and to contain such other provisions as may be approved by the Officers whose signatures are affixed thereto, such signatures to be conclusive evidence of their approval.

RESOLVED, that the Officers of the Company be and they hereby are authorized and empowered, for and on behalf of the Company, to take or cause to be taken any and all such other and further action, and to execute, acknowledge and deliver any and all such instruments, as they, in their discretion, may deem necessary or advisable in order to carry out the purpose and intent of the foregoing.

RESOLVED, that messrs. __(Name of Counsel)__ be and they hereby are appointed counsel for the Company to make any writ-

_____
*Courtesy of A. G. Becker.

ten opinion required to be given to said bank, banks, banking institutions, commercial paper dealers or other financing agencies pursuant to the provisions of said notes, joint bank loan agreement or other instruments.

I FURTHER CERTIFY that the foregoing resolutions have not been rescinded, modified, altered or amended in any way and are now in full force and effect.

WITNESS my signature and the seal of the said Company at _____ this _____ day of _____ , 19_____ .

_____
                                            Secretary

SEAL

SAMPLE SIGNATURE CARD

Name _____ Location _____

To: **A.G. Becker**
Incorporated

You are hereby authorized to recognize any of said signatures below in the transaction of all business for our account. Please Sign Footnote

Mr .	will sign	
Mr .	will sign	President
Mr .	will sign	Vice President
Mr.	will sign	Secretary
Mr .	will sign	Treasurer
Mr .	will sign	Ass't Secretary
Rule out spaces not used and indicate below the number of signatures authorized.		Ass't Treasurer

Date _____ 19____   The ____ signatures above written are the duly authorized signatures of this Corporation.

Title of Corporation _____

_____   _____
President   Secretary

Note—Kindly have the names either printed or typed and a speciment of the signature appear before the title.

APPENDIX TWO*

OPINION OF COUNSEL

Attention:

Dear Sirs:

You have requested my opinion as an attorney duly admitted to the practice of law in the State of...and counsel for..., a corporation (the Company), with respect to certain matters relating to the proposed issuance and sale by the Company to or through you, from time to time, of unsecured promissory notes (the notes), in bearer form and having a maturity date at the time of issuance of not more than nine months, exclusive of days of grace. The notes will not be advertised for sale to the general public but will be sold to or through you for purchase by institutional investors and other entities and individuals who normally purchase commercial paper in large denominations, and will not be issued in denominations of less than $100,000.

The proceeds to be received by the Company from the issue and sale of the Notes are intended to be used for current general corporate purposes.

In connection with the foregoing, I have examined and am familiar with such corporate records, certificates and other documents, have supervised such corporate proceedings, and have examined such questions of law and fact, as I have considered necessary or appropriate for the purposes of the opinions hereinbelow expressed. Based upon the foregoing, I am of the opinon that:

1. The Company is duly incorporated and validly existing as a corporation in good standing under the laws of the State of ... and has all necessary corporate power and authority to create and issue the Notes.
2. The issuance and sale of the Notes has been duly and validly authorized by all necessary corporate action, and such Notes, when executed, issued, and delivered against payment therefor, will constitute legal, valid, and binding obligations of the Company in accordance with their terms.

---

*Courtesy of A. G. Becker.

3. The issuance and sale of the Notes will not conflict with or result in any violation of the certificate of Incorporation or By-Laws of the Company or of any indenture, agreement, or other instrument to which the Company is a party or by which it is bound.
4. The Notes may be issued and sold in the commercial paper market without registration thereof under the Securities Act of 1933 in reliance upon the exemption contained in Section 3(a) (3) of such act.

I hereby confirm that I have advised representatives of the Company responsible for the issuance and sale of the Notes of the basis for the exemption of the Notes from the registration requirements of the Securites Act of 1933 and of the continuing need to comply with the requirements of such exemption, particularly the requirement that the Notes must either arise out of a current transaction or the proceeds of such Notes must be used for current transactions.

Very truly yours,

APPENDIX THREE*

APPLICATION FOR RATING REVIEW

_____
(Date)

Mr. Edward Z. Emmer
Vice President
Standard & Poor's Corporation
25 Broadway
New York, New York   10004

Mr. Thomas J. McGuire
Executive Vice President
Moody's Investors Services Inc.
99 Church Street
New York, New York   10007

Mr. Richard Cacchione
President
Fitch Investors Service, Inc.
5 Hanover Square
New York, New York   10004

Mr. Frederick B. Whightman
Vice President
Duff and Phelps, Inc.
Suite 4000
55 Monroe Street
Chicago, Illinois   60603

Dear Mr. _____

The Board of Directors of _____ Company has authorized the issuance of up to $_____ million of commercial paper. Accordingly, we are requesting that __(Rating Agency)__ evaluate the enclosed for the purpose of assigning its commercial paper rating.

A. G. Becker has been designated the dealer for the commercial paper program; _____ Bank will be acting as issuing/paying agent.

The following officers of our Company and A. G. Becker can be contacted to answer any questions your staff may have:

NAME	TITLE	TELEPHONE NUMBER
	Treasurer	
	Vice President	

We will be pleased to meet with you and your associates to answer any questions.

Sincerely,

_____

*Courtesy of A. G. Becker.

CHAPTER FIVE

EURODOLLARS

Eurodollar is a generic term referring to dollar-denominated deposits made by foreign entities to banks and loaned internationally to corporate and government borrowers. The loans are made in U.S. dollars and repaid in U.S. dollars. A borrower whose indigenous currency is not dollars sustains a foreign exchange exposure when converting the local currency back to dollars for repayment.

Although deposits originate from many countries, such as Hong Kong, the United Kingdom, and Singapore, the Eurodollar rate is established in London and is referred to as LIBOR, an acronym for London Interbank-Offered Rate. The rate is set according to economic conditions impacting supply and demand for Eurodollars. Rates are quoted in 30-day increments up to six months. Occasionally, these loans may exceed six months when companies are willing to make deposits for longer periods. Banks may make commitments to fund loans with Eurodollars for periods beyond six months and simply roll over or refinance the loan at maturity at the prevailing rate. Like acceptances and prime loans, a bank may commit to fund loans with Eurodollars for any period. This is not always the case with commercial paper, since the market is incapable of issuing commitments to fund and only funds up to 270 days.

Although Eurodollars and acceptance rates are quoted up to 180 days, banks may commit to fund beyond 180 days. If the bank's commitment exceeds one year, the loans, irrespective of the funding periods, may be considered long-term debt. This procedure improves the current ratio and working capital since the loan is no longer in current liabilities. Commercial paper usually does not enjoy this feature, since the market is unable to execute commitments. However, if a bank makes an unconditional commitment to support commercial paper beyond one year, the CPAs may consider this long-term debt.

Unlike acceptances or commercial paper, Eurodollar loans are not discounted and interest is paid in arrears. No discount interest adjustment is required representing the opportunity cost of paying for funds before the use of proceeds.

The following flowchart diagrams the life cycle of a Eurodollar loan. The numbers correspond with the narrative that follows.

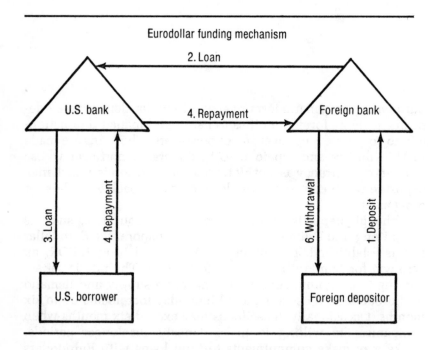

Eurodollar funding mechanism

1. Foreign entity deposits dollars in foreign bank or U.S. foreign branch.
2. Foreign bank loans deposit proceeds to U.S. bank.
3. U.S. bank adds a spread and reserve costs if applicable and reloans funds to U.S. borrower.
4. At maturity, U.S. borrower repays U.S. bank or rolls over Eurodollar loan at prevailing rates.
5. U.S. bank repays foreign bank.
6. Foreign depositor maintains deposit or withdraws funds to pay for foreign purchases made in U.S. dollars.

HISTORY

Dollar deposits made abroad, giving rise to Eurodollar loans, originated from international trade and foreign government transactions. Overseas entities retained dollars because of the economic and political stability of the U.S. dollar; to purchase U.S. goods; and in some cases, to avoid U.S. tax on repatriated dollars from foreign sales.

Dollar deposits are generated from foreign trade where foreign concerns prefer payment in dollars. This was particularly true in the 1970s when OPEC countries required dollar payment, or petrodollars, for oil sales. Dollar payments were required for two reasons: (1) OPEC wanted a stable hard currency that was freely exchangeable, and (2) OPEC required deposits to be tied to the dollar, economically and politically stable compared to their indigenous currencies impacted by potential instabilities in the region—that is, Iraq and Iran. Also giving rise to U.S. deposits in foreign countries are dollars generated by overseas subsidiaries of U.S. corporations. To avoid accounting treatments for foreign exchange fluctuations, many U.S. firms with foreign operations require invoicing in dollars.

Eurodollar loans have grown substantially since the 1970s, reaching close to $1 trillion in 1982. The relative global acceptance of Eurodollars with attractive rates and large petrodollar deposits had facilitated the growth of this "stateless" money. The following table shows the growth over the last decade.

Until December 1981, U.S. banks loaning Eurodollars were unable to provide competitive rates with other offshore lenders, since the Federal Reserve, under regulation D, required reserves on the dollar deposits from abroad. These deposits and loans were made through offshore facilities located in the Bahamas and Cayman Islands, where U.S. banking and tax considerations were not in effect. Rarely were these offices staffed with U.S. bank employees, and, in most cases, the physical building was the office of a bookkeeper with numerous brass plaques on the front, with the names of the various banks represented. In essence, Eurodollar loans are strictly paper transactions without a corresponding physical movement of dollars. The actual disbursement of funds is through U.S. banks to borrowers.

In December 1981, the Federal Reserve opened the door for Eurodollar deposits and loans within the United States. The Fed allowed the establishment of International Banking Facilities (IBFs) to take Eurodollar deposits and make loans to foreign entities without maintaining reserves or paying minimum interest on deposits. The IBFs may not make Euroloans directly to U.S.-domiciled companies without imposing reserves. To avoid re-

CHART IV
Eurodollar Global Outstandings

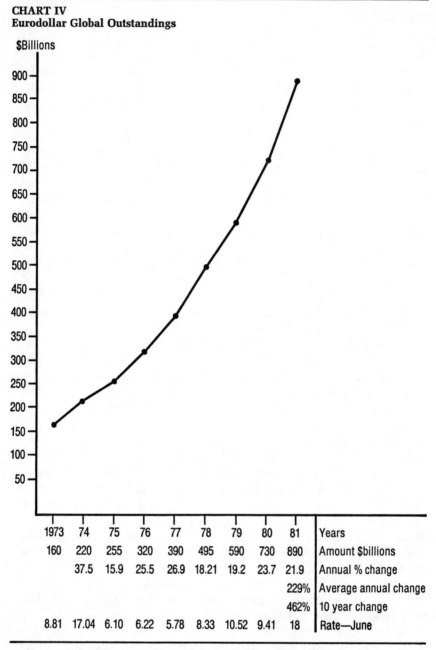

Years	1973	74	75	76	77	78	79	80	81
Amount $billions	160	220	255	320	390	495	590	730	890
Annual % change		37.5	15.9	25.5	26.9	18.21	19.2	23.7	21.9
Average annual change									229%
10 year change									462%
Rate—June	8.81	17.04	6.10	6.22	5.78	8.33	10.52	9.41	18

Sources: Federal Reserve statistics; World Financial Markets: Morgan Guaranty.

serves for U.S. loans, funds are transferred to the U.S. company's overseas subsidiary, which in turn transfers the funds to the U.S. parent. Again, there is no actual physical transfer of funds, but the legal documents show the borrower to be an overseas operation for the purpose of avoiding reserves. Actual funding is made to the U.S. company by the IBF through its parent bank, for example, Citicorp, Continental Bank, Chase. Eurodollar loans made directly to U.S. borrowers bear reserves which are added to the prevailing base rate and quoted to the borrower as an all-in rate.

Aside from the reserves added to U.S.-made loans, the other restriction for IBFs is that deposits and withdrawals must exceed $100,000. Because of the general lack of government control over Eurodollars, these funds are referred to as stateless currency. IBFs operating in New York, Connecticut, Maryland, Florida, and Georgia do not pay state and local taxes.

As we will explore in the next chapter, Eurodollar loans outside the United States represent a foreign currency loan to the borrower which must be repaid in dollars. Any currency fluctuation between the indigenous currency and the dollar will directly impact the amount of repayment. Specifically, if the dollar revalues (strengthens) against the currency, the borrower will pay more for the principal repayment because it will require more of the foreign currency to purchase the same amount of dollars. Conversely, if the U.S. dollar devalues against the foreign currency, the borrower will pay less for the principal repayment because it will require less of the foreign currency to purchase the same amount of dollars for repayment. This process is known as foreign exchange exposure and is a fully speculative position when the borrower is long in dollars. The next chapter explains various hedging procedures reducing the risk.

Some companies prefer not to hedge the exposed position because they believe (hope) the indigenous currency will strengthen against the dollar, resulting in a reduction in principal payback. These speculative positions may be performed by the seat-of-the-pants approach or through elaborate analysis and probability/simulation models. In any event, the vagaries affecting money are not all known at the time of the borrowing, and the longer the term, the more uncertain the influencing factors will be.

Although Eurodollar loans are committed up to 180 days on a fixed-rate basis, depositors may be prepared to maintain deposits for longer periods at fixed rates. These deposits may be loaned for the corresponding period at a fixed rate. This rarely occurs in a period of rising rates, when corporations wish to borrow for longer fixed-rate periods but depositors do not wish to lock in rates and sacrifice future higher returns. Conversely, when rates are falling, depositors are willing to deposit for longer periods to lock in higher rates.

MECHANICS

Unlike commercial paper, where numerous steps are taken to establish the borrowing program, a Eurodollar loan facility is easily incorporated in a bank loan agreement. An example of the actual language follows:

> Sixty million dollar loan to be drawn under prime plus 1 percent or the prevailing Eurodollar rate plus 1 percent at the borrower's option on a best-efforts basis.

The language states the options available to the borrower and the rate. The "best-efforts basis" implies that, unlike prime borrowings, the bank cannot commit to the availability of funds.

Bank Selection

The bank selection is important since the LIBOR rate paid by the bank reflects the depositor's risk perception of the bank. The daily rates quoted in *The Wall Street Journal* apply to the most creditworthy money center banks. Other banks will pay more, and this is passed on to the borrower. The borrower will enjoy the most favorable rates when borrowing from the strongest banks. Also, large banks have immediate access to the Eurodollar community and avoid broker-dealer commissions which range from ⅛ to ¼ percent and are usually passed on to the borrower. Some U.S. corporations have established joint venture relations with foreign Eurodollar dealers. They not only place deposits for other banks but enjoy the best rates by direct access to the Eurodollar deposit and avoid commissions and spreads.

In the event a bank wishes to access the Eurodollar market, it may either go through brokers or establish a direct relationship with a major bank dealing in Eurodollars. This bank relationship is identical to the normal correspondent relationship and includes one bank borrowing Eurodollars from a money center bank. The disadvantage for the borrower is that it pays more, reflecting added handling fees. The advantage of dealing with a reputable broker is that the borrowing bank's name is broadly exposed to the Eurodollar community. This will eventually result in lowering the rates and provide alternative Eurodollar sources.

Dealer Selection

When a bank selects a Eurodollar dealer it should consider the following:

1. The general reputation and ability to market the borrowing bank's name.
2. The understanding of the Eurodollar market and ability to quickly attract funds.
3. The quality and frequency of dealer counseling regarding rate trends.
4. The level of asset and management commitment to Eurodollars.
5. The dealer's responsiveness to placing deposits, irrespective of the size.

Unlike commercial paper where the dealer underwrites the issue, Eurodollar dealers do not underwrite or engage their liability. These dealers simply act as a conduit for placing deposits in behalf of their client banks. Once the deposit is placed, the lending bank and borrowing bank deal directly.

When the borrower repays the Eurodollar loan to a U.S. bank, the payment is made to the order of the bank for the account of its IBF. This is an accounting treatment separating U.S. dollar loans from Eurodollar loans.

The credit analysis for Eurodollar loans made to U.S. corporations is identical to the analysis performed for conventional loans. When Eurodollar loans are made to non-U.S. companies, a country analysis is performed, and, where currency flow is restricted, the bank will require the acknowledgement of the appropriate government authority (central bank) that funds will be available for repayment at maturity.

The loan agreement (between the borrower and the bank) for Eurodollar loans includes repayment instructions to the account of the IBF as well as a hold-harmless agreement. The hold-harmless absolves the bank from any responsibility if reserves are later imposed retroactively by the U.S. bank regulatory agencies. Many major U.S. corporations have established overseas shell subsidiaries which receive Eurodollar loans and transfer the funds to the U.S. parent, avoiding reserves.

CHARACTERISTICS

Eurodollars are fixed-rate and fixed-term loans that may or may not be secured, depending on the borrower's creditworthiness.

In select cases the loans are made on a revolver-term basis, where the company borrows as needed but may convert these loans to longer terms at its option. Given the term convertibility, these loans are shown as long-term debt improving the current ratio and working capital.

The rates are established in London (LIBOR) and are quoted in 30-day increments up to 180 days. Occasionally, a depositor will place longer-term Eurodollar CDs which have maturities and rates for periods exceeding 180 days.

Unlike acceptances and commercial paper, where the loan proceeds must fund short-term requirements, Eurodollar loan proceeds may fund working capital or long-term fixed-asset investments.

Since Eurodollars rates are fixed when the loan proceeds are disbursed, the borrower must assess rate trends over the anticipated financing period. Like commercial paper, the borrower is not required to fund a specific transaction as is required for acceptance financing. Eurodollar loans provide flexibility, enabling the borrower to select financing periods corresponding to trend expectations. Since Eurodollars are a form of fixed-rate, matched funding, there is a rate fluctuation risk in a declining rate environment compared to the floating prime.

Matched funding is an interest rate hedge, but the borrower may pay more interest in a declining rate environment compared to floating prime borrowings that fluctuate according to moves in the prime rate. Our assertion is that money is a commodity whose price, the interest rate, is influenced by innumerable variables, not all of which are known at a given time. Trend analysis and simulation models are necessary to determine rate fluctuation probabilities against which funding decisions are made.

Eurodollars may be hedged in the futures market in $1 million increments. This relatively new approach allows the borrower to offset its future borrowing against moves in the Eurodollar futures market. Naturally any hedge sacrifices probable gains while minimizing probable losses. The borrower must consider three factors before taking a hedged position: (1) Is the borrower taking a speculative position by borrowing and not offsetting with a hedge? (2) Does the borrower wish to speculate? and (3) What are the rate trends?

When the rate trends appear to be rising, the fixed-rate Eurodollar borrowings are obviously an advantage over floating rates that will rise. When rates are declining, the fixed-rate Eurodollar locks in the position and the borrower's rate is not reduced, compared to the downward floating prime.

There are three variables impacting the decision to fix the rate or use the floating rate: the comparable rate spread between Eurodollars and prime borrowings, the time period, and the velocity of the floating prime moves.

Rate spread. The borrower first identifies the rate differential between the Eurodollar rate and the floating all-in prime rate. This difference may be as much as 2 percent in favor of Eurodollars at any given time. Holding the time and velocity variables constant, the higher the rate differential, the lower the probability that the weighted average prime rate will fall below the fixed Eurodollar rate. The prime rate must float to a point below the Eurodollar rate offsetting the time it took for the rates to become equal. Therefore we calculate the weighted average prime.

Time. The second variable to consider is the time involved. The longer the time, up to 180 days, the greater the probability that the weighted average prime may fall below the fixed-rate Eurodollar in a declining rate environment. This is less likely to occur during a short financing period, reducing the attractiveness of using the floating prime under such circumstances.

Velocity. The third variable affecting the financing decision is the expected velocity of the prime move. As already discussed, when the price of a commodity is disproportionate to supply-and-demand considerations, the more volatile the price changes. When rates are low or moderate, the velocity of change is less than when rates are disproportionately high.

An example will amplify the point. A company is considering a 30-day Eurodollar loan with a rate differential of 2 percent and prime of 20 percent. We conclude the following:

1. The 2 percent rate differential is high; therefore the probability is low that the weighted average prime will fall below the Eurodollar fixed rate.

2. The 30-day finance period is short; therefore the probability is low that the weighted prime will fall below the fixed-rate Eurodollar rate.

3. The general rate environment is disproportionate to commodity supply and demand. Therefore the probability is high that the weighted average prime will fall below the fixed-rate Eurodollar.

In this case, two variables, rate differential and time, provide low probabilities for the shift to prime, and the probability of velocity is high for the shift to prime. Our experience shows that the order of influence is usually rate differential, time, and velocity. Extremes in any variable will change the degree of influence.

Like commercial paper or bank matched funding, Eurodollars may be refinanced at prevailing rates. A company can fix the rates for 30-day periods and refinance as rates drop, or, if rates are expected to rise, the company may lock in longer fixed rates. For future borrowings, the company may hedge in the Eurodollar futures market.

Irrespective of future moves, the hedge eliminates gains from rate drops and minimizes losses from rate gains. Specifically, if the company expects to borrow $10 million over a 90-day period, it will hedge by buying 10 $1 million Eurodollar futures contracts. If the rate rises, the company will gain when it sells the futures contract, which will offset its increased borrowing costs. Conversely, if rates drop, the company will lose on the futures contract, which will be offset by lower borrowing costs. The offset is rarely exactly equal, but the futures contract and the actual cash market trend will be the same. In this case, the corporation is not concerned about which direction rates will move, since the borrowing cost is offset by gains or losses in the futures market.

The *pricing components* for Eurodollars are the LIBOR, or base rate; market risk adjustment; spread; and dealer commission. The lending bank may require compensating balances.

LIBOR is a function of supply-and-demand considerations and is quoted in 30-day increments up to 180 days. Rates and terms may exceed 180 days.

The *risk adjustment* is an added factor which reflects the market's risk perception of the borrowing bank. Prime bank names pay the LIBOR rate and less creditworthy banks pay a higher rate.

A *dealer commission* of ⅛–¼ percent is added if the U.S. bank obtains the Eurodeposits through a dealer.

A *spread* is added by the U.S. bank reflecting its loan processing costs and risk perception. Like acceptances and conventional loans, a bank may reduce the fixed spread and charge balances, or it may increase the spread and reduce balances. This is predicated on the bank's return on equity and asset criteria, but the trade-off should yield the same return for the bank. Various banks have differing approaches.

Assuming the bank will charge a customer LIBOR plus X percent without balances, it may be willing to eliminate the X percent spread but add compensating balances providing an equivalent return. There are certainly cases where the bank charges less than prime, or LIBOR, but the borrower is required to maintain large noninterest bearing deposits. When this opportunity cost is calculated, the all-in rate should be equivalent to the prime, or LIBOR rate plus the spread. From the corporate viewpoint, the decision to pay the spread or maintain balances is a function of alternative returns or cash flow requirements.

The bank will apply an internal funds rate to the balances. If this rate is less than other opportunities for the corporation, the decision is to pay the spread. The internal rate usually approximates the CD rate.

Unlike the floating prime, where rate fluctuations impact the balance or spread return for the bank and interest expense for the borrower, Eurodollar loans are fixed-rate for the term. Therefore the bank's return and company's interest expense are known for the short-term. The formulas for determining the balance-spread equivalent are:

1. $\dfrac{\text{Spread} \times \text{Principal} \times \text{Days}}{360} = \text{Spread cost}$

When the spread is 2 percent and the principal is $1 million for 90 days, the calculation is:

2. $\dfrac{2\% \times 1{,}000{,}000 \times 90}{360} = \$5{,}000 \text{ Spread cost}$

To calculate the balance equivalent, we introduce the bank's prevailing internal rate or CD rate. Assuming the CD rate is 8 percent, the calculation is:

3. $\dfrac{\text{CD} \times \text{Balance required} \times 90 \text{ Days}}{360} = \text{Spread cost}$

4. $\dfrac{8\% \times X \times 90 \text{ Days}}{360} = \$5{,}000$

5. $.08 \times X \times 90 \text{ days} = \$1{,}800{,}000$

6. $7.2X = \$1{,}800{,}000$

6b. $X = \$250{,}000 \text{ Balances}$

This equates to 25 percent balances when dividing $250,000 balances by the $1 million principal. In other words, the company will sacrifice $5,000 when maintaining $250,000 balances for 90 days at 8 percent. If cash flow is a critical issue, the company will pay the 2 percent spread equalling $5,000 rather than maintain $250,000 in balances, resulting in an equivalent $5,000 opportunity cost. In this case the borrower has three options: (1) pay a $5,000 fee plus the prime, (2) pay the prime plus 2 percent, or (3) pay the prime and maintain 25 percent balances.

Although this approach is identical for the company whether borrowing under a fixed or floating rate, the bank's return differs. This is a result of applying the fixed spread or balance requirement to a varying cost of funds. The higher the cost of funds, the lower the percentage of a fixed-spread or fixed-balance requirement. Conversely, as the bank's costs decline, the fixed spread or balance requirement generates a higher return for the bank.

A solution for the bank is to quote a fixed percentage of LIBOR, for example, 120 percent of LIBOR. In this case, the return to the bank is constant, irrespective of LIBOR. If LIBOR is 10 percent, the bank will charge 120 percent of LIBOR, or 120 percent of 10 percent; which is 12 percent, resulting in a 20 percent return on LIBOR. When LIBOR is 20 percent, the bank will charge 120 percent × 20 percent, or 24 percent. Again, the spread is 20 percent return on LIBOR. Naturally, as rates rise, the borrower pays more under this approach, compared to a fixed spread. Conversely, the borrower pays less when rates fall. The following table shows the fixed spread relative to fixed percentage.

Spread comparison

LIBOR + 2	LIBOR × 120%
8% + 2 = 10	8% × 1.20 = 9.6
10 + 2 = 12	10 × 1.20 = 12
12 + 2 = 14	12 × 1.20 = 14.4
14 + 2 = 16	14 × 1.20 = 16.8
16 + 2 = 18	16 × 1.20 = 19.2

The breakeven point for both calculations is when LIBOR is at 10 percent. As LIBOR rises, the fixed spread is less costly for the borrower, and when LIBOR falls below 10 percent, the LIBOR spread is more attractive for the borrower. Since Eurodollars are not quoted on a floating basis, the bank's return is not volatile during the term of the borrowing. This approach also applies to floating prime loans where fixed spreads generate different returns when the cost of funds is changing.

Like acceptances, a standard approach for determining the spread is suggested. If the borrower is rated by one of the major rating agencies, the rate is convertible to a spread.

Where the company is not rated, a credit scoring approach is recommended. The company is scored against credit criteria which are weighted according to the importance of the category. The final score is converted to a LIBOR spread. This approach provides continuity and substantiates the spread.

LIBOR Spread Table

Company Rating	Spread
A-1	½%
A-2	¾
A-3	1
B	1–1¼

With this insight into the various LIBOR rate components, we will compare the all-in rate for the borrower with the three alternatives: prime, acceptances, and commercial paper. The rates are on a 90-day basis and assume the borrower is rated B. Certain adjustments must be made reflecting the perceived risk. We also assume that the funding bank is a money center bank and directly accesses the Euromarket, omitting the dealer's commissions. Rates are quoted as of November 19, 1982.

90-Day Rate Comparison (B-rated company)

Rate Components	Prime	Alternatives Acceptances	Alternatives Commercial Paper	Alternatives Euro-dollars
Base/discount rate	12.0	9.00	9.00	10.25
Risk adjustment	0	0	.25	0
Bank commission	0	1.00	0	0
Dealer commission	0	0	.12	0
Balances/spread	1.0	0	.60	1.00
Discount adjustment	0	.20	.20	0
Total all-in cost	13.0	10.20	10.17	11.25

The above calculations show that for the 90-day period, Eurodollars were 1.75 percent cheaper for the borrower compared to prime, but more expensive than acceptances or commercial paper. If the company had borrowed under a Eurodollar facility, it would have saved $17,500 compared to prime but paid $10,500 more than acceptances and commercial paper, assuming $1 million borrowed for one year. Other issues must be considered; specifically, of the four options, only prime and Eurodollars would allow the firm to apply proceeds to fixed capital expenditures. What is clearly pointed out is that other more attractive options are available to the corporate borrower than the traditional prime rate.

As was shown in Chapter Four, only 1,400 companies are rated to issue commercial paper. The vast majority of borrowers do not have access to this option. Corporations borrowing in small amounts, in other words, under $500,000, usually will not be encouraged to use acceptances or Eurodollars.

In the event the quality of the borrower's or bank's credit changes, the cost components will change. If the company's performance was rated below B and the bank is a regional bank, the spread would be higher and a risk adjustment would be added, reflecting the bank's creditworthiness. Also, a regional or local bank will pay a dealer commission for access to the Eurodollar market. Any adjustments must be uniformly applied to all the options in order to make an accurate comparison and proper decision.

The following table provides a 10-year history of the four alternatives. Certain adjustments must be made if the borrower is not rated B or if second- or third-tier banks are providing funds.

APPLICATION AND REGULATIONS

Eurodollar loans are more flexible than acceptances or commercial paper, and proceeds may apply to any corporate need and for extended periods beyond one year. The primary limitations focus on the 15 percent credit a bank may extend to a customer and the application of reserves if funds are directly disbursed within the United States.

Like acceptances and commercial paper, Eurodollars are fixed-rate and fixed-term borrowings. A declining interest environment may result in the floating weighted average prime falling below the Eurodollar rate. However, since Eurodollars may be rolled over for 30-day periods, the rate will follow the declining rate trend. This is not the case with acceptances.

Eurodollars may be prepaid without regulatory penalty, but this policy differs for each bank. For large money center banks, the customer can often prepay the Euroloan. This is predicated on the bank's ability to replace the funds either by repaying the overseas originating bank or by relending the funds to a second borrower. In the event the bank accepts prepayment, a rate adjustment will be made, reflecting the prevailing rate change compared to the original LIBOR rate when the funds were disbursed.

BENEFITS

Eurodollars offer numerous benefits for banks, corporate borrowers and investors.

TABLE 5-1
Rate Comparison "B" Rated Company (90 Days, June 1973–1982)

	90-Day Rate	Bank Commission	Bank Balances	Discount Adjustment	Market Adjustment	Dealer Commission	Total Rate
1973							
Prime	7.75	0	1.16	0	0	0	8.91
Acceptances	7.90	.75	0	.19	0	0	8.84
Commercial paper	8.00	0	.80	.19	0	.13	9.12
Eurodollars	8.81	.75	0	0	0	0	9.56
1974							
Prime	11.75	0	1.76	0	0	0	13.51
Acceptances	10.79	.75	0	.32	0	0	11.86
Commercial paper	11.18	0	1.12	0	0	.13	12.43
Eurodollars	12.04	.75	0	0	0	0	12.79
1975							
Prime	7.00	0	1.05	0	0	0	8.05
Acceptances	5.70	.75	0	.09	0	0	6.54
Commercial paper	5.67	0	.57	.09	0	.13	6.46
Eurodollars	6.10	.75	0	0	0	0	6.85
1976							
Prime	7.25	0	1.09	0	0	0	8.34
Acceptances	5.77	.75	0	.09	0	0	6.52
Commercial paper	5.58	0	.56	.09	0	.13	6.36
Eurodollars	6.22	.75	0	0	0	0	6.97
1977							
Prime	7.00	0	1.05	0	0	0	8.05
Acceptances	5.39	.75	0	.08	0	0	6.22
Commercial paper	5.42	0	.54	.08	0	.13	6.17
Eurodollars	5.78	.75	0	0	0	0	6.53

TABLE 5-1 (concluded)

	90-Day Rate	Bank Commission	Bank Balances	Discount Adjustment	Market Adjustment	Dealer Commission	Total Rate
1978							
Prime	9.00	0	1.35	0	0	0	10.35
Acceptances	7.48	.75	0	.12	0	0	8.23
Commercial paper	7.75	0	.78	.12	0	.13	8.75
Eurodollars	8.33	.75	0	0	0	0	9.08
1979							
Prime	11.50	0	1.72	0	0	0	13.22
Acceptances	9.79	.75	0	.25	0	0	10.79
Commercial paper	9.77	0	.98	.25	0	.13	11.13
Eurodollars	10.52	.75	0	0	0	0	11.27
1980							
Prime	10.04	0	1.51	0	0	0	11.55
Acceptances	8.31	.75	0	.21	0	0	9.27
Commercial paper	8.27	0	.82	.21	0	.13	9.43
Eurodollars	9.41	.75	0	0	0	0	10.16
1981							
Prime	17.87	0	2.68	0	0	0	20.55
Acceptances	16.21	.75	0	.40	0	0	17.36
Commercial paper	16.24	0	1.62	.40	0	.13	18.39
Eurodollars	18.00	.75	0	0	0	0	18.75

Bank Benefits
1. Access to an alternative and reliable source of funds providing liquidity relief.
2. Given rate advantages, banks may use Eurodollars to develop new business relations.
3. Banks may use Eurodollars to maintain a relationship in the face of competition.
4. Eurodollars, for non-London depository banks, are an efficient funding source because the demand is matched to the supply.

Bank Obstacles
When a bank has excess liquidity, it prefers to loan in-house funds, which otherwise may be idle. Occasionally, a bank will add exorbitant spreads to Eurodollars, encouraging the company to borrow under the prime-related facility.

Corporate Benefits
1. Since Eurodollars are often less costly than prime, corporate borrowers may save substantial interest expense.
2. Eurodollars provide the borrower with a reliable alternative source of funds.
3. During periods of rising rates, fixed-rate Eurodollars can lock-in lower prevailing rates for a longer period.
4. Eurodollar proceeds may finance general working capital and long-term investments.
5. Eurodollars may be committed for periods beyond 270 days.

Corporate Obstacles
The primary disadvantage of Eurodollars is the fixed-rate/term aspect during periods of declining rates, as is the case with acceptances and commercial paper. As previously discussed, the treasurer must weigh the three influences: rate differential, time, and velocity.
Like commercial paper, Eurodollars may be refinanced for 30-day periods. The time variable is minimized, and the borrower may follow a declining rate trend.

Investor Benefits
1. Foreign dollar depositors are provided with relative stability with dollar deposits.
2. Depositors may enjoy more attractive returns compared to indigenous deposits.

CHAPTER SIX

MULTICURRENCY

LOANS

This chapter is provided to introduce the reader to a relatively new source of funds for U.S. corporate borrowers. In fact, foreign currency loans have been available for some time, but hedging procedures—minimizing risks—are comparatively new.

Multicurrency, or foreign currency, loans are funds provided to a U.S. borrower, which must be repaid in the foreign currency. Why would a U.S. company borrow in a foreign currency, and why would a foreign bank loan its currency to a U.S. borrower? There are rate advantages for both the borrower and lender. The borrower may pay considerably less for the funds, while the lender is able to earn more interest compared to local rates.

An excellent example is the Swiss franc, a strong and stable currency. As of December 3, 1982, the Swiss franc equivalent to prime was 6½ percent, compared to the U.S. prime of 11½ percent. Further, the Swiss franc was less expensive compared to commercial paper, acceptances, and Eurodollars. On the surface, it would appear that every U.S. corporate borrower should be fighting to borrow 6½ percent Swiss francs.

The primary obstacle is that the funds must be *repaid* in Swiss francs, and the borrower assumes a foreign exchange exposure when converting dollars to francs. If the dollar revalues against the franc, the U.S. company will need fewer dollars to buy the same amount of francs, which further reduces its borrowing cost. *However*, if the dollar weakens, devalues, against the franc, the U.S. borrower will need more dollars to purchase the same amount of francs to repay the loan, thus increasing its overall borrowing cost.

The Swiss lender will not incur this exposure, which is for the account of the U.S. borrower. Irrespective of the parity (exchange move), the Swiss bank receives the same amount. The following table summarizes this point, where the U.S. corporation borrows in a foreign currency. We will assume that on the day the foreign currency loan was made, it took one U.S. dollar to purchase two units of the foreign currency.

Dollar Devalues

	United States		Foreign	Charge
Borrowing parity	$1.00	=	$2.00	
Payback parity	1.00	=	1.50	– 25%

Dollar Revalues

	United States		Foreign	Charge
Borrowing parity	$1.00	=	$2.00	
Payback parity	.50	=	2.00	50%

In the first case, the dollar devalues by 25 percent against the foreign currency; therefore it will take 25 percent more dollars to buy the same foreign currency for repayment. If the corporation borrowed $1 million it would repay $1.25 million plus interest on the $1 million principal. In the case of the 6½ percent rate for the Swiss franc, the true cost of borrowing would be the interest rate plus foreign exchange adjustments, as shown below.

U.S. dollar principal	$1,000,000
+ 6½% Interest/year	65,000
+ 25% Rate charge	266,250
Cost of borrowing	$1,331,250

Therefore, the effective interest cost is 33.125 percent by dividing the $331,250 excess above principal by $1 million principal. This, clearly, is expensive money compared to the other dollar-denominated alternatives. We are reminded that the lender only realized the Swiss franc equivalent of the $1 million principal loaned and the 6½ percent interest, or $1,065,000 franc equivalent. The $266,250 difference is not for the account of the lender but merely represents the cost to the borrower for buying the foreign money. This is a parity cost or commodity charge cost where the trading rates of two commodities changed.

However, if the dollar revalues the foreign currency the reverse will occur. Our above table shows the dollar appreciating by 50 percent. Given the same example, the borrower will repay $532,500, as follows:

U.S. dollar principal	$1,000,000
+ 6½% Interest/year	65,000
Total	$1,065,000
50% Rate reduction	× .50
Cost of borrowing	$ 532,500

In this extreme and highly unlikely case, the U.S. borrower will pay $532,500 dollars to buy the currency to repay the loan. In this case the borrower has a 50 percent negative interest rate. Again, the foreign lender receives the same amount of francs, and the difference represents the parity charge.

Naturally, the last example is most attractive, while the example of a dollar devaluation is not at all appealing. We repeat a common theme of this book: *Money is a commodity whose cost is influenced by innumerable influences not all of which are known when the decision to borrow is made.* The U.S. corporation borrowing in a foreign currency is a full speculator and may earn substantial gains or sustain substantial losses. We assume the borrower has some degree of risk aversion and would prefer to minimize losses. In so doing, the borrower eliminates probable gains, but the point of borrowing in a foreign currency is to save on the cost of interest, not engage in commodity speculation.

When the foreign currency loan is made, the immediate question is: How much of a U.S. dollar devaluation must occur before the payback offsets the interest rate advantage? In our example, the dollar must devalue by 5 percent, representing the difference between the U.S. 11½ percent prime and the Swiss franc 6½ percent prime. Any devaluation exceeding 5 percent would result in a comparative loss for the borrower. When this difference is identified, the borrower must decide whether to borrow and speculate or to hedge the exposure, eliminating gains and losses.

HEDGING

There are three fundamental hedging options available: (1) foreign exchange contracts provided through banks, (2) futures market hedges in select foreign currencies, and (3) multicurrency swaps.

Foreign exchange contracts. These are provided by U.S. money center banks acting as brokers through their treasury or foreign currency departments. The borrower may engage these banks to buy the foreign currency needed to repay the loan, preventing parity changes between the dollar and foreign currency. Any change in parity will not impact the borrower when it buys the foreign currency to repay the loan. However, the cost of this procedure approximates the interest rate differential between U.S. dollar loans and foreign loans. In our Swiss franc example the cost to hedge will be 5½ percent, the difference between the U.S. prime at 11½ percent and the franc prime at 6½ percent. Therefore, there is no interest rate advantage.

We introduce this concept to dispel the misconception that the hedge will enable the U.S. borrower to enjoy attractive foreign interest rates without exposing the company to principal repayment foreign exchange swings. Although the foreign exchange exposure will be minimized, the cost offsets any rate advantages.

The primary purpose of a foreign exchange contract is to protect principal, not participate in interrest rate arbitrage. When a company anticipates future payments in a foreign currency, such as when foreign goods are bought and the invoice is in the foreign currency, the U.S. buyer may purchase the currency for future delivery on the date of the expected sale. This establishes the exchange and eliminates ambiguity. In this case, the U.S. buyer is not concerned about interest rate differences, merely the fixing of the exchange for repayment. However, if the buyer does not hedge, it is speculating, and any gain or loss in the foreign currency will be realized by the buyer when payment is required.

Futures market. The futures market provides for hedging in a number of hard (easily exchangeable) currencies, including the British pound, Japanese yen, and West German mark. The purpose of these hedges is not interest rate arbitrage but to minimize exchange rate fluctuations impacting foreign currency payments to foreign entities.

Both the futures market and the bank hedging procedures are

for relatively short periods. Foreign payments beyond one year become more difficult to hedge.

A swap program offered by select banks and some investment and brokerage houses can eliminate principal repayment exchange fluctuations and provide attractive rates. Two corporations borrowing in each other's currencies contractually exchange debt repayment. For example, if Company A in the United States borrows Swiss francs at 6½ percent, and Company B, operating in Switzerland, has U.S. dollar obligations from loans its U.S. subsidiary must repay, the two companies swap obligations. Company A in the United States will repay Company B's U.S. dollar obligations, and Company B in Switzerland will repay Company A's Swiss franc obligation. This eliminates future foreign exchange purchases, and therefore no currency fluctuation impacts principal repayment.

The critical issues here are that the repayment schedules should coincide, the repayment amounts should coincide, and the companies must be comfortable with the credit risk of each other. In some cases, a bank familiar with both companies will guarantee the performance of the companies, eliminating the credit risk for them.

The swap does not eliminate foreign exchange fluctuations covering interest repayment, and the rates are not swapped without penalty. One alternative to avoid this exposure is to discount the interest from the principal disbursement at the outset or to prepay the interest. This process incurs a discounted interest adjustment cost reflecting the opportunity cost for not having access to the full amount of the loan and sacrificing investment opportunities. It appears, depending on the opportunity cost, that the cost of this approach more than offsets the foreign exchange exposure, which may be significant. Also, this cost is easily calculated and identifiable and may allow the U.S. company to enjoy favorable foreign rates. The calculation is:

$$\frac{R \times CD \times Days}{360}$$

where

$$R = \text{Interest rate}$$
$$CD = \text{Prevailing CD rate}$$
$$Days = \text{Financing period}$$

For example, a U.S. company borrowing Swiss Francs at 6½ percent with an 8 percent CD opportunity cost for 90 days, will incur the following added expense for interest hedging through interest prepayment.

$$\frac{6.5\% \times .08\% \times 90}{360} = .13$$

The U.S. borrower's total cost will be the 6.5 percent rate plus .13, or 6.63 percent. If the period is one year, the 90-day period is changed to 365 days and the adjustment is .527, or a total rate of 6.5 percent plus .527 percent (7.027 percent), which is cheaper than the 12 percent U.S. prime.

When the interest is paid up front to hedge currency fluctuations, the foreign bank realizes a greater return, since funds are received at the outset and not in arrears. Just as the corporate borrower incurs an opportunity cost, the lender incurs an opportunity or windfall gain. This gain should be considered by the foreign bank and the rate reduced proportionately. The corporation's opportunity cost will not be completely offset by the lender's windfall gain, but any negotiated interest reduction, reflecting the windfall gain, further reduces the borrower's interest expense.

The swap program is primarily used by major corporate borrowers, with minimal borrowings of approximately $15–20 million. The documentation for the swap is identical to the conventional loan except for the actual swap agreement between the two companies.

Aside from principal swaps and interest rate hedges, there are various interest rate swaps. In this case, one company exchanges its variable rate interest schedule for a fixed-rate schedule of a second company. Each company is responsible for its respective principal repayment. A bank intermediary may guarantee the interest repayment of the two swapping companies, depending on their creditworthiness. For purposes of this section, we assume that the two companies do not have a foreign exchange exposure covering principal repayment. They either swapped the foreign currency loan repayment or the borrowed currency, for they are the same.

SITUATION

For a number of reasons a company may have an interest rate schedule (floating or fixed) that it elects to swap. The company may have a floating rate but, as a matter of policy, elects to have a fixed rate to avoid a rate fluctuation exposure; or the company may have a fixed-rate schedule but wishes to enjoy rate advantages of lower prevailing floating rates. In any event, the two companies elect to exchange their rate schedules. An example will amplify the application.

In August 1982, a BBB-rated company negotiated a $60 million, seven-year Eurodollar loan with a floating rate. At the time the loan was made, the all-in rate was approximately 13½ percent, with rate changes every six months reflecting the prevailing six-month LIBOR base rate. The company was uncomfortable with the floating nature of the loan, which could fluctuate down or up, depending on the commodity nature of money rates. Wishing to eliminate the speculative rate fluctuations, the company was willing to pay a higher fixed rate over the seven-year term. However, given its BBB-credit rating, the tight Eurobond fixed-rate environment, and relatively high rates of 17 percent for the loan, the company settled for the lower short-term variable LIBOR rate.

Expecting rates to stabilize or possibly increase, a major European bank arranged for a seven-year, 15.37 percent fixed-rate Eurobond issue for its own use. As rates continued to decline, the European bank envied the lower floating rates.

Through a U.S. bank intermediary, the European bank swapped its 15.37 percent fixed rate for the U.S. company's lower floating rate. The European bank now enjoys lower rates while synchronizing these rates with maturities of other liquid assets and liabilities. If the floating rate rises, the European banks will pay more, offset by higher rates it charges borrowers. The U.S. company is paying more at the outset for fixed-rate money, compared to the floating rate it traded, but it has achieved its objective of hedging against rate changes. Further, it is paying 15.39 percent, reflecting the creditworthiness of the European bank, compared to 17 percent the company would have paid in the fixed-rate Eurobond market with its BBB rating.

CHAPTER SEVEN

OTHER

APPLICATIONS

While reviewing short-term borrowing alternatives, we would be remiss not to elaborate on innovative applications. In the management of corporate short-term borrowings, there are approaches that reduce the debt-to-equity ratio and improve working capital for corporations with erratic earnings or with significant inventory or long-term asset investments. This management approach falls under the heading of "off–balance-sheet financing," where certain assets and counterpart debts are not shown on the financial statements.

Before elaborating, we must caution that, although the following examples have been successfully employed, there are severe legal and accounting implications which must be carefully reviewed and approved by the corporate counsel and certified public accounts. Improper structure will result in a failed attempt to implement these highly sophisticated and technical approaches. The programs must not violate accepted accounting treatments, and complicated credit exposures must be minimized.

PURPOSE

The fundamental purpose of off–balance-sheet finance is to remove debt from the financial statement or improve cash flow. By removing debts and assets, the company's current ratio, working capital, debt/equity, return on assets, and interest-expense coverage ratio will improve. Banks, rating agencies, and even stockholders will look more favorably on the corporation. With the definition of interest relative to risk, we can see that off–balance-sheet financing could conceivably reduce borrowing costs as performance is improved.

The critical issue in all the examples is that *the risk of ownership for the assets removed may not be with the benefactor or borrower.* The benefactor may not provide contractual comfort to the lenders in the form of take-or-pay contracts or guarantees. Lenders must be comforted with the structure of the program and the underlying transaction, not the creditworthiness of the creditor.

APPLICATION

We will review three structures that have been employed for different reasons. Other hybrid applications are possible.

1. *An inventory off-balance sheet* removes abnormally large inventory assets and offsetting debt. The first example covers a major soybean processor which purchases large amounts of soybeans during the harvest period and stores the commodity for its full year's usage. For high-inventory investment periods, the debt/equity and return on assets ratio is abnormally high. By removing the soybeans while maintaining access to the commodity, the performance ratios are smoothed for the operating cycle.

2. *A new plant off-balance sheet* removes debt and improves working capital, debt/equity, and the return on assets during the construction stage of a plant when it is a noncontributing asset. The second example covers a major manufacturer that held new plant construction off the balance sheet during the construction phase.

3. *An international receivables off–balance* sheet improved cash flow, debt/equity and the return on assets. The third example shows how a major corporation with international sales eliminates its international receivables and foreign risk.

Inventory Off–Balance-Sheet Financing

Situation.   A major agribusiness corporation purchases large quantities of soybeans during the peak October–December harvest period. The purchase dramatically increases the soybean inventory, which is used throughout the year to produce consumer products. As soybean purchases occur, payment is made from bank credit and commercial paper. As debt rises, the period cash flow is distorted and the debt/equity and return on assets are impacted and appear to reflect poor performance.

Solutions. In order to improve and smooth out the operating performance and maintain attractive interest rates, the company established an off–balance-sheet program.

Structure. A third-party nominee was established by the trust department of a major bank. The nominee corporation purchased soybeans from farmers with proceeds of bankers' acceptances provided by the bank. The soybeans were shipped to the benefactor's warehouse, which was leased by the nominee and subleased to a warehouse company that provided the warehouse receipt to the bank.

The warehouse receipt provides two functions: (1) it protects the bank, which is loaning millions of dollars to a trust which is negligibly capitalized, and (2) it allows for eligible acceptance financing required under the Federal Reserve Act. The benefactor cannot guarantee the debt obligation of the trust to the bank, and the full risk of ownership rests with the trust and the lending bank.

The trust and, therefore, the bank have an exposed commodity position, since the trust is long in soybeans purchased. In the event the benefactor does not buy the beans, the bank will foreclose on the trust and sell the beans to pay off the acceptances. For this reason, the trust enters the futures market and sells or shorts the soybean market. This reduces commodity fluctuation risks. Therefore, if the benefactor defaults, the trust will have the option of actually delivering the beans under a futures contract, ensuring the bank of repayment. The margin account for this transaction is provided by the bank.

All costs associated with this transaction are passed on to the benefactor when the beans are ultimately purchased. When needed, the benefactor purchases the beans from the trust, which pays off the acceptance. Since the benefactor incurs no direct financing charges, which are incorporated in the trust's invoice, the benefactor's cost of goods sold increases, but its interest-expense coverage ratio, debt/equity and return on assets ratios, improve.

IMPACT

The bank no longer enjoys the credit comfort of the benefactor, its exposure is to the trust. The bank's position is protected with the execution of the futures contract, which guarantees the price of the beans and provides an avenue for sale of the beans if the benefactor fails to buy the commodity.

The company's performance will significantly improve. Further, the company is not tying up needed commercial lines of credit, and its rating is not distorted, since the debt does not appear on its financial statement.

The legal structure and accounting reviews are extensive, ensuring the program's viability. The cost of implementing such a program is quite high, approximately $200–350,000; therefore the cost benefit must be obvious. In essence, this structure introduces into the picture a soybean broker, who acts as a financial shock absorber.

A basic fact should provide comfort to the lenders: Soybeans to the benefactor are like insulin to a diabetic; the benefactor needs the product in the short-run. Further, any default by the benefactor will certainly impact its future ability to obtain credit.

This form of inventory off–balance sheet has been employed by other industries. The 1978 coal strike encouraged select utilities to purchase abnormally large stocks of coal. These purchases proportionately increased debt or reduced cash flow, which negatively impacted performance, which could lead to higher interest rates and reduce stock prices.

By implementing an inventory off–balance-sheet program, the utility smooths its performance while maintaining adequate coal stocks meeting consumer demand. Utilities have also employed this approach to hold nuclear fuel cores off the balance sheet. The approach may be modified to apply to the airline industry covering jet fuel or spare engines.

Documents
    Trust agreement.
    Trust loan agreement.
    Documentary acceptance agreement.
    Futures market agreement with dealer.
    Margin account agreement.
    Warehouse lease agreement.
    Warehouse sublease agreement.
    Warehouse receipt.

New Plant Off–Balance-Sheet Financing

Situation. A major company wished to expand its production capacity by adding a $70 million plant. During the three-year construction period, the company would increase its debt to pay for various stages of completed construction. However, during the construction stage the plant is a noncontributing asset. The debt actively contributes to the debt-equity ratio, reduces the return on assets while increasing assets, and disproportionately reduces profits.

Solution. In order to hold debt, covering new construction in abeyance pending the operation of the plant, the company (benefactor) implemented an off–balance-sheet program.

Structure. A third-party nominee corporation was incorporated as the general contractor. A major insurance company with an "A" commercial paper rating issued its bond in favor of dealers supporting the nominee's commercial paper. The rating agencies applied the same "A" rating to the general contractor nominee's commercial paper because the ultimate recourse was to the insurance company.

The general contractor nominee issued commercial paper as invoices were presented, representing work completed. During the three-year period the nominee's assets and commercial paper debt grew in proportion to the work completed. As the paper matured, it was rolled over until the plant was completed. When finished, the company purchased the plant from the general contractor nominee for a price which included the interest expense and insurance bond. This invoice was used to calculate future depreciation and the investment tax credit.

The primary risk in this program rests with the intent of the benefactor to purchase the plant when completed. In the event there are contingencies discouraging the benefactor from buying the plant, the insurance company will own a nonoperating $70 million plant. As stated, the benefactor may not issue its guarantee to the insurance company, supporting the debt of the general contractor, without the CPA's noting the contingent liability.

To encourage the insurance company to issue its bond, the company contractually agreed with a long-term lender to finance the completed plant. The long-term lender issued its unconditional take-out to the insurance company issuing the bond. Therefore the issuer's source of repayment was the long-term lender.

An alternative to the bond supporting commercial paper is the use of a bank's standby letter of credit. In this case, the bank's take out is the long-term lender. Also, the insurance company could have committed itself to the long-term take-out.

Impact. This structure improved the key performance ratios of the benefactor by removing interim debt covering construction.

When the plant was completed, the benefactor purchased the plant with proceeds from the prearranged long-term debt. For the insurance company the bond is not a direct liability but a contingent liability, as in the case of a bank's standby letter of credit. The important benefit for the benefactor is that the plant and term debt were taken on the balance sheet when the plant was actively contributing to the overall financial performance.

International Receivables Off–Balance-Sheet Financing

Situation. A major corporation has $6 billion in sales, of which $3 billion are to overseas customers. At any given time, $750 million were outstanding international receivables financed with a combination of bank debt and commercial paper. The firm had expansion plans and was looking for long-term debt. However, the debt-equity ratio was high relative to industry standards, which resulted in a higher-term debt interest rate.

Solution. The company removed $400 million of the $750 million debt covering international receivables.

Structure. The company was selling most of its goods to international buyers against confirmed letters of credit. These L/Cs engage the opening bank's obligation to pay the U.S. company, irrespective of the foreign buyer's ability to perform. The company's financial advisor arranged for the receivable to be assigned to the U.S. bank which confirmed the Letter of Credit. The bank was obviously comfortable with the foreign bank's creditworthiness, otherwise it would not have confirmed the letter of credit in the first place. The confirming bank agreed to purchase the receivables from the company without recourse. The bank's exposure was covered by the commitment of the foreign banks to pay in 30 days. The result was nonrecourse, international discounted receivable financing, off the balance sheet.

Impact. The elimination of $400 million of debt significantly improved the debt-equity ratio and reduced the long-term interest expense for new acquisitions. Further, the company's performance improvement was reflected by an increase in its stock price. When the company made its acquisition, it offered a combination of cash provided by cheaper long-term debt and a stock swap in its favor, since the price per share had increased due to improved performance, partially due to debt reduction and a better return on assets.

Conclusion. Although the three examples of off–balance-sheet financing have taken place, the application of each will not immediately apply to all corporations. The legal and CPA procedures may be quite complicated, and our brief summation ignores the complicated and sometimes intricate maneuvers that must be managed to ensure success. The important point is that short-term debt management, which played a critical role in the implementation of these programs, had a positive impact for the benefactors.

CHAPTER EIGHT

MANAGING

CORPORATE

SHORT-TERM DEBT

We have witessed the growth and importance of short-term debt in the last decade. This resulted from disproportionately high long-term rates and increased emphasis on cash flow. Unlike long-term debt and equity issues, short-term debt impacts every aspect of financial performance and, by its short-term nature, supplements cash flow, the corporate life blood.

With the global economic flux, liability management is reemerging as a key to survival and success. The proper management of short-term debt may stimulate performance while mismanagement may lead to financial ruin. The responsibility of the corporate treasurer is to orchestrate short-term borrowing to maximize financial flexibility and minimize interest expense.

Our objective is to provide the practitioner and student of finance with the fundamentals of short-term debt alternatives while introducing state-of-the-art applications. As seen, there are different features, benefits, and applications for the alternatives, which, when properly managed, will significantly contribute to more efficient use of short-term debt and impact the aggregate economy. The primary trade-off between these options is cost versus flexibility.

Prime-related loans are the most costly but provide maximum flexibility. Commercial paper and bankers' acceptances are less expensive but are limited as to whom and what transactions qualify for these financing techniques. Eurodollars are moderately priced above acceptances and commercial paper but below prime and enjoy significant flexibility. While foreign currency loans may be competitively priced, the inherent foreign exchange risk may eliminate any advantages. The following table highlights and compares the differences which may change, depending on the structure or the bank.

Characteristic	Prime	Acceptances	Commercial Paper	Eurodollars	Multicurrency
Price competitive		Yes	Yes	Yes	Yes
Fund working capital	Yes	No	Yes	Yes	Yes
Fund long-term	Yes	No	No	Yes	Yes
Fund speculation	Yes	No	No	Yes	Yes
Reserves	Yes	No	No	No	No
Funds beyond 180 days	Yes	No	Yes	Yes	Yes
Funds beyond 270 days	Yes	No	No	Yes	Yes
Underlying transaction	No	Yes	No	No	No
Rollover	Yes	No	No	Yes	
Fixed rate	No	Yes	Yes	Yes	Yes
Balances	Yes	No	Yes	No	No
Prepayment	Yes	No	No	No	Yes
Extensive regulations	No	Yes	No	No	No
Foreign exchange risk	No	No	No	No	Yes

The text has reaffirmed the commodity nature of money and emphasized the importance of recently introduced hedging techniques, protecting borrowers from rate fluctuations. Fixed-rate funding for acceptances, commercial paper and Eurodollars, is a hedge against rate fluctuations. This minimizes interest expense when rates are rising and eliminates gains when rates are falling. The decision to fund with hedged fixed rates is obvious when rates are increasing. However, when rates are falling, the funding decision is more elusive, requiring probability analysis.

To assume that the floating prime will ultimately be less costly when declining, compared to fixed-rate alternatives, is without foundation. This is because the fixed-rate alternatives are generally less than prime at any given time. Therefore, to be advantageous the floating prime must not only move downward, but it must move to a point below the fixed rate, offsetting the time it took to equal the fixed rate. As discussed, the treasurer must weigh three influencing variables: spread differential, time, and velocity of prime moves, determining the probability of the weighted average prime floating below fixed-rate alternatives.

Since Eurodollars and commercial paper may be refinanced every 30 days, the time influence is diluted compared to acceptances which may not be refinanced.

When considering future borrowings, the company may elect to hedge through various futures market alternatives. In essence, actual rate fluctuations will be partially offset by moves in the futures market: the loss or gain in the actual borrowed rate will tend to be offset by moves in the futures market. When minimizing future rate fluctuations, the borrower buys a long position in the financial futures market which is sold back to the market when borrowings occur. Some borrowing instruments may be directly hedged, and some borrowing must be offset by a complementary contract. The following amplifies.

ᵛinancial Futures

Borrowing Instrument	Futures Contract
Prime	CDs or commercial paper
Subprime	CDs or commercial paper or T-bills
Acceptances	Commercial paper
Eurodollars	Eurodollars
Commercial paper	Commercial paper
Multicurrency	Multicurrency

Past and Future

While summarizing the growth of borrowing alternatives over the last decade, we note that the stateless nature of Eurodollars makes it difficult to identify U.S. corporate borrowings. The $900 billion outstanding in 1981 reflects global government and corporate borrowings.

Chart 1 shows the total outstandings of all the alternatives, while charts 2–5 show each alternative, identifying the outstandings graphically and numerically, the per year percentage growth, nine-year percentage growth, and annualized rate.

Although Eurodollars reached $900 billion in 1981, representing global outstandings, the 462 percent, nine-year growth followed the 686 percent expansion of bankers' acceptances, which grew from $8.8 billion in 1973 to $69.2 billion in 1981. This was followed by commercial and industrial loans of $360 billion for 1981, expanding 118 percent over nine years; and commercial paper, reaching $165.5 billion, an increase of 297 percent.

Acceptances also lead the alternatives for the weighted average annual growth, at 32.39 percent, followed by Eurodollars,

22.7 percent; commercial paper, 19.48 percent; and commercial loans, 12 percent. It is speculated that bankers' acceptances outpaced Eurodollars because of the rate advantage in favor of acceptances. Further, acceptances grew faster than commercial paper because of the competitive rates and general corporate accessibility to acceptance finance compared to the comparatively few (1,400 issues) commercial paper issues. Acceptances increased faster than commercial loans because of the consistent and significant rate advantage.

Chart 6 compares the all-in cost of the alternatives for a B-rated company and identifies the incremental pricing components that contribute to the total costs. It is noted that for 1973, prime was slightly below acceptances and commercial paper—a temporary phenomena, since acceptances and commercial paper are usually less expensive. Given the responsiveness of acceptances and commercial paper to economic considerations, moves in these rates precede moves in the prime rate. Therefore these higher rates indicate an upward rate environment, to be followed by the prime rate. The rates for 1974 clearly show the increasing trend and prime moved higher than acceptances and commercial paper.

We suspect that acceptance financing will maintain its growth lead over the alternatives. This will result from recently enacted legislation increasing bank limits, flexibility through the elimination of a bill of lading (title document) for domestic shipping transactions, and new bank participation allowances. The key to managing short-term debt is awareness of the alternatives and insight into proper application, given the rate environment, hedging alternatives, and structure.

CHART I
Total Outstandings

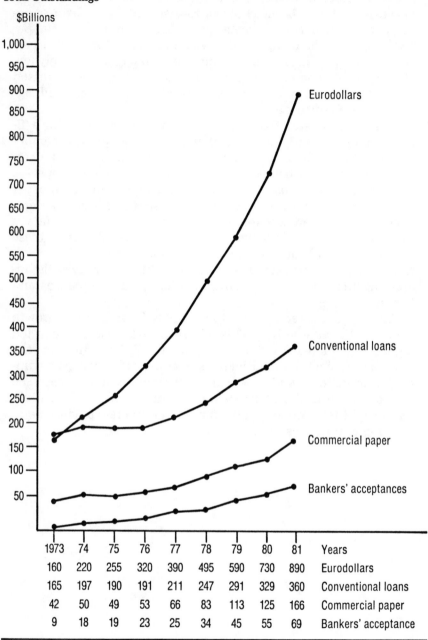

Source: Federal Reserve statistics.

CHART II
Bankers' Acceptance Outstanding

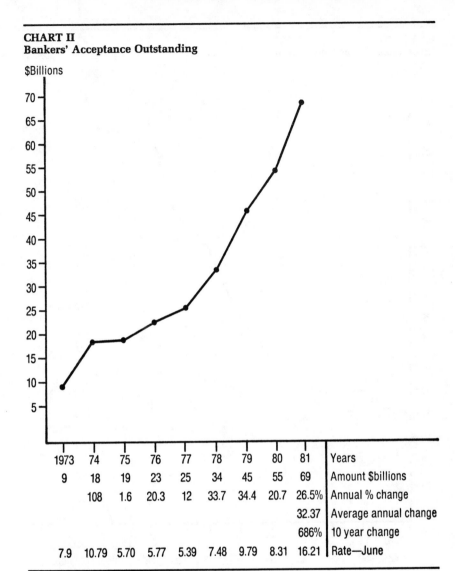

Years	1973	74	75	76	77	78	79	80	81
Amount $billions	9	18	19	23	25	34	45	55	69
Annual % change		108	1.6	20.3	12	33.7	34.4	20.7	26.5%
Average annual change									32.37
10 year change									686%
Rate—June	7.9	10.79	5.70	5.77	5.39	7.48	9.79	8.31	16.21

Source: Federal Reserve statistics.

CHART III
Commercial Paper Outstanding

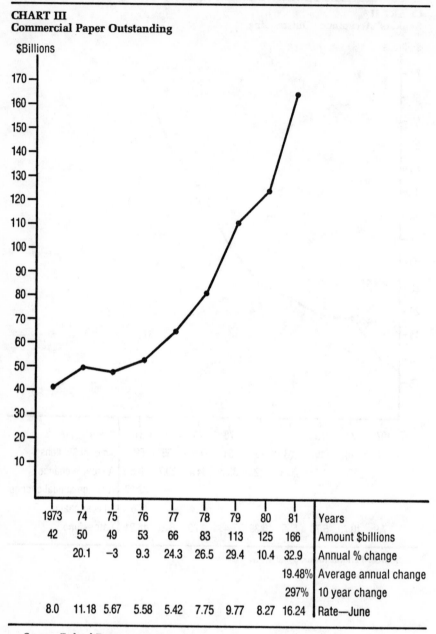

Years	1973	74	75	76	77	78	79	80	81
Amount $billions	42	50	49	53	66	83	113	125	166
Annual % change		20.1	−3	9.3	24.3	26.5	29.4	10.4	32.9
Average annual change									19.48%
10 year change									297%
Rate—June	8.0	11.18	5.67	5.58	5.42	7.75	9.77	8.27	16.24

Source: Federal Reserve statistics.

CHART IV
Commercial Loans Outstanding

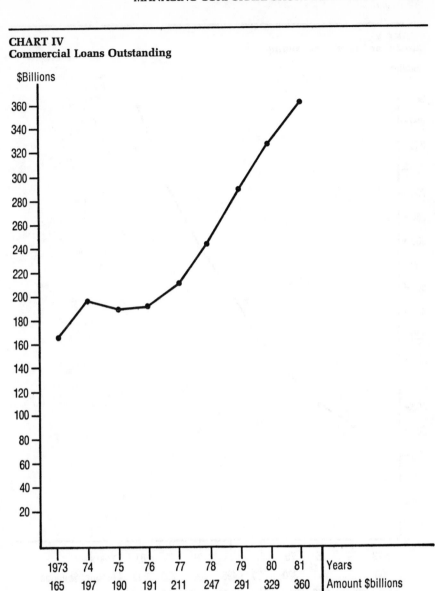

	1973	74	75	76	77	78	79	80	81	Years
	165	197	190	191	211	247	291	329	360	Amount $billions
		31.7	−3.8	.7	10.5	16.7	17.8	13.2	9.5	Annual % change
									12%	Average annual change
									118%	10 year change
	7.75	11.75	7.0	7.25	7.0	9.0	11.50	10.04	12.89	Rate—June

Source: Federal Reserve statistics.

CHART V
Eurodollar Global Outstandings

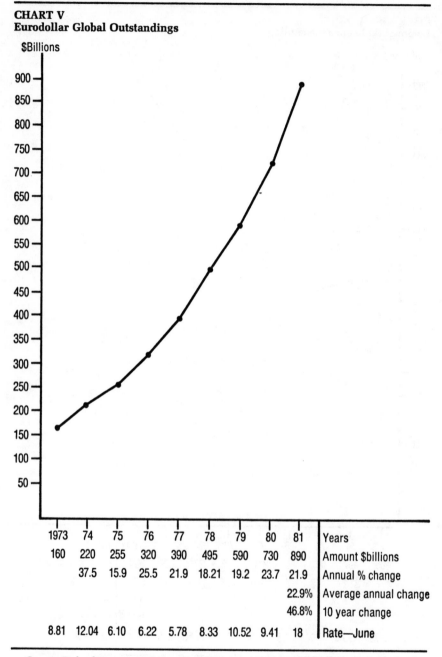

$Billions

Years	1973	74	75	76	77	78	79	80	81	
Amount $billions	160	220	255	320	390	495	590	730	890	
Annual % change		37.5	15.9	25.5	21.9	18.21	19.2	23.7	21.9	
Average annual change									22.9%	
10 year change									46.8%	
Rate—June	8.81	12.04	6.10	6.22	5.78	8.33	10.52	9.41	18	

Source: Federal Reserve statistics; World Financial Markets: Morgan Guaranty.

CHART VI
Commercial Loans Outstanding

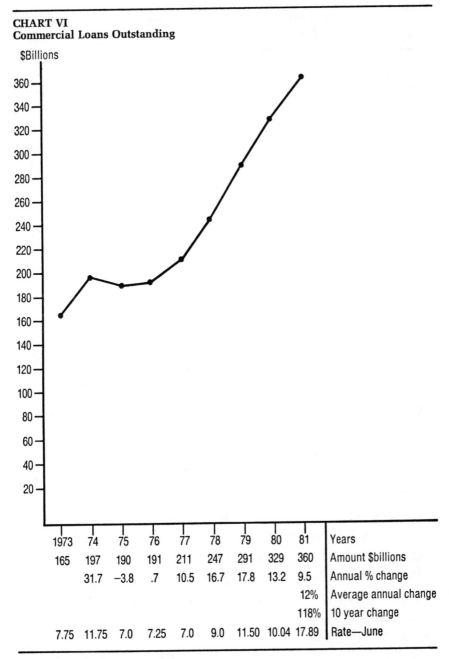

	1973	74	75	76	77	78	79	80	81	Years
	165	197	190	191	211	247	291	329	360	Amount $billions
		31.7	-3.8	.7	10.5	16.7	17.8	13.2	9.5	Annual % change
									12%	Average annual change
									118%	10 year change
	7.75	11.75	7.0	7.25	7.0	9.0	11.50	10.04	17.89	Rate—June

Source: Federal Reserve statistics.

GLOSSARY

Account party. Buyer or importer opening letter of credit.

Advance. Prime-related loan.

Advised letter. Letter of credit not engaging the advising bank's liability.

Advised line of credit. Amount of credit a bank agrees to commit.

Agent bank. A lead or managing bank of a group of banks extending credit.

All-in costs. The quoted rate to borrowers plus related costs, i.e., balances or dealer rate.

All-in rate. The base rate plus spread or commission, not including associated costs; i.e., balances or fees.

Back-up lines. Bank credit, supporting commercial paper.

Bankers' acceptances. A time draft or bill of exchange drawn on and accepted by a bank.

Basis point. One hundredth of 1 percent; there are 100 basis points in 1 percent.

Beneficiary. Seller or exporter of goods in whose favor a letter of credit is executed.

Blended cost. A weighted or melded cost of funds for a bank.

Borrowing base. A percentage of assets against which a bank will make loans, i.e., 80 percent of receivables under 30 days.

Cash/spot. Prevailing price of a commodity.

Collection. A procedure where banks transfer documents to buyers covering goods and payment to sellers.

Commercial paper. Short-term unsecured promissory notes issued by companies to investors.

Commission. Bank spread above the acceptance discount rate.

Confirmed letter of credit. Advising bank agrees to pay exporter (seller) when proper documents evidencing shipment are presented.

Compensating balances. Noninterest-bearing cash deposits maintained at the bank in consideration of a line of credit.

Current ratio. Measure of current liabilities as a percentage of current assets (Current assets ÷ Current liabilities).

Dealer. Purchases (underwrites) corporate-issued commercial paper not directly issued by the corporation.

Debt-equity ratio. Measures the contribution and relationship of debt and equity (Debt ÷ Equity).

Devalue. Decline in the exchange of one currency (commodity) against another.

Discount. Principal less interest associated with acceptances and commercial paper.

Discount adjustment. Measure of opportunity cost for paying interest at the outset, compared to paying interest in arrears.

Draft. An order to pay funds.

Eligible acceptance. Collateral qualified for securing a Federal Reserve loan to a member bank; meets regulation A.

Eurodollars. Dollar deposits made in foreign countries.

Federal funds. Fed funds; funds valued the same day.

Fixed rate. Where the borrower's rate does not change.

Floating rate. A variable rate where the borrower's rate fluctuates with the prime rate.

Foreign exchange contract. A commitment to buy or sell a foreign currency for future delivery.

Futures contract. A commitment to buy or sell a commodity for future delivery.

Guidance line of credit. Total amount of credit approved by a bank, a portion of which is not advised to the company, pending future needs.

Hedging. Protection against commodity price fluctuations.

In arrears. Interest paid after usage of principal.

Ineligible acceptance. Also referred to as a finance bill; an acceptance that is unqualified as collateral in securing a loan from the Federal Reserve to a member bank. If discounted, these acceptances bear reserves.

Intrabank rate. Price of internally transfered bank funds from one department or profit center to another.

Interest. Bank's cost of funds plus a spread reflecting risk.

Interest coverage. The measure of debt service ([Net profit − Interest] ÷ Interest).

Issuing bank. The buyer's (importer's) bank that opens a letter of credit.

Letter of credit. A bank's legal promise to pay the seller (exporter) of goods upon presentation of documents representing shipment.

LIBOR. London interbank-offered rate: interest rate of Eurodollar deposits made between "London" banks.

Line of credit. Amount of bank credit available to a company.

Long-term debt. Debt payable after one year.

Matched funds. Loans made against specific funds, e.g., CDs.

Melded costs. A weighted or blended cost of funds reflecting the aggregate cost of bank funds.

Negotiating bank. The seller's (exporter's) bank, through which the letter of credit is advised and to which the documents are presented for payment.

Open account. Unsecured or supported trade credit.

Open line of credit. Unsecured bank credit often supporting commercial paper.

Participation. Two or more banks agreeing to provide credit to a company.

Petro dollars. Dollars paying for OPEC (Organization of Petroleum Exporting Countries) oil sales.

Prime. A most favorable rate offered to corporations. (See Subprime.)

Purpose statement. Corporate certification that goods exist and qualify for acceptance financing.

Quick ratio. Measures the relationship between the most liquid current assets and current liabilities: (Current assets—inventories) ÷ (Current liabilites).

Rate differential. The difference between two rates, e.g., acceptances and prime.

Rating. A rank of corporate creditworthiness applied by private agencies, such as Moody's or Standard & Poor's, to corporations.

Regulation A. Federal Reserve guidelines for creating eligible bankers' acceptances.

Reserves. A percentage of bank deposits maintained with the federal reserve system.

Return on assets. Measures the efficiency of asset management (Profits ÷ Assets).

Return on equity. Measures the efficient application of investor's funds (Profits ÷ Equity).

Revolver. A line of credit used at the customer's convenience. The outstandings move up or down as funds are needed, but the amount committed remains the same.

Rollover. Refinancing.

Secondary market. The investment community providing money market funds.

Short-term debt. Debt payable within one year.

Speculation. An unprotected or open position subject to commodity price fluctuations.

Spread. An amount above the bank's cost of funds, including risk perception.

Subprime. Interest rates below prime, usually tied to an established deposit or matched funding.

Syndicate. Two or more banks contractually agreeing to provide credit to a company.

Swap. A contractual agreement between two companies to exchange principal and/or interest repayment.

Two-name paper. A debt obligation issued by a corporation and endorsed by a bank.

Trade acceptances. Time draft (bill of exchange) drawn by the buyer on and accepted by the seller of goods.

UCC-1. Uniform commercial code form no. 1 securing assets for loans; legally filed with the secretary of state.

Underwriting. Dealers unconditional promise to purchase commercial paper (and other securities) from corporate issuers.

Velocity. The speed at which interest rates change.

Weighted cost of funds. A blended or melded cost of funds for the bank.

Weighted prime. The average prime rate over a given period of time.

Working capital. A measurement of liquidity identifying the current assets over current liabilities (current assets – current liabilites).

INDEX